The Organizational Culture Perspective

The Organizational Culture Perspective

J. Steven Ott
University of Maine
Orono, Maine

Brooks/Cole Publishing Company
Pacific Grove, California

Sponsoring editor: Leo A. W. Wiegman
Project editor: Mary Lou Murphy-Luif
Production manager: Ann Cassady
Cover design: Leon Bolognese & Associates
Compositor: Eastern Graphics
Typeface: 10/20 Century Schoolbook
Printer: Malloy Lithographing, Inc.

Library of Congress Cataloging-in-Publication-Data
Ott, J. Steven.
    The organizational culture perspective / J. Steven Ott
        p.   cm.
    Bibliography: p.
    Includes index.
    ISBN 0-534-10918-7
    former ISBN 0-256-06319-2
        1. Corporate culture. 2. Organizational behavior. I. Title
HD58.7.087 1989
302.3'5—dc19   88–9574

Printed in the United States of America
10 9 8 7 6 5 4

Dedicated to Virginia E. Ott

Preface

Since about 1980, a sizeable and growing body of the literature on organizations has expressed dissatisfaction bordering on frustration with the inability of standard, respected views of organization and traditional organizational research methodologies to produce substantive answers—or ways to find answers—to pressing contemporary questions of organization. The segment of the literature that moves beyond bemoaning the inadequacies of existing theory, empirical data, and research methods to propose alternatives is involved in a high stakes competition to gain positioning as the "cutting edge" in the "next wave" of organization theory and investigative approaches. Since about 1982, members of the organizational culture or symbolic management perspective have been among the most visible and articulate proponents of their alternative to traditional theory and methods.

Organizational culture is the newest and has been perhaps the most controversial of the organization theory perspectives. Instead of viewing an organization as a goal-oriented structure (formal or informal), functions, information systems and decision processes, or groups of members, the organizational culture perspective puts on a different set of "lenses" through which to "see" an organization. When we look through these special organizational culture lenses, we see a mini-society made up of social constructions. These social constructions vary in different areas of an organization (there are sub cultures), but consistent threads are woven across the organization which clearly identify the existence of an "umbrella" organizational culture. Although the organizational culture clearly mirrors aspects of the broader societal culture, it is relatively unique.

As in *all* cultures, *all* facts, truths, realities, beliefs and values are *what the members agree they are*—they are perceptions. Interestingly, these social constructions are not created explicitly or consciously. Members come to agreement on them slowly, implicitly and subconsciously. They develop as people work together and successfully overcome problems of survival. New members learn them (are enculturated) through nonverbal communications (cues) and through repeated retelling of organization myths, stories and sagas, complete with heroes, crises, and happy endings. "Old members" often do not even realize they are in the process of passing a culture along to the next generation of members. It is the gestalt—the holistic composite interweaving—of these ways of seeing things, assumptions about the nature of things and relations, patterns of doing things, beliefs, values, and realities, that together comprises the identity, or in the language of this book, the structure or contents of an organizational culture.

Some beliefs and realities of an organizational culture are very useful. They let members know what is expected of them: what and how they should deal with certain situations, thereby eliminating the need for formal information and control systems. In this sense, organizational culture could be a key element in the answer to the thorny questions being raised regularly today about how to make American organizations more competitive in the world markets (Kilmann & Covin, 1988; Mitroff, 1987; Ouchi, 1984). Organizational culture may be an important key for revitalizing—restimulating the quality and quantity of American organizational productivity.

Then again, by forging common perceptions of truths, "shoulds" and realities, a strong, pervasive organizational culture can lead to organizational rigidity—to strategic or tactical decision making by leaders who are wearing mental blinders. If organizational culture predisposes an organization to certain patterns of behaviors (including decisions), and if it is possible to decipher that culture (if our investigative methods are capable of doing so), is it not more than remotely possible that outsiders (competitors or "enemies") can become able to predict its strategic decisions?

And, what about those people in organizations who do not choose to "see" truths and realities as they are prescribed in a particular organizational culture, or to accept its beliefs and values? What should happen to them? Should we try to mold them into conformity? Or, should we celebrate their uniquenesses and tolerate their disruptive views? Are we on a thirty-year cycle heading back toward William Whyte, Jr.'s *Organization Man* (1956)?

These are a few of the types of issues, questions, and themes addressed in *The Organizational Culture Perspective*. This perspective of organizations contributes significantly to our ability to explain and predict the behavior of organizations in some circumstances. However, it is not the *alpha and the omega* of organization. I doubt that there is or ever will be a single set of answers (or source of a single set of answers) to the complex social phenomena that we call organizations. The organizational culture perspective is one more, very important, building block in our arsenal of knowledge, theory, and methods of organization.

My purpose for this book is to expose the reader to the nature, structural elements, and functions of organizational culture, and to the ways of thinking—the realities, truths, beliefs, approaches, and methods of the organizational culture perspective. If I am successful, the readers will be able to make informed decisions about the advantages and disadvantages of using management and research techniques from the organizational culture perspective. My purpose is not to gain converts—to win managers, consultants, and students over to the use of organizational culture lenses. Rather, it is to present my interpretation of one useful alternative to the more traditional ways of thinking about and seeing organizations. In this sense, I consider *The Organizational Culture Perspective* to be a call for balance; a plea for the acceptance of diverse views about and approaches to studying organizations; a cry for breaking out of the information systems/logical-positivist/quasi-experimental mold that has placed a mental and emotional straight jacket on organization theory and theorists for too many years.

Despite the controversies surrounding the first years of the organizational culture perspective's existence, it is more than just another trendy fad of modern business management. The perspective has long, deep, and rich roots in a variety of very respectable disciplines, including cultural anthropology, ethnoarchaeology, social psychology (most typically, cognitive social psychology), artificial intelligence, sociology (particularly phenomenological sociology), organizational communication, psychology, business administration, public administration, and educational administration. And, regardless of the future of the perspective, organizational culture itself is a permanent feature of organizations. It affects organizational behavior. It will not disappear. It cannot and should not be ignored by serious managers or students of organizations.

ACKNOWLEDGMENTS

First, this book is for Jay Shafritz, who recently moved to the University of Pittsburgh. As a professional colleague and a close friend, he both required and helped me to shape, refine, and organize my semi-free floating concepts into a coherent set of contents that followed a reasonable logic. Without Jay's constant assistance, cajoling and encouragement, I seriously doubt this book ever would have been completed.

Many others have contributed more to this effort than they realize. Sam Overman, at the University of Colorado–Denver, planted the notion of "lenses" for seeing organizations and opened my awareness to many of the methodological issues and questions that became Chapter 5. Ed Schein, at the M.I.T. Sloan School, has contributed so much to my thinking about social organization over the years. John Buechner, at the University of Colorado, helped me rekindle my

long-dormant interest in organizational socialization and enculturation. John Sherblom, in the University of Maine's Department of
Speech Communication, introduced me to the then-foreign world of
organization communication. David Rosenbloom, at the University of
Syracuse's Maxwell School, provided timely support. Mary Davis, in
the Department of Community Health at the University of Northern
Colorado, helped me clarify areas of logical inconsistency.

And special appreciation to Pat, Daren, and Terry who tolerated
my turbulent times of authorship, which extended from Colorado to
Maine, and for all of the highway and emotional miles between them.

J. Steven Ott

Contents

LIST OF FIGURES

LIST OF TABLES

CHAPTER 1

The Organizational Culture Perspective

This book is about organizational culture, a phrase that means two different but related things. First, it is the culture that exists in an organization. When the phrase is used in this sense, it means something similar to the culture in a society and consists of such things as shared values, beliefs, assumptions, perceptions, norms, artifacts, and patterns of behavior. It is the unseen and unobservable force that is always behind organizational activities that can be seen and observed. According to Kilmann and associates (1985), organizational culture is a social energy that moves people to act. "Culture is to the organization what personality is to the individual—a hidden, yet unifying theme that provides meaning, direction, and mobilization" (p. ix).[1]

Second, organizational culture is a way of looking at and thinking about behavior of and in organizations, a perspective for understanding what is occurring. When used in this sense, organizational culture refers to a collection of theories that attempt to explain and predict how organizations and the people in them act in different circumstances. For clarity, *organizational culture* is used in this book to mean the culture of an organization, and *the organizational culture perspective* means the use of organizational culture as a frame of reference for the way one looks at, attempts to understand, and works with organizations.

The organizational culture perspective represents a counterculture within organization theory. Its assumptions, theories, and approaches are very different from those of the dominant structural

---

[1]A thorough examination of what organizational culture is, and what it consists of, is presented in Chapters 2 and 3. The brief statement here is intended for introductory purposes only.

and systems perspectives. The organizational culture perspective is challenging the views of the structural and systems perspectives about basic issues: for example, how organizations make decisions, and how and why people in organizations behave as they do.

Organizational culture is the newest and perhaps the most controversial of the organization theory perspectives. Its theories are based on assumptions about organizations and people that depart radically from those of the mainline perspectives. One important difference is that the organizational culture perspective does not believe that quantitative, experimental-type, logical-positivist, scientific research is especially useful for studying organizations.

In the structural and systems perspectives of organization theory, organizations are assumed to be institutions whose primary purposes are to accomplish established goals. Goals are set by people in positions of formal authority. In these two schools of thought, the primary questions for organization theory involve how best to design and manage organizations so that they achieve their declared purposes effectively and efficiently. The personal preferences of organizational members are restrained by systems of formal rules, by authority, and by norms of rational behavior. In a 1982 article Karl Weick, a leading writer about symbolic management, argues that four organizational conditions must exist in order for the basic assumptions of the structuralists and systemists to be valid:

1. A self-correcting system of interdependent people.
2. Consensus on objectives and methods.
3. Coordination is achieved through sharing information.
4. Organizational problems and solutions must be predictable.

However, Weick is forced to conclude that these conditions seldom exist in modern organizations.

ASSUMPTIONS OF THE ORGANIZATIONAL CULTURE PERSPECTIVE

The organizational culture school rejects the assumptions of the modern structural and systems schools. Instead, it assumes that many organizational behaviors and decisions are almost predetermined by the patterns of basic assumptions existing in the organization. Those patterns of assumptions have continued to exist and influence behaviors because they have repeatedly led people to make decisions that usually worked for the organization. With repeated use, the assumptions slowly drop out of peoples' consciousness but continue to influence organizational decisions and behaviors—even when the organization's environment changes. They become the underlying, unquestioned—but virtually forgotten—reasons for "the way we do things here," even when the ways are no longer appropriate. They are so basic, so pervasive, and so totally accepted as the truth that no one thinks about or remembers them. Thus a strong organizational culture controls organizational behavior; for example, it can block an organization from making changes needed to adapt to a changing environment.

From the organizational culture perspective, the personal preferences of organizational members are not restrained by systems of formal rules, authority, and norms of rational behavior. Instead, they are controlled by cultural norms, values, beliefs, and assumptions. In order to understand or predict how an organization will behave under different circumstances, one must know what its patterns of basic assumptions are—its organizational culture.

Every organizational culture is different for several reasons. First, what has worked repeatedly for one organization does not for another, so the basic assumptions differ. Second, an organization's culture is shaped by many factors, including, for example, the societal culture in which it resides; its technologies, markets, and competition; and the personality of its founder(s) or most dominant early leaders. Some organizational cultures are more distinctive than others. Some organizations have strong, unified, pervasive cultures, whereas others have weaker cultures; some organizational cultures are quite pervasive, whereas others have many subcultures in different functional or geographical areas.

RESEARCH BIAS OF THE ORGANIZATIONAL CULTURE PERSPECTIVE

Knowledge of an organization's structure, information systems, strategic planning processes, markets, technology, goals, etc., provides clues about an organizational culture—but not accurately or reliably. As a consequence, an organization's behavior cannot be understood or predicted by studying its structural or systems elements: its organizational culture must be studied. And, the quantitative quasi-experimental research methods used by the structural and systems perspectives *cannot* identify or measure unconscious, virtually forgotten basic assumptions. Van Maanen, Dabbs, and Faulkner (1982) describe a growing wave of disenchantment with the use of quantitative quasi-experimental research methods for studying organizations, mainly because such methods have produced very little useful knowledge about organizations over the last twenty years. Yet quantitative research using quasi-experimental designs, control groups, computers, multivariate analyses, heuristic models, and the like are the essential "tools" of the structural and systems perspectives. More and more the organizational culture perspective is turning to qualitative research methods such as ethnography and participant observation.

The reasons for terming the organizational culture perspective a *counterculture* within the field of organization theory should be becoming evident. The organizational culture perspective believes that the mainstream structural and systems perspectives of organization theory are using the wrong "lenses" to look at the wrong organizational elements in their attempts to understand and predict organizational behavior. Their tools are as ineffective as a hammer is for fixing a leaking pipe. In effect, they are wasting their time.

RADICAL CHANGE IN ORGANIZATIONS

It takes courage to challenge the basic views of a mainstream perspective in any profession or academic discipline. Yet this is just what the organizational culture perspective is doing when it advocates radically different ways of looking at and working with organizations. For example, from the organizational culture perspective, AT&T's basic problems since deregulation and court-ordered splintering of the Bell System are not in its structure, information systems, or people.[2] Rather, they rest in an organizational culture that no longer is appropriate for AT&T's deregulated world. The longstanding AT&T culture has been centered on assumptions about:

- The value of technical superiority.
- AT&T's possession of technical superiority.
- AT&T's rightful dominance in the telephone and telecommunications market.

Working to improve AT&T's goals, structure, differentiation and integration processes, strategic plans, and information systems will not solve AT&T's monumental problems. The solution requires changing an ingrained organizational culture: changing basic unconscious

---

[2]All cases and reportings of field data in this study depict true situations in real organizations. Identities of people and organizations have been concealed except recipients of media coverage—such as in the case of the breakup of the Bell System and Mr. Iacocca's experience at Chrysler Corporation. Factors and events have been omitted from the examples to maintain brevity and focus attention on important variables.

assumptions about what makes for success in a competitive telephone and communications market.[3]

Lee Iacocca (1984) faced a similar problem (but different in its content) when he took over leadership of the Chrysler Corporation. Chrysler was a "loser" in just about every way imaginable—in the eyes of employees, potential employees, investors, car dealers, financiers, suppliers, and car buyers. It was simply *assumed* that Chrysler could not compete head-on. Iacocca had to change not only an organizational culture but also just about everybody's perception of that culture. Chrysler needed and got in Iacocca what Bennis (1984); Bennis and Nanus (1985); Tichy and Ulrich (1984); and Tichy and Devanna (1986) have called a *transformational leader*. A transformational leader is a person who can literally transform an imbedded organizational culture by creating a new vision of and for the organization and successfully *selling that vision* by rallying commitment and loyalty to transform the vision into a reality.

The organizational culture perspective is especially useful for describing, explaining, and, to a limited extent, predicting behavior when organizations are facing fundamental changes, particularly changes involving their identities. This is what I refer to in this book as *radical change*. In order to make this point more real, the chapter appendix presents and briefly analyzes three case studies about radical change in organizations.

The usefulness of the organizational culture perspective is not limited to radical change in organizations. It also is helpful for understanding and predicting a host of other types of holistic organizational phenomena and behaviors involving, for example, employee commitment and loyalty, leadership effectiveness, leadership succession, creativity, and innovation and organizational survival strategies. Furthermore, it seems logical to expect that there are strong relationships between aspects of organizational culture and an organization's productivity and quality of outputs—but the existence of culture-productivity relationships has yet to be established.

Other perspectives of organizations (in other words, other groupings of organization theories) are not well suited for explaining or predicting these kinds of holistic organizational phenomena. Moreover, they are least useful during periods of major organizational change, especially when change in an organization's identity is involved. For now, please accept the unsubstantiated and

---

[3]AT&T's organizational culture is described and discussed further in a case in this chapter's appendix.

oversimplified assertion that other existing perspectives of organizations do not provide the correct "lenses" through which to "see" organizational culture nor the analytical methods for working with it. By analogy, using any other perspective to work with organizational culture is like trying to watch a three-dimensional movie without those special "3-D glasses."

The organizational culture perspective is important to practicing managers as well as students of organizations, for it provides a new approach for viewing, thinking about, analyzing, understanding, explaining, and predicting organizational behavior. For example, the organizational culture perspective is ideal for understanding what happened at AT&T and Chrysler.

Despite its usefulness, the organizational culture perspective has major problems and limitations. First, it is only one of many ways of looking at organizations. It is not the ultimate answer—the magic key for understanding all complexities of organizations. Second, the organizational culture perspective has many problems that reflect its youthfulness. Although the phrase "culture of a factory" was used by Elliott Jaques as long ago as 1952, and "organizational culture" was used by Philip Selznick in 1957, few students of management or organizations paid much attention to organizational culture until about 1978. Even then, the subject typically was addressed narrowly, and the writings did not receive much notice. The turning point for the organizational culture perspective came in 1981 and 1982, when it suddenly became a very "hot" topic in books, journals, and periodicals aimed at both management practitioners and academicians.[4]

The perspective's problems and limitations of youthfulness remain today. Minimal consensus exists about much of anything concerned with organizational culture, even among its proponents. The disagreements start with what an organizational culture is.[5] So, it is no surprise that the debates are even more pronounced and heated about its nature, components, and the appropriate situations and methods for applying the perspective. Lack of agreement about these very basic issues causes serious problems for those inclined to use the organizational culture perspective for managing or studying organizations. It creates doubts about the very legitimacy of the perspective.

To be more concrete: consider a few conflicting views about changing an organizational culture. Should a manager even try to do

---

[4]The References contain myriad examples.

[5]The widely divergent published views about the nature of organizational culture are examined in Chapter 3.

so? If so, what change strategy should be used? For example, Allen and Kraft (1982) are proponents of changing organizational cultures by changing behavioral norms. Davis (1984) disagrees, arguing for chief executive officer-imposed, top-to-bottom, organizationwide change efforts. Schein (1985); Sathe (1985); and Martin and Siehl (1983) all predict failure for any single-strategy organizational culture change program. Schein (1985) cautions that attempts to change organizational cultures can be harmful and, in many situations, should not even be tried.

Leadership provides an excellent second example of the debates. Can a manager change existing leadership styles and practices in an organization by changing the organizational culture, or does one modify the organizational culture by changing leadership practices? Or both? Some writers, including Davis (1984), postulate that dominant, charismatic, organizational founders and chief executive officers are the primary sources, transmitters, and maintainers of organizational cultures. On the other hand, Sergiovanni (1984) describes organizational leadership and the leaders' decision patterns as cultural artifacts. He believes that leaders, leadership styles and practices, and patterns of decisions are created and shaped more by organizational culture than by the leaders themselves.

The youthfulness of the organizational culture perspective is evident in the dearth of comprehensive and integrative writing about it.[6] Schein (1985) and Sathe (1985) bemoaned the problem:

> Unfortunately, most of the writers on organizational culture use different definitions, different methods of determining what they mean by culture, and different standards for evaluating how culture affects organizations. These conceptual and methodological differences make it almost impossible to assess the various claims made (Schein, 1985, p. x).

> Although the importance of corporate culture is now widely acknowledged in both business and academic circles, the available literature leaves something to be desired. . . . This literature is also generally not well grounded in systematic theory and research (Sathe, 1985, p. 1).

Depending on one's viewpoint, the first comprehensive and integrative studies of organizational culture did not appear until 1984 or 1985. There are now only a few such studies. Schein's (1985) *Organizational Culture and Leadership* is the most notable. Sathe's

---

[6]The term *integrative* is used throughout this study in its ordinary sense, meaning multidisciplinary in approach, sources, and methods, and not directed toward justifying, supporting, or proving a single viewpoint.

(1985) *Culture and Related Corporate Realities* is a theoretically sound textbook with readings and cases. Sergiovanni and Corbally's (1984) *Leadership and Organizational Culture* is a stimulating collection of theoretical papers mostly concerned with educational administration.[7] There are several excellent chapters in H. P. Sims, D. A. Gioia, and Associates' (1986) reader, *The Thinking Organization: Dynamics of Organizational Social Cognition.*

As useful as these works are, there has been no serious attempt to present a historical analytical study of the organizational culture perspective in its totality. The situation is equally bleak relative to methods for identifying or deciphering organizational cultures.[8]

Why is there a dearth of good comprehensive integrative writing about organizational culture? The answer requires some reasoned speculation. The first reason has been discussed previously. The perspective is young, and there are few good precedents for researchers and writers to follow and build on. Second, since the late 1960s, the dominant, mainstream perspectives on organizations have assumed that organizations are rational, goal-oriented institutions whose behaviors can be understood by studying their goals, structures, and processes for making decisions. For example, the dominant mainstream perspective, usually termed the *structural and systems school* or the *structural/systems framework* (Bolman and Deal, 1984, chs. 9, 10, and 12) relies on quantitative analytical methods to analyze structures, information, information systems, and decision processes. In contrast, the organizational culture perspective does not assume that organizations are necessarily rational, goal-oriented entities. Whereas the mainstream perspectives tend to work with hard, tangible, quantifiable, organizational variables—often using computer models—the organizational culture perspective focuses on soft, less tangible, more ethereal variables such as basic assumptions, cognitive patterns, values, myths, and unspoken beliefs. Using another analogy, organizational culture is like ordinary air. Usually, it cannot be touched, felt, or seen. It is not noticed unless it changes suddenly. The mainstream perspectives of organizations are not comfortable with air-like variables and concepts. Computerized information systems and statistical, quasi-experimental research methods of the structural and systems perspectives are not designed to mea-

---

[7]Bolman and Deal (1984) provides an excellent but brief overview of the "symbolic framework." Kilmann, Saxton, Serpa, and Associates (1985) contains excellent articles but makes no effort to integrate the information.

[8]Martin and Siehl (1983); Siehl and Martin (1984); Sathe (1985); Harrison (1972); Pettigrew (1979); Van Maanen, Dabbs, and Faulkner (1982); and Van Maanen (1983) have contributed usefully to aspects of the issue.

sure ethereal concepts such as values, myths, and preconscious underlying assumptions.

Thus, the organizational culture perspective is a counterculture within organization theory. The assumptions, theories, and approaches of countercultures are not readily accepted by members of dominant cultures (Kuhn, 1970a, ch. II). They are challenging existing assumptions and beliefs about what is important, how organizations function, and ways of designing and conducting research. It takes courage to advocate new and different ways of looking at and working with organizations—just as the organizational culture perspective is doing.

Third, a comprehensive and integrative study of organizational culture requires analyzing and synthesizing theories and research findings from a wide array of academic disciplines. The task is formidable. Just for starters, the fields of organization theory, archaeology, anthropology, psychology, social psychology, sociology, organizational communication, and even biology contain knowledge, theories, and research methods that are important for understanding organizational culture and using the organizational culture perspective. When one also considers contributions from subdisciplines such as material anthropology, cultural anthropology, learning theory, cognitive social psychology, social constructionism, clinical psychology, and transactional analysis, it becomes readily apparent why few attempts have been made to synthesize it, to "pull it all together."

Despite the problems, or, more important, because of the problems, the need for an integrative, pulling-it-all-together study is evident. The perspective holds too much potential to be ignored or to remain in its current state of rampant disagreement about even its most basic concepts.

The overall purpose for this book is to make usable sense out of organizational culture and the organizational culture perspective by analyzing and synthesizing information from a broad array of existing published sources and from field data collected in several very different institutions. This purpose is ambitious. It can only be accomplished by taking small steps, one at a time. These steps or subpurposes and the chapters in which they are addressed are:

1. *To clarify what organizational culture is, what makes it up, and the functions it performs.*

This purpose is accomplished in several steps. First, Chapter 2 examines the elements that make up different levels of organizational culture, the functions they perform, and their relationships to other elements of organizational culture. Chapter 3 then compares and contrasts, analyzes, and synthesizes divergent viewpoints about the essence of organizational culture and the organizational culture perspective. A classification system or a typology (Miles & Huberman, 1984) is created and used to sort through different concepts, elements, and functions of organizational culture. The typology is the analytical framework used in Chapters 4 through 8.

2. *To analyze how organizational cultures form, develop, are perpetuated and changed, and transmitted to new organization members.*

Where do organizational cultures come from? Why do they differ between organizations engaged in the same line of work? How are they maintained and transmitted to new organization members? Chapter 4 focuses on these questions.

3. *To assess the applicability of different tools and methods for identifying and deciphering organizational culture for different purposes and under different circumstances.*

Selection of a research method for studying organizational culture needs to take such things into account as (a) the purposes for the investigation: for example, an urgent need to increase the viability of an organization facing a crisis that threatens its survival, versus academic research; and (b) the specific concept (or level) of organizational culture that is operational. These are the subjects of Chapter 5.

4. *To trace and analyze the historical evolution of the organizational culture perspective, its concepts, assumptions, methods, and language through the history of organization theory and other academic disciplines.*

In order to appreciate the depth, richness, and potential applicability of the organizational culture perspective, it is necessary to understand its roots and historical development. The historical analysis also raises numerous unanswered research questions. This purpose is addressed in Chapters 6 and 7.

5. *To explore some of the more important practical implications of the organizational culture perspective.*

Chapter 8 concludes this work by merging the theory and realities of organizational culture.

LIMITATIONS

Even if this book is successful in achieving some of these purposes, questions will remain after the last page has been read. Some unanswered questions will mean that things or concepts were not explained clearly. Others will illuminate the boundaries of what we know about the perspective. And some will reflect the limitations of the organizational culture perspective itself.

Children must crawl before they walk, walk before they run. They also must develop through a sequence of levels of moral reasoning ability (Kohlberg, 1968, 1969) and psychological or intellectual development (Piaget, 1973).

> Any development . . . supposes duration, and the childhood lasts longer as the species becomes more advanced; the childhood of a kitten and that of a chick are much shorter than that of the human infant since the human infant has much more to learn (Piaget, 1973, p. 1).

The development of schools of organization theory appears to go through analogous stages. The organizational culture perspective will need to pass through a sequence of developmental steps before it achieves its full potential or becomes a mature perspective. Reaching agreement about what organizational culture is, is the first level—akin to an infant crawling. A definition does not accomplish very much in and of itself, but just like crawling before walking, it is a necessary precondition for advancing to the second developmental level, the level at which organizational cultures can be identified other than through lengthy participant observation.

Once it has become possible to identify or decipher organizational culture with a reasonable amount of effort, the perspective's ability to explain and predict organization behavior—as well as its array of "action tools" for leading effectively and managing organizational change—should expand rapidly. Results of efforts to date to "run" with the organizational culture perspective (to apply it in complex practical situations) while it is still in an early stage of development are predictable (Allen & Kraft, 1982; Davis, 1984; Kilmann, 1984). As with a toddler, its legs are not strong enough; and its sense of balance is not adequate for the task. The organizational culture perspective per se usually is not the problem. Rather, the problem lies in attempting to use the perspective to accomplish that which is beyond its current stage of development.

While a child is in an early stage of moral development, he or she cannot comprehend moral reasoning from more advanced stages—it is beyond the child's mental grasp (Kohlberg, 1968, 1969). Likewise, not enough is known yet about organizational culture and its perspective to appreciate their full potential and, thus, to grasp all that we do not know about them. This book attempts to decrease what is not yet known.

Appendix to Chapter 1

THREE CASES DEPICTING RADICAL CHANGES IN ORGANIZATIONS

With Analyses From the Organizational Culture Perspective

PURPOSES FOR THE CASES

The three cases and the brief analyses serve two primary purposes: first, they demonstrate different aspects of organizational culture and the usefulness of the organizational culture perspective; and second, they provide examples that are used repeatedly throughout the rest of this book. They are presented here so they are ready for use when needed.

CASE 1: AN ORGANIZATIONAL CULTURE THAT BECAME A LIABILITY WHEN THE BUSINESS ENVIRONMENT AROUND AT&T CHANGED SUBSTANTIALLY[1]

The Case

For generations AT&T and its operating telephone companies (the Bell System) were regulated monopolies. Two of the dominant beliefs and basic assumptions that permeated the Bell System included: (a) it was important to provide telephone service to everyone indiscriminately—hence, market segmentation was not a common pattern of thinking or decision making; and (b) technical values were at the core of the Bell System's success—not marketing values.

Since the breakup of the Bell System and the demise of its regulated monopoly status in most of its product and service lines, AT&T and its ex-operating companies have not fared well in the telecommunications marketplace. AT&T's marketing problems have been reported widely in daily newspapers and in business trade journals. A

---

[1]All cases and reportings of field data in this book depict true situations in real organizations. Identities of people and organizations have been concealed except recipients of media coverage—such as in the case of the breakup of the Bell System and Mr. Iacocca's experience at Chrysler Corporation. Factors and events have been omitted from the cases to maintain brevity and focus attention on important variables.

multitude of firms, many of them considerably smaller than AT&T, have successfully cornered lucrative segments of AT&T's voice and data transmission and equipment markets, frequently outmaneuvering AT&T and leaving "Ma Bell" looking like a rather ponderous, uncompetitive dinosaur.

Analysis

From the organizational culture perspective, AT&T's primary problems are not size, structure, intelligence of personnel, or lack of sophistication. For example, AT&T and its former operating companies reportedly have spent millions of dollars developing sophisticated strategic marketing plans. The problem from the organizational culture perspective is AT&T's whole way of viewing and thinking about itself and its world—and thus the way it conducts business. In essence, AT&T's problem is the inapplicability of the old Bell System organizational culture in a new competitive world and AT&T's inability to change its longstanding organizational culture. The problem includes AT&T's unshakable belief in the central value of technical superiority, in its own technical superiority, and thus in its inevitable and "rightful place" in the telecommunications market. The problem is manifested in—but is neither caused by nor limited to—management recruiting and advancement policies, corporate information and control systems, personnel incentive and reward practices, the ways in which groups of customers and potential customers are organized in sales plans, and procedures for clearing new products and services through the organization to the market.

From the organizational culture perspective, AT&T's culture has permeated the organization so completely and for so long that its basic practices, beliefs, values, and ways of thinking have become unquestioned assumptions about the nature of reality. Those assumptions about reality become dysfunctional—counterproductive. When the world changed around the Bell System, the organizational culture did not.

CASE 2: A NEW LEADER'S INABILITY TO CHANGE THE ORGANIZATIONAL CULTURE AT THE MOUNTAIN STATE CHAPTER

The Case

Human Services, Inc., is a highly visible international nonprofit organization that provides recreational programs for people with certain types of disabilities through a network of volunteers. Human

Services, Inc., was originated by one very caring person and her immediate family. The growth of Human Services, Inc., into a national and international organization was accomplished through a network of the founder's friends. During its early years, Human Services, Inc., looked and acted like an extended family.

The growth of the Mountain State Chapter of Human Services, Inc., paralleled that of the national organization. A dedicated handful of relatives and friends of people with the disability formed the Chapter in 1968. Most of the founders became members of the Chapter's first Board of Directors; but they also continued as working volunteers, helping with programs and clients, selling souvenirs and clipping coupons to raise money, distributing flyers, driving people to programs—whatever needed to be done. In 1984, six of the Chapter's thirteen directors were Chapter founders. One founder became the Chapter's first paid executive director in 1972 and remained in that position until 1984.

Prior to 1983, selection of new directors was by recommendation of staff or existing directors. All directors were expected to help out in running Chapter programs. Board of Directors meetings were casual —almost social—events held every two to four weeks. Discussions about family problems and postprogram parties often extended well into the scheduled meeting time. Agendas were still being created as directors arrived for Board meetings, and new items of business frequently were introduced from the floor without warning and often on substantive issues. The paid executive director acted like a member of the Board of Directors. She participated actively in all discussions, refraining only from voting.

Open disagreements among directors were not permitted. When opinions were divided at meetings, the issue in question was simply dropped. Motions were not tabled formally. If the executive director could engineer consensus prior to the next meeting, it was reintroduced. If not, the issue was avoided and not discussed until consensus could be reached.

In 1981, John Thomas, a rapidly climbing manager in a large firm, approached the Mountain State Chapter and asked to become a director. He had no prior involvement with Human Services, Inc., the Chapter, or its client population but thought it was a worthwhile cause and organization for which he would like to volunteer his leadership and managerial skills. He is a highly intelligent, aggressive, energetic, and articulate person whose professional specialties are strategic planning and quantitative analytical methods. The directors were nervous about accepting someone on the Board who had not been involved previously but, by their description, "did not know how to tell him 'no' to his face" when he appeared in person to apply.

In January 1982 Mr. Thomas maneuvered himself adroitly into the Chapter presidency and hand-selected a compliant vice president. On taking office, he announced his intention to "pull the Chapter's management and the Board of Directors into the twentieth century." His priorities for improving Chapter management included introducing computer technology; strategic planning; management by objectives (MBO); financial planning; cash management; staff performance reviews; an incentive-based employee compensation system; and expanded media coverage. The amount of private funding and the number of disabled persons participating in Chapter programs also were to increase substantially.

He announced that the Board of Directors would "start working like a business," using a system of committees to focus its efforts on fund-raising and broad policy issues. It would disinvolve itself from programs and thus from client-related issues. Applicants for the Board of Directors would be solicited from organizations such as the Chamber of Commerce and the Junior League. All candidates would be considered competitively. The Board of Directors would meet only quarterly, relying on the system of committees to conduct business in the interim. Agendas would be distributed at least ten days prior to meetings, and no issue would be discussed unless it was on the agenda. Issues not involving policy or broad strategy would not be discussed at Board meetings.

A scheduled "Board rotation" procedure would be implemented under which no director could remain on the Board for more than one three-year term. Presidents would rotate off the Board after completing one term in office. Two years after rotating off the Board, ex-directors and ex-presidents could apply and compete for another three-year term.

By fall 1982 it was clear that John Thomas could not implement all of his priorities before the expiration of his term (January 1983), so he pushed the end of his term back to June 30, 1983. By May virtually all of his management improvements had been implemented, and he had engineered passage of several of his Board changes, including the very controversial Board rotation policy.

John Thomas resigned from the Board at the expiration of his term in order to demonstrate his commitment to the Board rotation policy. In August 1983 a Board of Directors resolution was introduced from the floor and passed that permitted all existing directors to fill another three-year term. Of the four directors scheduled to rotate off the Board in 1983, only one did so (not including Mr. Thomas). The directors again started to meet several times a month. By November all of Mr. Thomas's management improvements had withered, except an MBO-based employee performance review procedure (because the staff liked it). An obviously never-used microcomputer sat in the back of the Board meeting room with boxes of outdated posters and plastic coffee cups symbolically strewn on and around it.

During John Thomas's term in office, the Mountain State Chapter had increased its income and capital holdings by more than 100 percent, income from improved cash management procedures and investments by more than 75 percent, media coverage of Chapter events by more than 100 percent, the number of disabled persons participating in Chapter programs by 25 percent, staff size by 50 percent, and staff salaries by an average of 14 percent. The Chapter's accomplishments were recognized formally by Human Services, Inc., and Chapter representatives were invited to make presentations at national and regional meetings and conferences. The Chapter received several requests to provide volunteer "consultants" to assist other chapters.

In March 1985 John Thomas submitted a letter asking to be a candidate for the Board of Directors. His name was not among those the nominating committee submitted to the Board of Directors. No one nominated him from the floor.

Analysis

From the organizational culture perspective, John Thomas tried to change the Mountain State Chapter from a caring, nurturing, extended family/support group into an effective and efficient, businesslike organization. While he was physically present he was able to take advantage of the Chapter's behavioral norms to accomplish his ends but not to change the organizational culture. It simply went underground. For example, by forcing votes on controversial changes, he took advantage of the norm that prohibited directors from disagreeing with each other. Although Thomas regularly violated that norm, the others would not. Votes went Thomas's way regularly, but, with few exceptions, other directors' votes did not signal agreement —only conformance to the norm. His programs for improving the Chapter reflected a system of beliefs and values—*a Chapter identity* —that was incompatible with the Chapter's deep and strongly held organizational culture.

What would have happened if John Thomas had not voluntarily rotated off of the Board of Directors in 1983, or if he had appeared in person again to apply for Board membership in 1985? The directors would have had to choose among three alternatives:

1. Violate their norm and fight to protect the Chapter's culture.
2. Continue to conform to the norm and allow the Chapter's culture to be altered.

3. Withdraw from the Chapter, which probably also would have resulted (eventually) in a changed Chapter culture.

CASE 3: INCOMPATIBILITY OF TWO ORGANIZATIONAL CULTURES IN THE PLAINS STATE HEALTH DEPARTMENT

The Case

The Plains State Department of Health ("State Health") has a long and highly respected tradition of honestly and vigorously trying to protect the public from health hazards, substandard and fraudulent health care practices, and excessive health care costs. State Health has regulated providers of health care tightly through a very detailed system of rules and regulations based on very comprehensive state statutes, typically drafted by State Health personnel. There is an unstated but pervasive belief at State Health that health care providers such as hospitals, clinics, nursing homes, and practicing physicians cannot be trusted to act in the public's interest. Only public sector regulatory organizations that do not provide health care can be so trusted.

From 1972 through 1982, the U.S. Public Health Service administered a program of competitive grants for the development of Emergency Medical Services (EMS) systems across the nation. The Public Health Service's EMS program had an entirely different set of beliefs; and the ability of state health departments (and other organizations within states) to obtain grants depended on their acceptance of the Public Health Service's EMS beliefs and values. Primary among them was that only practicing physicians were capable of designing and making systems of medical care work. Government agencies were to fill subordinate administrative roles. Practicing doctors were to be the decision makers. A second (but unspoken) belief was that health care cost containment was less important than the development of a highly sophisticated system of strategically located, expensive, tertiary medical centers (Guillemin & Holmstrom, 1986).

The incompatibility of State Health and Public Health Service EMS values and beliefs caused the Public Health Service to reject State Health's first several grant applications. The applications clearly communicated State Health's antipathy toward Public Health Service EMS beliefs and values. After three years without grant funding, in-state political pressures finally forced State Health to make the necessary "paper concessions."

When State Health's first EMS grants were awarded, serious internal problems began. The EMS Office (in State Health) was designated to administer the grants. In order to comply with Public Health Service EMS grant requirements, the Office invited practicing physicians to help make medical policy decisions: for example, identifying and designating hospitals and physicians capable of treating the most critically ill and injured patients. Potentially, those decisions could affect hospitals' and doctors' abilities to attract patients and also to collect from private and government insurers. Another example of physician involvement in policy decisions was the allocation of EMS grant funds among medical care providers.

A subculture formed rapidly in the EMS Office that was incompatible with State Health's organizational culture. In less than one year the EMS Office and its employees had been socially and professionally isolated from the rest of State Health. The Office director could not obtain even perfunctory support from State Health executives. Requests for meetings were ignored, and scheduled meetings were canceled without notice. Documents requiring timely executive action sat unsigned. State Health executives were "too busy" to make even ritualistic welcoming speeches at EMS meetings and conferences. When avoidance of public forums was impossible, they would speak only to issues unrelated to EMS. State Health executives repeatedly invoked questionably applicable rules and regulations to delay EMS Office activities. The EMS Office was mandated to develop its own comprehensive set of rules to control those health care providers who had been recruited and coopted into the EMS system development processes.

As the EMS Office became more and more deeply involved in the Public Health Service program, even its language and jargon became that of Public Health Service EMS. By 1979, communications between EMS Office employees and other State Health personnel were being impeded by a language barrier as well as by incompatible beliefs and values.

No EMS Office employees were promoted out of the Office between 1978 and 1985 despite the Office's undeniable success in administering a series of large and complex grants. During the same seven-year period, two State Health executives from other offices who had fallen out of higher management's favor were demoted and "pigeonholed" in the EMS Office where "they couldn't cause any harm."

Analysis

From the organizational culture perspective, the problems and their eventual resolution were obvious and predictable. There was a clash between two strong cultures, the dominant State Health culture and the EMS subculture or counterculture. The subculture could survive only as long as Public Health Service grant funds were flowing and, therefore, in-state political pressure was maintained on State Health executives to comply at least superficially with Public Health Service EMS thinking. As the end of the EMS program of grants approached, pressure on the EMS Office to reenter the State Health organizational culture became overwhelming. The Office director resigned. By 1985, no vestiges of the EMS subculture remained—not its beliefs, values, practices, or language. The EMS Office and its programs now are completely reintegrated into the State Health culture.

CHAPTER 2

The Essence and Functions of Organizational Culture

THE IMPORTANCE OF LANGUAGE

Every culture, discipline, perspective, organization, profession, school, and theoretical frame has its own unique set of conceptual components and elements on which its language or jargon is built. The language, then, becomes the medium through which the perspective's concepts, elements, values, and beliefs are communicated. In this sense, a language serves purposes beyond basic communication. Perhaps most important, language controls cognitive patterns—it affects the way people think about things. Morgan, Frost, and Pondy (1983, p. 10) and Evered (1983, p. 126) assert that language defines and shapes reality. Goodall (1984, p. 134) proposes:

> the words and other symbols we use to generate understanding . . . attain the quality of powerful, literal truths. Powerful truths, because they can be used to explain a situation, induce cooperation, or control outcomes, and literal truths because once they are used to inform a perspective they tend to become it.

Greenfield (1984, p. 154) goes further: he contends that "language is power. It literally makes reality appear and disappear. Those who control language control thought, and thereby themselves and others."

For example, the Navajo language contains no words meaning *superior, subordinate, boss,* or *hierarchy.*[1] Navajos historically did not think about and obviously did not respect hierarchical organizational relations. The absence of words for *boss* and *subordinate* symbolizes the Navajo belief that a person is a person. One does not accept orders

---

[1] The information was obtained in a series of personal conversations with managers from the Navajo Nation that took place over the course of about one year.

from another simply because of his or her relative position in an organizational hierarchy. This language/reality has caused serious problems as the Navajo Nation has attempted to develop its economy by attracting and retaining manufacturing enterprises from the non-Navajo world. One would also presume that it has strongly influenced the organizational culture of Caucasian-owned industries that have located in the Navajo Nation. On the other hand, the absence of such words in the language helps the Navajo maintain a core element (basic assumption) of the culture.

The organizational culture perspective is no exception. It possesses its own language and jargon for communicating its concepts, components, and elements that also function to define and maintain its unique realities. The concepts and elements of organizational culture shape the language of the organizational culture perspective, and the language in turn solidifies the perspective's concepts of organizational realities. Thus, the language of organizational culture is both an artifact of the organizational culture perspective and a shaper or controller of its assumptions, thoughts, beliefs, and concepts. "Kenneth Burke once said he was suspicious of communication studies done in the 'Burkeian tradition' because they 'focus on what people do with symbols, rather than on what symbols do to us'" (Goodall, 1984, p. 134). (Language is discussed more completely in the "Artifacts" section later in this chapter.)

This chapter examines the most important elements and functions of organizational culture, what Vijay Sathe (1985) calls "the stuff" of organizational culture. The chapter is organized into sections that correspond to the levels of organizational culture defined in Chapter 3, starting with the most concrete level (artifacts) and working up to the most abstract level (unspoken basic assumptions). However, it is impossible to appreciate the significance of any organizational culture elements and functions without an understanding of symbols and symbolism. Thus the discussion begins with an introduction to these two concepts.

SYMBOLS

Symbols are signs that connote meanings greater than themselves and express much more than their intrinsic content. They are invested with specific subjective meanings. Symbols embody and represent wider patterns of meaning and cause people to associate conscious or unconscious ideas that in turn endow them with their deeper, fuller, and often emotion-invoking meaning. A sign may be anything: a word or phrase, policy, flag, building, office, seating arrangement, picture of a chief executive officer, or computer terminal. Any sign can be the raw material for symbol creation when a group of people subjectively invest it with broader meaning and significance (Morgan, Frost & Pondy, 1983).

Consider a few signs-turned-symbols from the organizations described in the cases in the appendix to Chapter 1.

The Mountain State Chapter

Immediately after John Thomas maneuvered himself into the presidency of the Mountain State Chapter, he initiated a series of efforts designed to "pull the Chapter's management and the Board of Directors into the twentieth century." Management systems improvements and scheduled rotation of members off the Board of Directors were two of Thomas's major focuses. Successful implementation of his "improvements" would have destroyed the Chapter's cultural identity as a caring, extended family-like, direct client-involved, support system.

Microcomputers became symbols, reminding people of John Thomas's change efforts—of a serious threat to the survival of the Chapter's culture—its very identity. Thus, a microcomputer was left sitting on a table in the back of the Board of Directors' meeting room as a highly visible symbol of John Thomas's efforts to destroy the caring, extended family-like culture of the Mountain State Chapter. It was an artifact of an unwanted, feared, counterculture. Shortly after Thomas voluntarily rotated off the Board, someone strewed outdated posters and styrofoam coffee cups on and around it. More than a year later, no one had removed the computer or the debris. It was never discussed or rearranged. Collectively the computer and the mess symbolized a successfully defeated enemy incursion, a victory for the cherished, caring, extended family-type organizational culture. It also was left untouched as a visible reminder for Board members to remain on guard against any future threats.

Whereas the computer with its piled debris was a tangible artifact-become-symbol, "Board rotation" was a verbal symbol that carried equally deep meaning. The phrase *Board rotation* signified the forced severance of longstanding personal bonds among members of an important support group. More than three years after the John Thomas resignation, a member of the Chapter's Board of Directors sat near me at a meeting of a different organization. When someone used the phrase *Board rotation,* the director flinched involuntarily, and red splotches appeared on his upper neck. He turned to look knowingly at me. Later at lunch, without my raising the subject, he told me about the horrible feelings he still experienced whenever he heard these words. It was with obvious discomfort that he uttered them out loud.

State Health

There is an unstated but pervasive belief at State Health that health care providers (such as hospitals, clinics, nursing homes, and practicing physicians) cannot be trusted to act in the public's interest. Only public sector planning and regulatory organizations that do not provide health care can be so trusted. Thus, for executives at State Health, a private physician sitting in the front of a room in the State Health Department building, chairing an official, State Health-sanctioned policy advisory committee meeting, carried intense symbolic meaning—core assumptions of the organizational culture were being violated.

In 1976, the Emergency Medical Services (EMS) Office of State Health started to pursue federal grants from the U.S. Public Health Service (PHS). PHS's fundamental beliefs, values, and assumptions were directly opposite those of the State Health culture: PHS believed that *only* practicing physicians were capable of designing and making systems of medical care work. Government agencies were to fill subordinate administrative roles. Practicing doctors were to be the decision makers. Thus, executives at State Health had resisted pursuing the EMS grants, yielding reluctantly only under heavy local political pressure.

State Health executives used actions as symbols. When the EMS Office was racing to meet a suddenly changed grant application deadline, a State Health executive "borrowed" one of two Office secretaries for a day to fold and staple copies of the State Health newsletter. The borrowing was done over a lunch hour when no other Office personnel were present to help the secretary object. By the time the Office director returned from lunch, the borrowing executive had left the building for the rest of the day. Her secretary refused to release the EMS Office secretary without permission from the executive.

The symbolic message was unmistakable. State Health did not want to have the EMS grants because of the negative counterassumptions and values associated with them. Protection of State Health's cultural values was more important than the $1.5 million dollars a year the grants would bring into the state for at least five years. However, in-state political pressures to get the grants prohibited State Health executives from overtly blocking the pursuit of them.

Obstructions had to be subtle. As in the case of the borrowed secretary, the obstruction could be explained away easily to an outsider (if necessary) as an oversight by another secretary or as an unfortunate consequence of understaffing at State Health: "If only the legislature would . . . these types of situations would never occur. It was not aimed at or unique to the EMS Office." Yet everyone inside State Health knew exactly what the symbolic message was.

Symbols and symbolism—the management of symbols in an organization—are central to organizational culture. They help create, maintain, and transmit shared meanings, realities, and truths within organizations. Because the meaning of a symbol goes beyond the intrinsic content of the readily visible or audible sign—and because meaning is created subjectively by members of an organization, often over a long period of time—the true significance of a symbol rarely is apparent to an outsider or organizational newcomer.

This introduction to symbols and symbolism provides a frame of reference to begin an exploration of the essence of organizational culture and the functions it performs. The exploration starts with relatively concrete artifacts and works up to the rather abstract basic underlying assumptions.

ARTIFACTS

Artifacts include material and nonmaterial objects and patterns that intentionally or unintentionally communicate information about the organization's technology, beliefs, values, assumptions, and ways of doing things. A few examples of material artifacts are documents (such as annual reports, internal memoranda, organizational brochures, and sales pieces); physical layouts or arrangements (for example of offices, distances between working areas, dividers or walls between offices, private or shared working spaces, open or closed doors, and leisure-time facilities); furnishings (such as carpeting, sizes of desks, and pieces of art on walls); patterns of dress or dress codes; company cars; and so on.

Some artifacts reflect and provide useful information about an organization's technology, such as computers on desks; centrally located equipment or machinery; the density and locations of filing cabinets (for example, centralized or dispersed in private offices); and the complexity of the telephone system—things that archaeologists and anthropologists would call the primeval carpenter's or the modern executive's tools of the trade.

Nevertheless, not all artifacts are tangible things. Patterned behavior can be an artifact and thus a symbolic representation of the culture. Organizational language, jargon, metaphors, stories, myths, and jokes can be artifacts. Patterns of administrative behavior and organizational leadership are beginning to be described as cultural artifacts rather than expressions of individual leadership styles or patterns of behavior (Sergiovanni, 1984). It is not difficult to make a convincing argument that organization charts often are nothing more than artifacts—symbolic representations used to satisfy expectations of important constituencies inside and outside organizations, such as environmental protection groups, minority protection groups, and womens' advocacy groups. They are not working descriptions of organizational realities (Meyer, 1984). Thomas Greenfield (1984) argues that organizations themselves—as totalities—are cultural artifacts, "systems of meaning that can be understood only through the interpretation of meaning" (p. 150).

Artifacts may be symbols or merely signs. When they are nothing more than signs, they serve rational-functional purposes: computers process information, and executives borrow others' secretaries to get needed work done. When artifacts are symbols, they serve symbolic purposes first and rational-functional purposes only secondarily or not at all. It is in this manner that symbols and symbolism are crucial to the organizational culture perspective. They help create, maintain, and transmit shared meanings and perceptions of truths and realities within organizations. This last point needs to be understood clearly. From the organizational culture perspective, meaning, reality, and truth are social constructions—they exist as meanings, realities, and truths only because members of the organization collectively have defined them as such.[2] If truth, meaning, and reality were absolutes, there would be no organizational culture perspective.

Chapter 3 concludes that there are "three and one-half" conceptual levels of organizational culture. One of these is *artifacts*. According to one school of thought, *artifacts are the culture* (Hodder, 1982). However, most proponents of the organizational culture perspective prefer to use one of the higher definitional levels, either *beliefs and values* or *basic underlying assumptions*. For them, artifacts are (a)

---

[2]Among those who have written on this point from the cognitive social psychology and/or social constructionist frame of reference are Ball (1972); Bates (1984); Belcher and Atchison (1976); Bleicher (1980); Bougon, Weick, and Binkhorst (1977); Duncan and Weiss (1979); Eiser (1980); Geertz (1973); Greenfield (1984); Hunt (1984); Martin and Siehl (1983); Meyer and Rowan (1977, 1978); Pfeffer (1981b), Pfeffer and Salancik (1974); Pondy and Mitroff (1979); Sergiovanni (1984); and Weick (1969, 1976, 1977, 1979). Many of these acknowledge Berger and Luckmann (1966) and, to a lesser extent, Rosenberg and Hovland (1960); Eiser (1980); and Festinger (1954) as their theoretical/conceptual sources.

the maintainers and transmitters of shared meanings and perceptions of truths and realities within organizations; and (b) the readily
visible; audible; and/or tangible products (or results) of the organizational culture, from which the culture may be inferred—if the investigator is careful and also uses additional information from the other
levels. From these perspectives, artifacts are not only the relatively
passive products or results of culturally influenced behavior but also
simultaneously the functionally and/or symbolically active support
systems for the culture.

These two roles of artifacts help to explain why seemingly non-
functional artifacts continue to survive in organizations. From an
organizational culture perspective, *nothing* survives in an organization unless it serves purposes. Therefore, artifacts that do not serve
rational-functional purposes but continue to survive, such as the
unused microcomputer covered with old posters and coffee cups in the
back of the Board meeting room at the Mountain State Chapter (and
the equally unused Equal Employment Opportunity [EEO] offices in
many organizations), almost undoubtedly are serving important
symbolic purposes.

To the extent that artifacts are relatively passive products or
results of an organizational culture, they are easily identified (but
unreliable) indicators of the organizational culture. For example, an
organization's programs usually are visible manifestations or representations of its cultural beliefs, values, and assumptions. They are
artifacts, and, according to Stanley Davis (1984), they are "like
pottery shards; each fragment has much to tell about the culture. . . .
This is why it is tempting to collect information about specific
programs and to shy away from the harder task of interpreting the
values and beliefs that lie behind them" (p. 12). (We will return to
this subject in Chapter 5.)

Language: An Artifact, Communicator of Culture, and Shaper of Thought Patterns

Language is an absolutely integral and complex element of
organizational culture. It fills two very significant theoretical and
practical roles. In its more obvious role, language is something that
must be learned by organization members in order to communicate
effectively and, therefore, "get along." An organizational newcomer
or an outside observer will find much communication incomprehensible and will be unable to communicate on an equal footing. Sometimes an organization's language resembles the language of its dominant technology, such as electronics engineering or accounting. At
State Health, a government agency that regulates health care provid-

ers, the language blends the languages of health care economics, legalese, and administrative practices. Most organizations' languages, however, have unique words, phrases, and acronyms that are unrecognizable even to others who have backgrounds in the same technology.

Most organizations have formal and informal ways to instruct newcomers in the language of the organization—the unique terminologies, codes, acronyms, and sign systems, as well as the symbols and metaphors that convey the culture of the particular organization. The more formal instructional methods include orientation sessions, apprenticeships or designated mentor relationships, and training programs. Thus police departments typically assign fresh recruits to ride with and be "broken in" by veterans (Van Maanen, 1976).

A common language also serves to quickly identify members of a social group or subgroup. Those who do not speak the language or the jargon are identified easily as outsiders. Kanter (1983) and Kanter and Stein (1979) have shown that many organizations have systematically excluded women and minority group members from participation in highly visible, upward mobility-promoting settings (such as interdivisional, multiple-level task forces working on significant organizational plans) because of race or sex. The exclusion has prevented members of these groupings from learning the language needed to be identified as having upward mobility potential, and thus they are excluded from subsequent upward mobility-promoting settings.

Cultural anthropologists have always viewed language as an artifact and as an active shaper or controller of thoughts and concepts. For example, currently there is wide consensus among American Indian educators that tribal cultures cannot be maintained without also preserving use of language. And, without words for *boss, supervisor, subordinate,* and *hierarchy,* Navajos cannot be expected to revere directives from higher organizational authorities.

The repeated use of the words *meaning, concept,* and *perception* in this chapter reflects the central importance of language in the organization culture perspective. Organizationally related concepts, meanings, and perceptions, all of which are *socially constructed,* are made available to the mind through language. They are communicated to others through verbal, written, or sign language.

According to Goodall (1984, p. 139), even

> the evolution of (organization communication) research seems to be characterized by a tortuous passage from managerially-informed, scientifically-constructed, hierarchically-consumed studies focused on *attitudes toward communications* . . . to a transition period marked by the introduction of phenomenologically informed, cultural anthropologic-

ally constructed studies of *meaning* as perceived by the researchers and occasionally by the experiencers. (Emphasis in original text.)

Without language, it would be impossible to communicate the concept of the color green. Without a concept (truth, meaning, or reality) of green, it would be impossible to determine that frogs are green.

Jones & Jones, CPAs, is an independent certified public accounting firm with about twenty-five employees.[3] At Jones & Jones, the word *client* is never used by itself. Within the company office (hopefully, but not always, with no clients present), clients are called "assholes." *Asshole* is used as a word by itself, in the context of: "An asshole just called and . . . ", or (a frequent phrase), "Clients are assholes." The word is used metaphorically, not analogously. Thus you do not hear, "That client acts like an asshole." The language metaphor reflects a fundamental truth at Jones & Jones: clients *are* assholes, they don't just act like them. New members of the firm learn the language—and the company's truth—quickly.

Language affects thought patterns and concepts: it can require or prevent patterns of thought. Language, as symbolic representation, has strange effects on us. At Jones & Jones, the language virtually requires organization members to think of clients as assholes. In Navajo Land, the language prevents people from thinking about hierarchical reporting relationships. This is why Greenfield (1984) asserts that language is power, a force that makes reality appear and disappear. "Those who control language control thought, and thereby themselves and others" (p. 154).

Like the tangible artifacts, language is both a product of the culture and a maintainer and transmitter of it. However, as was described earlier, language is most central to the organizational culture perspective because of its power or influence over thought and perceptions of reality.[4]

---

[3] All cases and reportings from field research presented in this book depict true situations in real organizations. Identities of people and organizations have been concealed except those that have received media coverage—such as in the Bell System case, which was presented in the appendix to Chapter 1.

[4] Many of the works that stress the significance of language in the organizational culture perspective acknowledge the cognitive social psychologists, such as Eiser (1980) and Rosenberg and Hovland (1960), and social constructionists, such as Berger and Luckmann (1966). Additional frequently cited influential sources include Hayakawa (1953, 1961); Edelman (1964, 1971, 1977); and Pondy (1978).

A few organization theorists who have emphasized the importance of language include Pondy and Mitroff (1979); Ackoff and Emery (1972); and Pfeffer (1981b). Pondy and Mitroff (1979) view language and the creation of shared meanings as the key elements in the cultural model of organization. Ackoff and Emery (1972) have extended

Jargon: The Shorthand of Language. *Jargon* concentrates meaning into a few words that do not mean the same thing in the language of the organization as they do in everyday English. Jargon is, in essence, the shorthand of an organization's language, cramming as much meaning as possible into a word or phrase that tends to be incomprehensible to those not members of the organizational culture. Jargon simplifies the process of communicating among those who know it—but it complicates things for outsiders and newcomers.

At State Health, where it is believed that health care providers cannot be trusted to act in the public interest, *physician involvement* is a jargon phrase meaning "token representation of private practitioners in groups and meetings that do not deal with policy issues." At Scenic Mountain State College,[5] a small rural state college (and with increasing frequency at other institutions of higher education), *college relations* means "a more acceptable term for fund-raising and public relations in a college or university" (Ott & Shafritz, 1986, p. 77).

Metaphors. *Metaphors,* such as *asshole* at Jones & Jones, CPAs, are powerful forms of organizational language because they communicate symbolic meaning beyond the obvious content of the words. *The Random House Dictionary of the English Language: The Unabridged Edition* defines a metaphor as "the application of a word or phrase to an object or concept which it does not literally denote, in order to suggest comparison with another object or concept, as in 'A mighty fortress is our God.'" Metaphors are more potent communicators of symbolic meaning than analogies. Analogies simply denote a partial similarity between parallel features of two things on which a comparison may be based, for example, "a heart is similar to a pump." The metaphoric phrase is stronger: "the heart is a pump," and "clients are assholes."

Metaphors are basic to the intellectual processes humans use to determine truth, facts, and meaning (Nietzsche, 1968). They help people organize and make meaning out of experiences. Metaphors help organization members put meaning into things they experience

---

Boulding's (1968) "level 7 systems" to include human "level 7 systems" as self-conscious language users. Pfeffer (1981b) identifies language, symbolism, and rituals as the important elements in the process of developing shared systems of belief and meaning.

Recent contributions also are appearing in the literature of organizational communication. See for example, Goodall (1984); Ott (1987); and Pacanowsky and O'Donnell-Trujillo (1983).

[5]See Footnote 3

and resolve apparent contradictions and paradoxes they encounter. Metaphors help organizations tie their parts together into meaningful wholes. That is, they "help to organize the objective facts of the situation in the minds of the participants" (Pondy, 1983, p. 157). On the downside, metaphors are potent controllers of thought. "They may also act like fly bottles, to keep us trapped in invisible prisons" (Bates, 1984, p. 264).

While I was interviewing a manager at Jones & Jones, the telephone intercom started to buzz repeatedly. When the manager finally could not ignore it any longer, he picked up the phone, listened to the secretary for a moment, and said, "Tell the asshole I'll call back." The interviewee turned to me apologetically and said, "Sorry. It was a client. I *told* my secretary not to interrupt us." Accountants at Jones & Jones did not use analogies nor did they qualify or condition the metaphor. Its use was not restricted by organization level, functional area, or sex of the utterer or recipient. I observed its use in the presence of new organization members. Reportedly, it has been used loudly in the halls when clients were present in the offices.

Jones & Jones provides a wonderful example of a clear relationship between the metaphor *asshole* and several basic organizational culture assumptions.[6] As one would expect, the assumptions had grave negative consequences. Jones & Jones's high rate of client turnover has been its single most serious business problem. Conceivably, high client turnover caused the metaphor to be coined. More likely, however, it was the other way around. Regardless of which came first, the metaphor and the negative beliefs/values it communicates clearly are causing problems. But no member of the firm was

---

[6]For example, I administered Mark Alexander's *Organizational Norms Opinionnaire* (1977) to the employees of Jones & Jones. (A copy of the instrument is in Chapter 5, Appendix 1.) The *Opinionnaire's* lead-in question asks: If an employee in your organization were to . . . most other employees would:

    A. Strongly agree with or encourage it.
    B. Agree with or encourage it.
    C. Consider it not important.
    D. Disagree with or discourage it.
    E. Strongly disagree with or discourage it.

Item #27 (of 42) states:

    "sometimes see the customer or client as a burden or obstruction to getting the job done. . ."

The responses at Jones & Jones universally were either *B* or *A*, which reinforced the interview findings about the pervasiveness of the use of the pejorative metaphor—and the value/attitude it communicates clearly.

aware of the possibility of a connection between the metaphor and client turnover until I suggested it.

As is the case with all artifacts, metaphors are both products of and maintainers/transmitters of the organizational culture. Geertz (1973) describes them as models of the situation and models for the situation. Bates (1984) places so much emphasis on the importance of metaphors that he defines organizational culture as "the links between language, metaphor, and ritual and their celebration of particular social ideals or myths" (p. 268).

Myths: Extended Metaphors.   *Myths* are extended metaphors. The story contained in a myth has a metaphoric relationship to real events (Pondy, 1983, p. 159). In order to qualify as a myth, part of its story must be questionably historically accurate, and its content must focus on the origins or development of the beliefs and values of the organizational culture (Cohen, 1969). Myths are about events alleged to have taken place long ago and thereby serve to link the past, present, and future (Levi-Strauss, 1963, p. 208). Interestingly, organizational myths often depict pure fantasies; and members know they are inaccurate but continue to relate them (Pondy, 1983). The known falsehood appears to add to rather than detract from the cultural functions of myths. Those functions include maintaining and expressing solidarity among organization members; legitimating practices (like violating rules); and "validating the rituals of the tribe" (Martin, 1982, p. 263).

People at the Community Center (a nonprofit agency that arranges for the provision of human services to persons with developmental disabilities and that is funded exclusively with public monies) smiled knowingly and laughed while relating rather outrageous organization myths to each other in my presence, clearly communicating that they knew they were perpetuating falsehoods, and they were not concerned about hiding their deceit. *Myths are too important for people to be embarassed about factual inaccuracy.* One of the most frequently heard myths at the Community Center is about a woman manager who would arrange to sleep with the administrator of a state agency who had the power to allocate discretionary funds whenever the Community Center was short on funds (which was the case frequently). The myth conveys important messages about organizational beliefs and values to new members and functions as an important reminder to veterans. The messages include the irrationality of the Community Center's environment (including its primary funding source); that facts and logic are not useful tools for dealing with the environment (obtaining funds); creative self-sacrifices are required of staff to help keep the Community Center afloat; and violations of formal channels, procedures, and rules are encouraged, if they benefit the Community Center and its clients.

Stories. *Organizational stories* are anecdotes about sequences of events in an organization's history. They are similar to myths in form and function but are, or are perceived to be, historically accurate (Wilkins, 1983). Current or past organization members play the leading roles; and the stories always have morals that reflect important organizational beliefs, values, and basic assumptions (Martin & Siehl, 1983, p. 59). Typically, stories communicate their morals metaphorically; and the morals usually speak to core elements of an organization's culture, philosophies, policies and/or practices.[7] In order to qualify as an organizational story, the narrative should have a plot or plots complete with crises and happy endings; central characters including heroes; and an organizational context (Bower, 1976).

Stories communicate their core messages implicitly, metaphorically, and usually symbolically. They tend to have greater impacts on attitudes than most other forms of verbal communication. Their messages are retained longer by organization members when they are transmitted in stories than through more explicit and less vivid communication modes. Thus Martin (1982) contends that stories should be used when new employees are learning the ropes of an organization (p. 261), or when an attempt is being made to form a counterculture or to change an organizational culture (Martin & Siehl, 1983).

All new employees in the Emergency Medical Services (EMS) Office at State Health—the Office that successfully pursued Public Health Service grants that violate State Health cultural beliefs and assumptions about physicians not acting in the public interest—are told the story about a senior State Health executive "borrowing" one of the EMS Office's two secretaries just before a grant application deadline, without asking or telling the Office Chief or anyone else in the Office (*a plot with a crisis*). Receipt of the EMS grant would require the EMS Office to regularly violate State Health's cultural beliefs and values (*establishment of a counterculture*); the grant was being pursued only because political pressure had been brought to bear on State Health executives (*organizational context*). The grant application was completed and submitted on time only because the EMS Office Chief (*hero*) used funds from a consulting contract to get

---

[7]For further discussions of organizational stories, see, for example, Martin (1982); Martin and Powers (1983); Martin and Siehl (1983); and Wilkins (1983).

and pay for part-time clerical help. Using consultant funds for clerical help was illegal (*another crisis*); so the part-timer worked at her home, and her involvement was successfully kept secret (*a happy ending*).

Heroes. *Heroes* are the leading actors in organizational stories. They personify the values and epitomize the strengths of an organization and its culture (or counterculture). They help to reinforce and maintain the culture by setting standards of behavior and providing performance role models. They provide living proof of the importance and viability of the morals embedded in organizational stories. The EMS Office Chief was the hero in the State Health story, the person who took substantial personal risks while steering the EMS Office through crises to successfully achieve a valued end.

Organizational Scripts. *Organizational script* is a phrase from cognitive social psychology that refers to the backbone of an organizational story, the core theme that makes a story more than just a story. A script is the stripped-down skeleton of a story. It contains a setting, an organizational context, a plot with a sequence of events, and central characters with roles. Most important, however, scripts are generalized and contain *slots* or general concepts that are filled with appropriate "instantiations of the content" (Martin, 1982b, p. 283). As conditions arise in which the basic script is applicable or needed, a story is created from it (or draped over the skeleton) that communicates morals reflecting beliefs, values, and/or basic assumptions specific to the incident or need of the moment.

The script for the story about a State Health executive "borrowing" an EMS Office secretary at a crucial time—just as a major grant submittal deadline was approaching—would read something like this:

> When State Health executives fear that basic tenets of the organizational culture will be violated but cannot overtly stop the threatening action, they will take steps to undermine the threat surreptitiously. The undermining will be a defensible action that cannot be directly challenged successfully. In order to make progress in this EMS Office counterculture, one must circumvent such blockages, illegally if necessary, and carefully conceal the circumvention. You have permission—indeed the obligation—to do the same.

Scripts are predictive: they are self-fulfilling prophecies. Abelson (1976) defines a script as "a coherent sequence of events expected by the individual" (p. 34), which highlights a most important function of scripts: allowing organization members to know or predict how people and/or the organization will act under different circumstances. While an organization is living out its script, members know what to expect; so it is safe to focus their attention elsewhere. Scripts provide previews of future incidents, individual and organizational responses, and the consequences of each. They function like the automatic pilot of an airplane, causing things to happen by predicting their occurrence.

The core element in a script is a *vignette,* which Abelson defines as "an encoding of an event of short duration, in general including both an image (often visual) of the perceived event and a conceptual representation of the event" (p. 34).

Sagas and Legends. *Sagas* and *legends* are collections of stories about organizations' histories that provide useful information about an organizational culture. In the premiere study to date of organizational sagas, Clark (1970) analyzed the sagas or legends that evolved during critical stages (turning points) in the histories of Antioch, Swarthmore, and Reed Colleges. Clark used sagas to assess why these three colleges became and remained distinctive. He focused on sagas as the primary method the three schools used to communicate their distinctive qualities effectively to employees, alumni/ae, the general public, and potential contributors. "The organization with a saga is . . . first of all a matter of the heart, a center of personal and collective identity" (p. 9).

Clark (1970) provides perceptive insights into how and why sagas not only communicate important information but also build allegiance, commitment, and emotional investment. *They fuse individual and organizational identities.* A saga, which Clark identifies as something in between an ideology and a religion, accomplishes these ends by capturing allegiance and committing the staff to the college and its central themes. "Deep emotional investment binds participants as comrades in a cause. . . . An organizational saga turns an organization into a community, even a cult" (p. 235).

Ceremonies and Celebrations

Ceremonies are *celebrations* of an organizational culture's values and basic assumptions. They celebrate the accomplishments of heroes and the defeat of threats to the organizational culture. Ceremonies place the culture on display. They are somewhat extraordinary experiences that usually are remembered vividly by employees. "Ceremonies are to the culture what the movie is to the script . . . or the dance is to values that are difficult to express in any other way" (Deal &

Kennedy, 1982, p. 63). Ceremonies and celebrations give meaning to organizational events.

Jones & Jones stages three major annual ceremonies to celebrate events. The first is a paid annual company trip for all employees and their spouses or significant others to celebrate the end of each tax season. The second is an annual party for all employees and clients to celebrate the company's move from second-rate to first-class office space. The move symbolizes the firm's successful establishment in the most prestigious (and profitable) segment of the public accounting profession. The third is a party open to employees only, celebrating the simultaneous resignations of a partner and a senior manager. The two had generated deep conflict and divisions while attempting to steer Jones & Jones into specializing in a different segment of public accounting.

Ceremonies are symbolic conveyors of meaning to important internal and external constituencies or stakeholders (Mitroff, 1983). The complex process of searching for and selecting a new university president communicates symbolic messages about the importance of the position and of the groups who participate in the search. Inaugural ceremonies (and firing ceremonies) often are used to placate powerful internal and external constituencies by symbolically communicating the reaffirmation of existing university directions and policies or a commitment to change them.[8]

Summary: Artifacts

Artifacts are material and nonmaterial objects and patterns that intentionally or unintentionally communicate information about the organization's technology, beliefs, values, assumptions, and ways of doing things. Artifacts may be symbols or merely signs. When they are only signs, they serve rational-functional purposes—as, for example, when computers process information or executives borrow secretaries to get work done. When artifacts are symbols, they serve symbolic purposes first and rational-functional purposes only secondarily (or not at all). It is in this way that symbols and symbolism are so crucial to organizational culture: they help create, maintain, and transmit shared meanings and perceptions of truths and realities.

Artifacts also are helpful for studying organizational culture. They can be identified readily, often just by looking or listening. They

---

[8]For extensive discussions of organizational ceremonies see, for example, Gephart (1978) and Pfeffer (1981b), or in a less academic vein, Deal and Kennedy (1982).

provide clues about the less tangible, more ethereal levels of organizational culture; but it is dangerous to rely on artifacts for inferring an organization's values, beliefs, or basic assumptions. There are too many opportunities to misinterpret the relationship between artifacts and the higher levels of organizational culture. "Artifacts are tangible, and it is possible to 'get your arms around them.' This is why it is tempting . . . to shy away from the harder task of interpreting the values and beliefs that lie behind them" (Davis, 1984, p. 12).

PATTERNS OF BEHAVIOR

Every organization has patterns of routinized activities, such as rites and rituals, which through repetition communicate information about the organization's technology, beliefs, values, assumptions, and ways of doing things. Patterns of behavior are things that members of an organizational culture continue to do (or that cause members to continue to do things), often without thinking. They include such familiar management practices as holding staff meetings, training, filling out forms, and conducting employee performance appraisals.

Rites and Rituals

Whereas ceremonies are conscious celebrations of values and basic assumptions, *rites* and *rituals* are more like habits with roots in those same cultural values and basic assumptions. They are the mundane, systematic, stylized, and programmed routines of daily organizational life that tell an alert observer much about an organizational culture. Bernstein (1975) and Popkewitz (1982) observe that rituals provide members with security, establish meaning and identity within organizations, and function as mechanisms of control.

The meanings and relationships represented in rituals often are both metaphorical and visible manifestations of relative power. Thus all personnel at the Community Center for Developmental Disabilities ritualistically route even the most mundane outgoing letters to the director, Bill Snow, a retired Army officer and a very authoritarian-style manager, for his signature. When they need to talk with him, they stand at his door silently until he invites them in. Even if he does not notice or acknowledge their presence for several minutes, they will not speak or enter until invited.

Bates (1984) found rituals to be so powerful and conformity to them so complete "as to govern movement, time, place, language, sequences of activity, participant's response, and the use of artifacts, their shape, the metaphors they utilize, and the symbols that guide responses" (p. 267). Frequently, the meanings and purposes of powerful rites and rituals are forgotten and take on lives of their own.

Pierre Boulle (1959) wrote a superbly believable fictional account of rites and rituals that took on lives of their own. The senior clerk at a British rubber plantation in North Africa continued to keep the most detailed and trivial corporate records even as the German army was approaching during World War II. He insisted upon taking along a large filing cabinet as the British plantation employees fled from the German army in small lifeboats. Life without corporate rituals, records, and files was unthinkable.

When rites and rituals take on lives of their own, their functional purposes become lost. They survive only for the symbolic purposes they serve—providing stability for members by communicating and perpetuating the organizational culture.

Behavioral Norms

While artifacts, rites, and rituals are objects and patterns that reflect, maintain, and communicate information about organizational culture, *norms* are more important. They are so pivotal to organizational culture that a few authors have defined norms *as* organizational culture (in fact or by inference) (Allen & Kraft, 1982; Hall, 1977).

Norms are prescriptions for behavior that exist in every social context, including organizations and work groups in organizations. Norms are behavioral blueprints for organization members in general and for people who fill specific roles. Schmuck (1971) contends that norms provide organizations with structure and coherence. Organization members behave in patterned and predictable ways "because their behaviors are guided by common expectations, attitudes, and understandings. . . . norms are strong stabilizers of organizational behavior" (pp. 215–216).

As standards of expected and allowed behavior and speech, norms may or may not reflect cultural beliefs and values. They deal with patterns of overt behavior. They are organizational sea anchors, providing predictability and stability.

For example, at the Mountain State Chapter, the nonprofit organization where its new president, John Thomas, tried to institute management changes that would have destroyed its extended family-like culture, open disagreements are prohibited at Board meetings. This is a norm. It reflects a deeply cherished and strongly held organizational culture value: the Board of Directors should be a supportive extended family, and open disagreements endanger the extended family. The norm was so strong that even though John Thomas was trying to change the very character or identity of the Chapter, the other directors would not violate it. A few other norms at the Chapter included: the executive director was expected to participate in Board discussions and had status and rights equal to the directors; Board meetings did not start until all directors were through discussing personal issues and problems; and, Board deliberations about problems involving participants in programs took priority over all other issues. Thus, much could be inferred about the Mountain State Chapter's organizational culture by observing its directors' norms.

Despite the importance of norms, they are not the organizational culture per se. They are artifacts—behavioral artifacts—that have evolved from and help maintain an organizational culture. They are part of the culture—but they are not the culture.[9]

Summary

Patterns of organizational behavior, including rites, rituals, and behavioral norms, have been separated from discussions of other artifacts because they represent a slightly higher level of organizational culture. They are somewhat more complex in nature and, from a managerial viewpoint, they perform perhaps more important functions in an organizational culture (particularly behavioral norms). Nevertheless, patterns of behavior are nothing more than high level artifacts. To reflect this, in Chapter 3 artifacts are labeled "Level 1A of organizational culture," and patterns of behavior are labeled "Level 1B."

BELIEFS AND VALUES

Beliefs, values, ethical codes, moral codes, and *ideologies* mean essentially the same things in the language of organizational culture as they do in ordinary English, so there is no need to discuss them as extensively as artifacts. Nevertheless, the shorter discussions should not be interpreted to mean they are less important to organizational culture than artifacts or patterns of behavior. Quite the opposite is true: beliefs and values are absolutely central to organizational culture. For example, Deal and Kennedy's (1982) research concluded that organizations become institutions only after they are infused with values (p. 40).

---

[9]The essence of organizational culture is addressed in-depth in Chapter 3.

Shared beliefs and values provide the reasons why people behave as they do. Vijay Sathe (1985) aptly labels them *justifications of behavior* (p. 10). As Chapter 3 explains, beliefs and values are so important to organizational culture that many organizational culture-oriented authors define them—and the broader system of ethical or moral codes in which they are embedded—as *the* organizational culture. For example, Davis (1984) describes *guiding beliefs* (a blending of beliefs and values) as the ethical underpinnings for why resources are allocated as they are and the ultimate principles by which organizational choices are made (p. 121).[10]

Beliefs are consciously held, cognitive (mental) views about truth and reality. Beliefs may be about almost anything: a belief that the world is round; a belief in God; the belief at the Mountain State Chapter that providing programs for people with disabilities will increase their self-images; and a belief at AT&T that strategic planning and other systems-type changes will make the companies more competitive.

Although many of us tend to use the words *beliefs* and *values* interchangeably, there is a difference. Values are conscious, affective (emotion-laden) desires or wants. They are the things that are important to people: the shoulds, should nots, and ought-to-be's of organizational life. As with beliefs, values may be associated with almost anything: the value that one should have a close personal relationship with God and that others should have similar relationships; the value of a supportive extended family-like relationship with the Mountain State Chapter; and the value that private health care providers should not participate in setting policy at the Plains State Health Department.

In essence, beliefs are what people believe to be true or not true, realities or nonrealities—in their minds. Values are the things that are important to people (including their beliefs)—what people care about—and thus are the recipients of their invested emotions. People come to their beliefs (to know things) in many ways (Gardner, 1987), including, for example, through faith, experimental research, intuition, and because respected others hold them. The processes through which values are formed are less clear and appear to vary more among people;[11] nevertheless, it is widely acknowledged that

---

[10]In contrast with *guiding beliefs,* Davis (1984) calls *daily beliefs* the "accumulated rites and rituals of experience" (p. 5).

[11]For more about beliefs in organizations see, for example, Eiser (1980); Morley (1984); Selznick (1957); and Sproull (1981). For additional information about values in organizations see, for example, Deal & Kennedy (1982); Peters (1981); Siehl & Martin (1984); and Selznick (1957).

cultures shape both beliefs and values (Jacobs, 1964, ch. 19; Kroeber, 1948, sect. 125).

Chester Barnard first argued in 1938 that the most important function of an executive is to establish and imbed a system of organizational values. Philip Selznick (1957) followed Barnard's lead and identified the construction and maintenance of a system of shared values as one of the critical tasks of management.

Why? Because beliefs and values influence patterns of organizational behavior, which, in turn, yield artifacts. The contents of the different levels of organizational culture are linked (artifacts, patterns of behavior, and beliefs and values); and beliefs and values are the shaping forces and energy sources for the other two levels. Beliefs provide cognitive justifications for organizational action patterns, and values provide the emotional energy or motivation to enact them. As Sproull (1981) argues, beliefs "can strongly influence organizational actions," (p. 214) for they underlie plans, they direct searches for information and thereby determine the reasoning patterns (systems of logic) that lead to action choices. To repeat an earlier assertion, beliefs and values provide the justification for organizational actions.

Ethical and Moral Codes

In the language of organizational culture, *ethical codes* and *moral codes* are the composite systems of beliefs, values, and moral judgments. *Philosophy* and *ethos* have been used to mean the same thing (Davis, 1984) and are reasonable substitute terms as long as the term *philosophy* is used in the sense of "philosopher"—not as it is commonly being used today, to mean "metaorganizational mission." Barnard (1938, 1968) describes the impact of moral codes with an example: *Doing things the "right" way* is the dominant moral code of musicians, artists, and other true professionals, and

> no other code on earth dominates their conduct in case of conflict (between codes). . . . It is not a matter of better or worse, of superior or inferior processes—a judgment rationally arrived at. It is a matter of *right* or *wrong* in a moral sense, of deep feeling, of innate conviction, not arguable; emotional, not intellectual, in character (p. 266). (Emphasis is in original text.)

Ideologies

Ideologies usually are defined as pervasive and dominant sets of interrelated systems of thoughts, beliefs, and/or values. They are integrative frameworks that allow members to piece together and make sense of the many different organizational beliefs and values (Sathe, 1985, p. 24). Ideologies, like ethical and moral codes, are "macro systems" that function to organize organizational beliefs and values and thereby justify patterns of organizational behavior. As Harrison points out (1972), organization theorists try to "keep their values from influencing their theories; people, for the most part, do not try to keep their values from influencing their organization ideologies. . . . If you change a man's organization theory, he usually ends up questioning his values as well" (p. 120).

It is very difficult to draw a clear distinction-in-practice between ideologies and moral or ethical codes. As Harrison (1972) observes, the term *organization ideologies* is "unfortunately ambiguous" (p. 119). Conceptually, moral and ethical codes connote systems of right and wrong, whereas ideologies tend to mean patterns of thinking. However, for example, Barnard's (1938, 1968) categorization of *doing things the "right" way* (p. 266) as a dominant professional moral code rather than as an ideology demonstrates how fuzzy the distinction can be in practice.

Summary

Shared beliefs, values, moral and ethical codes, and ideologies are central to organizational culture. They provide the justification for why people and organizations behave as they do. It is virtually impossible to understand the meaning and importance of artifacts and patterns of behavior or to predict them without knowing the beliefs and values that shape and drive them. It would be like trying to predict tomorrow's weather by studying yesterday's and today's weather but ignoring the movement of fronts and other causes of weather changes. Beliefs and values are pieced together into systems of moral and ethical codes and/or ideologies.

Beliefs and values are the elements of organizational culture where ethics, philosophy, and organization meet. As do persons, each organization has its own personality, character, and culture that cause it to think, feel, and behave uniquely.

BASIC UNDERLYING ASSUMPTIONS

The highest level of organizational culture is *basic assumptions,* a relatively new concept that only recently has begun receiving attention in the literature. Edgar Schein first defined organizational culture as its basic assumptions in a 1981 *Sloan Management Review* article entitled, "Does Japanese Management Style Have a Message for American Managers?" Since 1981, a few writers have pursued the concept, including Schein (1984, 1985), Caren Siehl and Joanne Martin (1984), and Vijay Sathe (1985). Reference materials on basic assumptions are sparse; nevertheless, some organization theorists now are defining organizational culture as its basic assumptions and are presenting convincing arguments for their position. (See Chapter 3.)

According to Schein, Sathe, and Siehl and Martin, basic assumptions are likely to have moved out of members' conscious into their preconscious, for they have yielded successful results repeatedly over time. It is like applying brakes while driving a car. After years of pushing the brake pedal and the car slowing, we quit thinking about brakes and braking: we just hit the brakes instinctively, *assuming* the car will slow down. If hitting the brakes works repeatedly, we cease thinking about braking. Our belief in the relationship between braking and slowing turns into a basic assumption.

Two important distinctions need to be made between beliefs and basic assumptions. First, beliefs are conscious and thus can be identified without too much difficulty; for example, we can interview people or administer diagnostic instruments. On the other hand, basic assumptions are likely to have dropped out of awareness—they are there but have moved back into the recesses of the mind. Second, beliefs are cognitions (*cognitions*), whereas basic assumptions include not only beliefs but also perceptions (*interpretations of cognitions*) and values and feelings (*affects*) (Schein, 1985). Thus, basic assumptions can be thought of as a comprehensive, potent, but out-of-conscious system of beliefs, perceptions, and values.

At first glance, there is an apparent contradiction in this conception of basic assumptions. If basic assumptions are likely to have dropped out of awareness, how can they be taught to new members? How does an organization socialize or enculturate its new members if the basic assumptions have dropped out of consciousness? The answer lies in the ways new members are taught. Seldom is such teaching done consciously or explicitly. Rather, it is accomplished somewhat unconsciously through stories and myths and by modeling patterns of behavior that new members must piece together like jigsaw puzzles in order to discover the basic assumptions lying beneath them. These teaching and learning processes are aided by the ever-present discrepancies between the morals of stories and modeled patterns of behavior, and stated organizational beliefs and values. These discrepancies force alert new members to look beyond stated beliefs and values for underlying patterns of unspoken basic cultural assumptions. In some organizations they are relatively easy to find—but not in others. Some new members find them and become enculturated quickly (or reject them quickly); whereas others do not.

As with beliefs and values, basic assumptions can be about almost anything that involves an organization's relationship to its environment, such as its view of its clients or customers, its competitive or collaborative posture in the marketplace or among other government agencies, or its openness to using technology from other industries to solve problems. They also can be about almost anything connected with an organization's internal integration processes. For example, Schein (1981) groups assumptions into categories dealing with the nature of human nature, the nature of human activity, and the nature of human relationships (pp. 64–65).

Consider some basic assumptions in the organizations we are getting to know. First, at Jones & Jones, CPAs, clients are inherently stupid (certainly about accounting matters, but really much more broadly); telephone calls from clients inevitably require the accountant to "straighten them out"; and (because they are stupid) that process takes time away from productive (billable) accounting work. Therefore, waste as little time as possible on telephone conversations, lunches, etc., with existing clients. While the geographic area in which Jones & Jones is located was experiencing unprecedented economic growth, the firm did not worry about the negative consequences of this basic assumption. But how can it be said that this basic assumption worked repeatedly for the firm? This is an easy question to answer. By minimizing nonchargeable conversation time with clients, income and profits were extraordinarily high. Although Jones & Jones lost many clients during those years, there always were new ones to replace them. Thus the replaceability of clients had developed as another basic assumption.

Every organization has its basic assumptions:

- At AT&T, technological superiority eventually will (would) prevail in the marketplace.
- At State Health, private health care providers do not act in the public interest.
- At the Mountain State Chapter, the primary purpose of the Board of Directors is to provide directors with a supportive extended family.
- At the Community Center, respite for parents of clients is the Center's most important responsibility.
- At Scenic Mountain State College, the faculty and administrators are not and never will be sufficiently competent for the College to be a full member of the academic world or to compete for financial resources in the state political arena.

Although it may not be immediately obvious, each of these basic assumptions has helped the organization cope with problems of external adaptation or internal integration—just like client stupidity and replaceability at Jones & Jones. Parents of clients at the Community Center for Developmental Disabilities are sources of political and financial support and, if unhappy, potentially vocal anti-Center activists: the developmentally disabled clients themselves are neither. Perhaps more important, virtually everyone who works at the Community Center is the parent of a disabled child. Similar functional and/or symbolic explanations exist for each of the basic assumptions presented.

Espoused Values and Values-in-Use

The people at Jones & Jones, State Health, the Mountain State Chapter, the Community Center, and Scenic Mountain State College unanimously and emphatically denied these basic assumptions when I first tried to discuss them.[12] The existence of these assumptions was acknowledged at Jones & Jones and Scenic Mountain State College only after several months had passed. Acceptance at the Community Center took about one year. Two years had gone by before even limited acknowledgment was made at the Mountain State Chapter. Officials at State Health never have been willing to acknowledge the presence or accuracy of their assumption about private providers—but ex-members of the EMS subculture have!

Why were the organization members so reluctant to acknowledge the existence and validity of these basic assumptions? The answer to this question has practical and theoretical importance. It is the reason why Sathe (1985); Schein (1981, 1984, 1985); Siehl and Martin (1984); and this book view organizational culture as basic assumptions rather than as beliefs and values. The assumptions were resisted because they vary dramatically from consciously held and publicly stated organizational beliefs and values. They are not *rational* (in the classical sense of the word); and they are not acceptable to important organizational constituencies. They are "secret coping devices" that help organizations deal with problems of external adaptation and internal integration but that, for many reasons, members do not want to face up to—somewhat akin to a person's deeply ingrained defense mechanisms.

Beliefs and values are what people will admit to. Basic underlying assumptions are what people actually believe and feel and what determine their patterns of behavior, whether or not they are aware of them. In Argyris and Schön's (1978) words, the difference is between "espoused theory" and "theory-in-use" (p. 11).

---

[12]The AT&T denial is based on newspaper and business journal reports.

Organizational Scripts

In transactional analysis, the subfield of clinical and social psychology popularized by Eric Berne (1964) and Thomas Harris (1969), there are cultural and organizational *scripts* just as there are personal scripts. Jongeward (1976) and James and Jongeward (1971) describe cultural and organizational scripts using concepts that sound very similar to organizational culture's basic assumptions. Jongeward (1976) asserts that scripts include the "institutionalized injunctions and permissions regarding expectations. . . . they are the dramatic patterns that give an organization its identity. . . ." (p. 8). James and Jongeward (1971) describe cultural scripts as:

> the accepted and expected dramatic patterns that occur within a society. They are determined by the spoken and unspoken assumptions believed by the majority of the people within that group. . . . The same drama may be repeated generation after generation. . . . Script themes differ from one culture to another (p. 70).

Because transactional analysis scripts appear quite similar to basic assumptions, they are discussed here with the basic assumptions. If assumptions and scripts are as similar as they seem to be, an entire body of applicable theory and research may exist that to date has been virtually untapped by organization theorists.

SUBCULTURES AND ORGANIZATIONAL CLIMATE

Before moving on to Chapter 3's definitions of organizational culture, two related concepts need to be introduced: *subculture* and *organizational climate*. They are in this separate section because they are not component elements of organizational culture.

Subcultures

Organizations and organizational cultures are not monolithic. All institutions of any size have subcultures, pockets in which the organizational culture varies to some degree from the culture in other pockets and from the dominant culture. Subcultures may develop in any organizational groups. Subcultures may exist in a building, a floor of a building, and among employees who take breaks in a lounge or ride in a car pool. They may form in groups that cross horizontal or vertical organizational boundaries. Thus an organization may have subcultures made up of people who work on a program or project, perform similar functions, share ethnic or religious backgrounds, have the same supervisor, service the same clients or customers, or were trained in the same professional cultures (for example, credit collectors, accountants, teachers, economists, or salespeople).

There are several subcultures with overlapping membership at Jones & Jones. Two of them have been formed by rank and age. One is made up of the partners and two senior managers, and the second is made up of junior accountants and one younger senior manager. Three functional subcultures also exist, consisting of respectively tax; audit and financial planning; and management advisory services (computer services) personnel. (Clerical and paraprofessional personnel tend to belong to the three functional subcultures, as they have not formed their own.)

The EMS subculture at State Health formed around a Public Health Service program of grants and consisted of the people in a single office. The dominant culture, based on assumptions about the value of regulating health care costs and the provision of services by private health care providers, demands that providers be carefully excluded from participation in public health policy formation. The EMS Office subculture had formed around directly contradictory assumptions: only private providers (particularly physicians) can design and implement systems of medical care; public bureaucrats should serve only minor supporting roles; and cost containment is secondary to developing effective systems of medical care.

Subcultures interlock, overlap, partially coincide, and sometimes conflict. Just as the dominant organizational culture, they may be strong, pervasive, and controlling; or they may be weak and hardly affect behavior. Siehl and Martin (1984, pp. 53–54) identify three types of subcultures: enhancing, orthogonal, and countercultural:

1. Assumptions, beliefs, and values in *enhancing subcultures* are compatible with and often are stronger and held with more fervor than those in the dominant culture. At Jones & Jones, the partners and senior managers make up an enhancing subculture.

2. Members of *orthogonal subcultures* accept the basic assumptions of the dominant organizational culture but also hold some that are unique. Jones & Jones tax accountants and support personnel are cautious, conservative, and detail-oriented; but the management advisory services subculture is somewhat more freewheeling, risk-taking, and marketing-oriented. Yet the Jones & Jones subcultures are consistent—orthogonal—with the dominant culture, which has been heavily influenced by professional accounting values and assumptions.

3. *Countercultures,* such as existed in the EMS Office of State Health, have basic assumptions that conflict with the dominant culture.

Thus, subcultures may enhance, refine, or challenge a dominant organizational culture. They may cause divisive behavior, such as at State Health; or they may provide pockets of creativity and innovation, as do the functional subcultures at Jones & Jones. Regardless of their consequences, they are inevitable facts of organizational life.

Organizational Climate

It was hard to decide where in this chapter to introduce *organizational climate*. The term has been used to denote many different concepts, both historically and currently.[13] Miles and Schmuck (1971) and Lippitt, Langseth, and Mossop (1985) conceptually interchange organizational climate and culture. Gellerman (1968) implies that organizational climate is something like an organization's personality, consisting of hopes, attitudes, and biases. Davis (1984) defines it as a "measure of whether people's expectations are being met about what it *should* be like to work in an organization" (p. 81). (Emphasis in original text.)

There appears to be as little agreement in the literature about the nature of organizational climate as there is about the nature of organizational culture. In the absence of any generally accepted definitions, this book uses *organizational climate* to mean an amalgamation of feeling tones, or a transient organizational mood. As such, organizational climate is not an element of organizational culture. It is a related but separate phenomenon.

SUMMARY AND CONCLUSIONS

Basic assumptions are beliefs, values, ethical and moral codes, and ideologies that have become so ingrained that they tend to have dropped out of consciousness. They are unquestioned perceptions of truth, reality, ways of thinking and thinking about, and feeling that develop through repeated successes in solving problems over extended periods of time. Important basic assumptions are passed on to new members, often unconsciously.

Beliefs and values are consciously held cognitive and affective patterns. They provide explicit directions and justifications for patterns of organizational behavior, as well as the energy to enact them. Beliefs and values also are the birthplaces of basic assumptions.

Artifacts and patterns of organizational behavior are material

---

[13]Interesting historical linkages exist between *organizational climate*, as the term was used by some writers in the 1950s and 1960s, and *organizational culture* of the 1980s. These ties are analyzed in Chapter 7.

and nonmaterial, visible and audible manifestations of organizational culture, as well as its maintainers and transmitters. The importance of artifacts cannot be appreciated without understanding the concept and functions of symbols and symbolism.

Organizational culture consists of elements from all levels. No level of organizational culture can continue to exist without the others. In this respect, arguments about what is the true organizational culture are moot and trivial. Nevertheless, the definitional question has major practical implications, such as when one needs to select a method for deciphering or identifying, strengthening, altering, changing, or managing in an organizational culture. Chapter 3 organizes the stuff of organizational culture (from this chapter) into a typology that provides the framework for considering alternative methods for identifying organizational culture (Chapter 5); analyzing the historical development of organizational culture (Chapters 6 and 7); and concluding with some practical implications of the organizational culture perspective (Chapter 8).

Organizational Culture: Concepts, Definitions, and a Typology

Organizational culture is not just another piece of the puzzle, it is the puzzle. From our point of view, a culture is not something an organization has; a culture is something an organization is. (Pacanowsky & O'Donnell-Trujillo, 1983, p. 126).

Many of the debates about organizational culture are caused by people's use of different concepts and definitions. This chapter seeks to clarify matters by examining just what organizational culture is. The overview of organizational culture in Chapter 1 and the discussion of its elements and functions in Chapter 2 provide the groundwork for this task.

There are two very basic ways to go about defining complex concepts: (a) inductively building a generalized theoretical definition from one's experiences, preferences, and assumptions; and (b) working deductively from a generalized theory, analyzing realities to see how they fit with theory, and modifying theory based on the results of the analysis.

While this chapter uses both deductive and inductive approaches, deduction predominates. Keesing (1974) and Schein (1981; 1984; 1985) provide the theory for creating an initial classification system, or a typology of organizational culture elements (Miles & Huberman, 1984, chs. III–VI), which then is used to analyze and compare a wide array of concepts of organizational culture that have been proposed by writers. The typology is used throughout the rest of this book as the analytical framework for understanding different aspects of organizational culture, such as the relationships between organizational culture, leadership, change strategies, and research methodologies.

It is useful to review the brief description of organizational culture that was presented in Chapter 1:

- Organizational culture is the culture that exists in an organization, something akin to a societal culture.
- It is made up of such things as values, beliefs, assumptions, perceptions, behavioral norms, artifacts, and patterns of behavior.
- It is a socially constructed, unseen, and unobservable force behind organizational activities.
- It is a social energy that moves organization members to act.
- It is a unifying theme that provides meaning, direction, and mobilization for organization members.
- It functions as an organizational control mechanism, informally approving or prohibiting behaviors.

These basic assumptions of the organizational culture perspective differ from those of other perspectives of organization theory.[1] As I asserted in Chapter 1, the organizational culture perspective is challenging the basic views of the structural and systems perspectives, about how organizations make decisions, and how and why people in organizations behave as they do. It is a counterculture within organization theory. Proponents of the organizational culture perspective believe that the structural and systems perspectives of organization theory are using the wrong lenses to look at the wrong organizational elements in their attempts to understand and predict organizational behavior.

The prior paragraph may make it sound as though there is consensus about organizational culture and unanimity of concepts among proponents of the organizational culture perspective. This is far from the case. There are very important substantive disagreements. The most fundamental of these involves the contents or composition of an organizational culture: what are the elements, constructs, and attributes of an organizational culture? The differences are more than semantic debates. They reflect serious disagreements about how one views, investigates, manages, and changes organizations.

The first step toward understanding the essence of *organizational culture* is to appreciate that it is a concept rather than a thing. This distinction is crucial. A thing can be discovered and truths established about it, for example, through empirical research. Unlike a thing, however, a concept is created in peoples' minds—that is, it

---

[1] More complete discussions are in Chapters 1 and 6.

must be conjured up, defined, and refined. Thus ultimate truths about organizational culture (a concept) cannot be found or discovered. There is no final authoritative source or experiment to settle disagreements about what it is or what comprises it.

Why is this important? Because when someone claims to have identified an organizational culture, that discovery represents nothing more than the results obtained from applying that person's concepts of organizational culture (via a concept-driven deciphering process) in a given organization.[2] Another discoverer who uses a different concept-driven deciphering process will find a different culture in the same organization (Van Maanen, 1979, 1983; Herbert, 1987, Preface). The concept of culture that is used to shape the discoverer's frame of reference determines what is looked for and how it is looked for; and it often predetermines what is found. Consider an analogy. It is easy to get people to agree that frogs are green once there is consensus about what constitutes green. Without agreement on green, there is no way to secure consensus on the color of a frog.

The second important thing to remember is that how one looks at organizational culture largely determines what it is. When you or I start thinking about organizational culture structurally (as in Figures 3–1, 3–2, 3–3, and 3–4) we create structural typologies that, in turn, cause us to forget that organizational culture is not just structural elements. It also is a *dynamic process*—a social construction that is undergoing continual reconstruction—as well as *the puzzle*, "not just another piece of the puzzle" (Pacanowsky & O'Donnell-Trujillo, 1983, p. 146).

Organizational culture's definitional problems mirror long-standing arguments in anthropology, archaeology, and cultural anthropology about the general concept of culture. In 1952, the cultural anthropologists Kroeber and Kluckhohn identified 164 different definitions of culture existing in their search of the literature. As recently as 1982, Ian Hodder described and bemoaned the problems caused by the continuing debate between anthropologically oriented and materially oriented archaeologists over what culture is. The

---

[2]For example, Allen and Kraft (1982) define organizational culture operationally as norms, describe how to measure norms, and then announce that the organizational culture has been identified. Davis (1984) identifies two levels of organizational culture, *guiding beliefs* and *daily beliefs*. He implicitly equates guiding beliefs with goals or strategies and proposes goal and strategy change tactics as though they were synonymous with tactics for changing organizational culture. He is more explicit about equating daily beliefs with existing rituals and management practices. Kilmann (1985) minimizes the importance of defining organizational culture, and seems to equate it with something akin to *organizational climate*. His "five tracks to organizational success" closely resemble an organization development program.

situation is perhaps even less clear relative to organizational culture.

There are very few areas of general consensus about organizational culture. They include the five assumptions stated earlier in this chapter:

1. Organizational cultures exist.
2. Each organizational culture is relatively unique.
3. Organizational culture is a socially constructed concept (Berger & Luckmann, 1966; Holzner & Marx, 1979, chs. 4 and 5; Mead, 1934).
4. Organizational culture provides organization members with a way of understanding and making sense of events and symbols.
5. Organizational culture is a powerful lever for guiding organizational behavior. It functions as "organizational control mechanisms, informally approving or prohibiting some patterns of behavior" (Martin & Siehl, 1983, p. 52).

But beyond these five basic points agreement is very limited, and the points say nothing about what organizational culture is. Consensus is restricted to its existence, relative uniqueness, and a few functions it performs.

The variety of views about the essence of organizational culture has been mentioned several times without substantiation. It is enlightening (and entertaining) to scan some of the definitions that have appeared in the literature. The chapter appendix contains excerpted definitions from fifty-eight books and articles on organizational culture and closely related topics. The references are representative but certainly not exhaustive. The key words and phrases from these definitions are presented in Figure 3–1. No words or phrases are included that describe sources, functions, transmittal, change, or maintenance of organizational culture—only what it is, and what elements constitute it.

Figure 3–1 lists seventy-three words or phrases used to define organizational culture from the fifty-eight different published sources listed in the chapter appendix. Figure 3–1 makes it easy to see why Kroeber and Kluckhohn (1952) found 164 definitions of culture. Clearly the concept has not been clarified very much since 1952, at least not by those who have written about organizational culture.

CLASSIFYING ELEMENTS OF ORGANIZATIONAL CULTURE

Typologies are simply classification systems. They are frameworks, much like file folders and drawers, where one puts sorted and grouped information (Miles & Huberman, 1984, ch. II). As with all

FIGURE 3-1 Alphabetical Listing of Elements of Organizational Culture

anecdotes, organizational
art
assumptions that people live by
assumptions, patterns of basic
assumptions, shared
attitudes
behavioral regularities
being
beliefs
beliefs, patterns of shared
celebration
ceremonies
climate, organizational
cognitive processes, patterns of
commitment to excellence
communication patterns
consensus, level of (about myriad
   organizational variables)
core
customs
doing things, way of
enactment (per Weick, 1977)
ethic, organizational
ethos
expectations, shared
feelings
glue that holds an organization
   together
habits
heroes
historical vestiges
identity
ideologies
interaction, patterns of
jargon
justification for behavioral patterns
knowledge
language
links between language, metaphor
   and ritual

management practices
manner
material objects
meaning, patterns of
meanings
meanings, intersubjective
mind-set
myths
norms
philosophy
physical arrangements
practical syllogisms
purpose
rites
ritualized practices
rituals
roots
rules, informal system of
scripts, organizational
sentiments
source of norms, rules, attitudes,
   customs, and roles
specialness, quality of perceived
   organizational
spirit
stories, organizational
style
symbols
thinking, way of
traditions
translation of myths into action and
   relationship
understandings, tacit
values
values, basic or core
values, patterns of shared
vision
way
worldviews

filing systems, useful typologies must have a sound theoretical framework or else they are not useful for grouping, storing, and extracting
information. The typology presented in this chapter was constructed

primarily from theories proposed by the cultural anthropologist Keesing (1974) and the organizational theorist Schein (1985).

Keesing (1974) described two schools of cultural anthropology that have strongly influenced current concepts of culture: the adaptationist and the ideationalist schools. These two schools provide a starting point for creating a typology to sort through the myriad conceptions of organizational culture. The *adaptationist* concept of culture is based on that which is directly observable about the members of a community, including socially transmitted patterns of speech, behavior, and uses of tangible (material) items such as tools. It is based on patterns of behavior that help communities relate to their environments. In contrast, the *ideationalist* concept of culture is based on that which is shared in the community members' minds, including their common beliefs, values, knowledge, meanings, and ideas.

The different concepts of culture held by the ideationalists and the adaptationists—by those who focus on behaviors and things, and those who are more concerned with shared ideas and meanings—help to explain why debates continue to rage about whether organizational culture consists of such things as artifacts, behavioral norms, patterns of behavior, and language, or of its shared assumptions, beliefs, understandings, and values.

Edgar H. Schein, a clinical psychologist turned organizational theorist, refined the distinction between the adaptationist and ideational views of culture by conceptualizing three levels of organizational culture: (Schein, 1981, 1984, 1985)

- Level 1—artifacts.
- Level 2—values and beliefs.
- Level 3—basic underlying assumptions.

Level 1 of organizational culture, *artifacts*, is consistent with the adaptationist view of culture. Level 2, *values and beliefs*, overlaps aspects of both the adaptationists and the ideationalists. Level 3, *basic underlying assumptions*, is consistent with ideationalist concepts. This conceptualization of the levels of organizational culture is diagrammed in Figure 3–2.

By now the reader should be questioning the usefulness of this definitional exercise: "Why bother to create a typology?" There are many practical reasons. Consider, for example, the different implications the three levels of organizational culture have for managers who want to make fundamental organizational changes—such as John Thomas, the new president of the Mountain State Chapter—or when the world changed around AT&T. How does a manager insti-

FIGURE 3–2 Schein's Three Levels of Organizational Culture
and Their Interaction

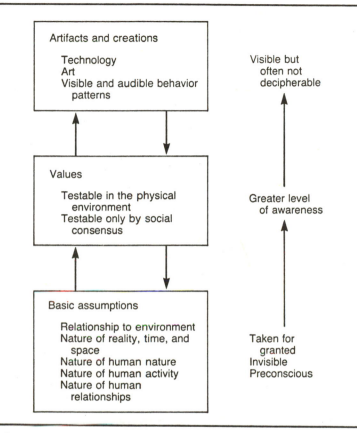

SOURCE: Reprinted from "Does Japanese Management Style Have a Message for American Managers?" by E. H. Schein, *Sloan Management Review*, Fall 1981, p. 64, by permission of the publisher. Copyright © 1981 by the Sloan Management Review Association. All rights reserved.

tute dramatic holistic changes? Where does one start? What "change
levers" should be used? The following discussion describes just one
example of the many practical applications for a typology of organizational culture.

If the Level 1 definition of organizational culture (artifacts) is
used as the frame of reference for holistic change, AT&T's management must alter longstanding patterns of behavior, including its
shared patterns of decision making. If this is the case, AT&T management should use whatever is known or theorized about how to
change patterns of behavior and decisions in organizations to induce
change in the company's culture. Presumably, management's strategy would include many complementary thrusts such as developing

strategic marketing plans; creating new organizational units with marketing-oriented goals and objectives; changing the rewards systems (the criteria for pay increases and promotions); and modifying the contents of management information and control systems. AT&T also might bring in teams of applied behavioral scientists to help alter patterns of behavior, perhaps using management training or instituting participative management techniques. New executives might be recruited from companies acknowledged for their marketing savvy. Management's levers for changing AT&T's basic orientation probably would include the company's strategic plans; organizational structures; management information and control systems; decision processes; policies and procedures; reward systems; management training; and behavioral norms (Allen & Kraft, 1982; Davis, 1984).

However, many newspaper and business journal articles have reported AT&T's apparently unsuccessful use of all of these change levers. For example, on October 26, 1985, the *Rocky Mountain News* carried a page three article headlined, "AT&T Plant in Westminster to Lay Off 400." The story announced that for the second time in four months, AT&T Information Systems was laying off workers from its Westminster (Colorado) manufacturing plant.

> Art Bouffard, public relations manager for AT&T in Denver, blamed the layoffs on slow orders for two business products. . . . The giant communications company, anticipating strong demand for the Merlin Communications Systems and PBX central telephone systems, had increased employment in plants nationwide, but orders have fallen short. AT&T is laying off employees at plants in other states.

The Level 1 perspective of organizational culture does not open the door to dramatic new strategies, tools, or approaches for changing the basic orientation of an organization. Yet some authors and consultants are exploiting the rising visibility of the organizational culture perspective by defining Level 1 as organizational culture and advocating the types of approaches described above as something new and innovative (Allen & Kraft, 1982; Davis, 1984; Kilmann, 1984). Their approaches and methods may be perfectly appropriate for the situations they describe, but to identify such approaches as the organizational culture perspective is misleading and creates unnecessary confusion.

In contrast, the use of Level 2 (values and beliefs) or Level 3 (basic assumptions) as the guiding theoretical framework for changing AT&T's (or any other organization's) organizational culture requires entirely different targets in an organization and a very different arsenal of change tools and approaches. The levers that can be used effectively to alter artifacts generally will not succeed in changing patterns of shared beliefs, values, attitudes, and assumptions. Many of the appropriate change levers have been around for a long time, and a few are the same ones as those that can be used in Level 1. However, they must be applied differently. The organization must be perceived differently. Managers must buy a new pair of "3-D glasses."

Some Older Tools for Creating Change

A few of the older but still applicable levers for creating employee readiness to modify their beliefs, attitudes, values, and moral codes include:

- The social psychological models for changing peoples' attitudes and thought patterns (Lewin, 1947; Zimbardo & Ebbesen, 1970).

- The subtle and not-so-subtle U.S. Forest Service strategies for gaining willing compliance among geographically isolated forest rangers (Kaufman, 1960).

- The thought and attitude change tactics used in total institutions such as asylums (Goffman, 1961) and prisoner-of-war camps (Schein, 1961).

- The processes organizations use to socialize new members and older employees promoted or transferred across organizational boundaries (Schein, 1968; 1978; Van Maanen, 1983b).

- The belief-controlling strategies used by cults (Festinger, Riecken, & Schachter, 1956).

- The value-altering strategies used by medical schools on future doctors (Becker, Geer, Hughes, & Strauss, 1961).

- The use of cognitive dissonance to change beliefs, perceptions, attitudes, and values (Festinger, 1957).

Some Newer Tools for Creating Change

Other Level 2- and Level 3-type organizational change targets and levers are relatively new, at least in terms of their application to changing organization culture. These change levers are used deliberately to alter perceptions of reality and the meanings of concepts and things central to peoples' patterns of cognitions. If AT&T's management should decide to use these levers to change the organizational culture, they would go beyond just modifying organization members' values and beliefs. They would work to alter perceptions of reality, truth, worth, meaning, and knowledge. Why? Because AT&T's longstanding technical value orientation is more than a set of shared beliefs and values. It is a pattern of thinking (basic assumption) rooted in basic perceptions about world realities and how AT&T meshes with those realities—the realities of the bygone world of monopolistic telephone service and telecommunications provided universally by the Bell System.

The tools needed to alter shared patterns of perceptions, meanings, and cognitions among organization members are neither mystical nor necessarily immoral. As with all tools of the social and physical sciences, they can be used for desirable or undesirable purposes. They may be used overtly and explicitly as, for example, President Reagan has done in an open effort to change U.S. perceptions about the impacts of liberal economic and welfare programs on both the rich and the poor. However, most attempts to change cognitive patterns in organizations are implemented with subtlety. A chief executive officer may become consistently unavailable for meetings about technological issues. The office of a once powerful, technologically oriented vice president may be reassigned to a recently recruited marketing-oriented person who knows little about the company's technology. The organizational stories told at informal gatherings and company retreats may start having new kinds of heroes and contain new morals that reflect the desired new conceptions of realities.

The tools for changing perceptions of reality that have received the most attention recently have been borrowed from several academic disciplines that are relatively new to organization theory. They include cognitive social psychology; social constructionism (a subset of sociology); and learning theory. The generic label being applied to them is *symbolism* or *symbolic management*.

Lee Bolman and Terrence Deal (1984, pp. 149–50) summarize the basic assumptions of the *symbolic frame*:

- The meaning or the interpretation of what is happening in organizations is more important than what actually is happening.
- Ambiguity and uncertainty, which are prevalent in most organizations, preclude rational problem-solving and decision-making processes.
- People use symbols to reduce ambiguity and to gain a sense of direction when they are faced with uncertainty.

A TYPOLOGY OF ORGANIZATIONAL CULTURE

The level of organizational culture that one uses as the frame of reference almost dictates how one studies, manages in, and goes about trying to change an organizational culture. These implications are sufficiently important to warrant the creation of a typology. There must be clear understanding when the phrase *organizational culture* is used, or else we will never be able to agree that frogs are green. Therefore, this chapter now returns to Schein's conceptualization of organizational culture (Figure 3–2) and adds more content to his three levels.

Level 1 of Organizational Culture: Artifacts

Artifacts are the behavioral patterns and the visible, tangible, and/or audible results of behaviors. Level 1 of organizational culture includes an organization's written and spoken language and jargon, office layouts and arrangements, organizational structure, dress codes, technology, and behavioral norms. According to Stanley Davis (1984), artifacts are tangible, and it is possible to "get your arms around them." This is why it is tempting to collect

> information about specific programs and to shy away from the harder task of interpreting the values and beliefs that lie behind them. . . . A living culture exists in beliefs and values more than in artifacts and documents. This makes managing the culture a very intangible undertaking, and it renders the job of analyzing culture equally frustrating at times (p. 12).

In addition, Vijay Sathe (1985) describes artifacts as relatively "easy to see but hard to interpret without an understanding of the other [two] levels" (p. 10).

To the Level 1 artifacts, we now add a *Level 1B*, patterns of behavior, a distinction first proposed by Joanne Martin and Caren Siehl (1983).[3] Following Martin and Siehl's logic, Level 1B of organizational culture includes such elements of organizational culture as habits, patterns of behavior, norms, rites, and rituals. These elements are consistent with the adaptationist concept of culture and do not appear to violate Schein's conceptualization.

Level 2 of Organizational Culture: Values and Beliefs

Level 2 of organizational culture consists of beliefs and values. They are the sense of "what 'ought' to be, as distinct from what is" (Schein, 1985, p. 15). Sathe (1985) describes Level 2 as revealing "how people communicate, explain, rationalize, and justify what they

---

[3]Martin and Siehl (1983) use the label *management practices*. I prefer the broader phrase, *patterns of behavior*.

say and do as a community—how they 'make sense' of the first level of culture. We will denote this level with the terms *cultural communications* and *justifications of behavior*, or *justifications*" (p. 10). (Emphasis in original text.) Beliefs and values are of interest to both the adaptationists and the ideationalists.

In addition to beliefs and values, the Level 2 constructs of organizational culture include ethos, philosophies, ideologies, ethical and moral codes, and attitudes. At first glance, Level 2 elements of organizational culture appear to represent an ideal, workable blending of the ideationalist and adaptationist concepts of culture. Indeed, it is tempting to label Level 2 the *true* organizational culture, and several organization theorists have done so.[4] Nevertheless, Level 2 elements cannot be trusted to provide accurate information about a *true* organizational culture (Level 3) because of prevalent incongruences between "espoused values" and "values-in-use" in organizations (Argyris & Schön, 1978). Espoused values often serve important symbolic functions and may remain in an organization for extended periods of time even though they are incongruent with values-in-use. Investigations of Level 2 elements of organizational culture often yield espoused values—what people will say—rather than values-in-use, which can be used to predict what people will do.

Despite the dangers inherent in using Level 2 elements, if in fact organizational culture (a) influences behavior in and of organizations; (b) increases understanding of organization members; and (c) can be used to predict behavior (at least in some circumstances), then (d) Level 2 elements of organizational culture (values and beliefs) should be better predicters of organizational behavior than Level 1 elements (artifacts and patterns of behavior)—because they are conceptually closer to Schein's *true* organization culture that resides in Level 3 (basic underlying assumptions).

Level 3 of Organizational Culture: Basic Underlying Assumptions

Schein defines basic assumptions as fundamental beliefs, values, and perceptions that

> have become so taken for granted that one finds little variation within a cultural unit. . . . What I am calling basic assumptions are congruent with what Argyris has identified as "theories-in-use," the implicit assumptions that actually guide behavior, that tell group members how to perceive, think about, and feel about things (Argyris, 1976; Argyris

---

[4]See Chapter 2 and Figure 3–5.

and Schön, 1974). Basic assumptions, like theories-in-use, tend to be nonconfrontable and nondebatable (Schein, 1985, p. 18).

Basic underlying assumptions are distinct from preferred solutions—"what should be"—in the sense of dominant values. Level 3 elements of organizational culture include spirit; truths (in the social constructionist sense); and possibly the transactional analysis concept of organizational scripts—but only if they are so completely accepted and deeply ingrained that they have moved into organization members' preconscious or unconscious.

Schein's three-level model provides the most useful typology published to date for classifying elements of organizational culture into usable groupings. Siehl and Martin (1984) and Sathe (1985) have acknowledged and utilized it in their analyses, perhaps indicating the beginning of a badly needed movement toward general agreement on a conceptual definition of organizational culture. Separating Level 1 into Level 1A (artifacts) and Level 1B (patterns of behavior) appears to make Schein's typology even more useful. Figure 3–3 presents the typology that serves as the analytical framework used for the remainder of this book.

SOME POTENTIAL USES FOR THE TYPOLOGY OF ORGANIZATIONAL CULTURE

How can the typology help one understand and use organizational culture? An example is provided in Figure 3–4, where the key words and phrases from various definitions of organizational culture (from Figure 3–1) are classified into the levels of culture from the typology in Figure 3–3.[5] The resulting matrix has many potential uses. For example, it provides a beginning point for a manager to match his or her reasons for changing an organizational culture with the lenses for seeing it and the tools for changing it.

Figure 3–5 takes the next logical step. It classifies various authors' writings about organizational culture into levels, which makes it easy to identify their conceptual and methodological preferences ("where they are coming from"). Thus, one would expect authors who write from a Level 1 slant of organizational culture (artifacts and patterns of behavior) to favor behaviorally oriented methods and instruments for identifying organization culture (for example, instruments that identify norms) and behavioristic strategies for

---

[5]All classifications were made by the author using the definitions and descriptions of levels presented in Chapters 2 and 3. When classification decisions were not clearly evident, I assigned the elements in question to more than one level.

FIGURE 3–3   Levels of Organizational Culture and Their Interaction

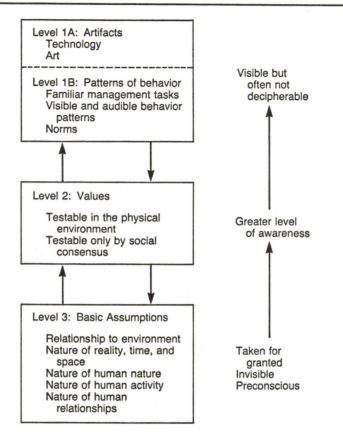

effecting changes in organizations (for example, strategies for altering behavioral norms). In contrast, writers who emphasize Level 2 of
organizational culture probably will approach organizational change
via strategies for changing members' beliefs and values and will use
research methods and instruments borrowed from psychology, social
psychology, and social constructionism.

Also, the matrix can assist a manager or a student to begin
matching alternative methods for changing or reinforcing an organizational culture with his or her purpose for doing so. A manager or
consultant who needs to effect rapid, tangible, demonstrable, organizational changes (such as doubling productivity levels) probably
should focus on Level 1 elements of organizational culture. In contrast, a macro organization theorist attempting to understand and
predict an organization's long-term policy or strategic decision pat-

FIGURE 3–4   A Typology of Elements of Organizational Culture

Elements of Organizational Culture	Level of Culture				
	Arti-facts 1A	Patterns of Be-havior 1B	Be-liefs & Val-ues 2	As-sump-tions 3	Not Clear
anecdotes, organizational	x				
art	x				
assumptions that people live by				x	
assumptions, patterns of basic				x	
assumptions, shared				x	
attitudes		x	x		
behavioral regularities		x			
being			x	x	
beliefs			x		
beliefs, patterns of shared			x		
celebration	x				
ceremonies	x				
climate, organizational					x
cognitive processes, patterns of			x		
commitment to excellence			x		
communications, patterns of	x				
consensus, level of			x		
core			x	x	x
customs		x			
doing things, way of		x			
enactment (per Weick, 1977)				x	
ethic, organizational			x		
ethos			x		
expectations, shared		x			
feelings			x		
glue that holds an organization together				x	
habits		x			
heroes	x				
historical vestiges	x				
identity			x	x	
ideologies			x		
interaction, patterns of		x			
jargon	x				
justifications for behavior			x		
knowledge			x		
language	x				
links between language, metaphor, and ritual	x	x			
management practices		x			
manner		x			

FIGURE 3–4 (*Concluded*)	*1A*	*1B*	*2*	*3*	*Not Clear*
material objects	x				
meaning, patterns of			x		
meanings			x		
meanings, intersubjective			x		
mind-set			x	x	
myths	x				
norms		x			
philosophy			x	x	
physical arrangements	x				
practical syllogisms			x		
purpose			x		
rites		x			
ritualized practices		x			
rituals		x			
roots					x
rules, informal system of		x			
scripts, organizational (cognitive social psychology)	x				
scripts, organizational (transactional analysis)				x	
sentiments			x		
source of norms, rules, attitudes, customs, and roles			x		
specialness, quality of perceived					x
spirit				x	
stories, organizational	x				
style		x			
symbols	x				
thinking, way of			x		
traditions	x	x			
translation of myths into action and relationship	x				
understandings, tacit			x		
values			x		
values, basic or core			x		
values, patterns of shared			x		
vision			x		
way			x	x	x
worldviews			x	x	x

terns would be expected to focus on Level 2 and/or 3 elements. Figure 3–5 demonstrates how the typology can be used to classify books and articles about organizational culture (and therefore authors). In it,

FIGURE 3–5   Typology of Publications on Organization Culture

Author and Work

Level 1A: *Artifacts*
Bates (1984)
Clark (1970)
Cohen (1969) (*)
Edelman (1971, 1977) (*)
Evered (1983)
Gephart (1978)
Hayakawa (1953) (*)
Hirsch (1980)
Martin (1982b)
Meissner (1976)
Pettigrew (1979)
Pfeffer (1981b)
Pondy (1978)
Steele and Jenks (1977)
Wilkins (1983)

Level 1B: *Patterns of Behavior*
Allaire and Firsirotu (1985)
Blake & Mouton (1969)
Clark (1970)
Davis (1984)
Deal and Kennedy (1982)
Gephart (1978)
Goffman (1959, 1967) (*)
Hall (1977)
Jaques (1952)
Martin and Siehl (1983)
Pettigrew (1979)
Ritti and Funkhouser (1982)
Schein (1968)
Tichy and Ulrich (1984)
Van Maanen (1976, 1979)

Level 2: *Beliefs and Values*
Allaire and Firsirotu (1985)
Barnard (1938, 1968)
Blake and Mouton (1969)
Buchanan (1975)
Clark (1970)
Davis (1984)
Deal and Kennedy (1982)
Duncan and Weiss (1979)

FIGURE 3–5 (*Concluded*)

        Hall (1977)

        Harrison (1972)

        Jaques (1952)

        Meyer (1984)

        Morley (1984)

        Ouchi (1981)

        Pascale and Athos (1981)

        Peters and Waterman (1982)

        Selznick (1957)

        Sergiovanni and Corbally (1984a)

        Smircich (1983)

        Sproull (1981)

        Tichy and Ulrich (1984)

        Weick (1977, 1979)

        Wharton & Worthley (1983)

Level 3:   *Basic Assumptions*

        Buchanan (1975)

        Duncan and Weiss (1979)

        Jongeward (1973)

        Sathe (1985)

        Schein (1981, 1984, 1985)

        Siehl and Martin (1984)

        Weick (1977, 1979)

Do Not Fit Cleanly into Levels, and Why

        Etzioni (1975) (Addresses all levels)

        Gold (1982) (A feeling of specialness)

        Lippitt, Langseth and Mossop (1985) (Organizational climate)

        Miles and Schmuck (1971) (Organizational climate)

        Tagiuri and Litwin (1968) (Organizational climate)

(*) The author was not writing specifically about organizational culture.

---

the authors and works that are listed in the chapter appendix (on page 70) are classified by their levels of primary focus.[6]

    Not all of the selected books and articles on organizational culture can be classified perfectly into one level. Nevertheless, almost all fit cleanly into either one or two adjacent levels. If the levels are

---

[6]I attempted to classify each work based on its overall slant and emphasis. This required going beyond the definitional statements presented in the chapter appendix and incorporating the context from which statements were excerpted. When there was doubt about the level to which an article or book should be assigned, it was classified in more than one level.

viewed as points on a continuum, virtually all of the works cited can be classified within a reasonable range. William Taylor (1984) provides a theoretical justification for viewing the levels of organizational culture as ranges on a continuum. He argues that the study of cultures is always a study of wholes.

> We can, and do, pick out particular features of cultural life, such as language, mythology, belief systems, conventional understandings, and so on for study and interpretation. But the reification that makes us comfortable with the methodologies and outcomes of structural analysis, the treating of social forms as objects, "out there" in the external world, created by man but possessing a superordinate reality and power of constraint, is more difficult to achieve in relation to cultural phenomena (p. 126).

Organizational culture is not something easily broken down into elements and placed in single boxes.

All except two of the listed works that do not fit neatly into a single or adjacent levels can be explained and dealt with. Etzioni's (1975) definition is so broad that it, in fact, addresses all levels. Similarly, Gold's (1982) "quality of perceived organizational specialness" can be interpreted to mean several different things. His intention is not clearly evident. Lippitt, Langseth, and Mossop (1985); Miles and Schmuck (1971); and Tagiuri and Litwin (1968) define organizational culture as the organizational climate, a concept akin to an organizational mood or feeling tone, which was introduced in the concluding pages of Chapter 2.

Figure 3–5 demonstrates how the typology can be used as the framework for analyzing and synthesizing organizational culture concepts, elements, tools for change, research methods, and empirical data.

A FUNCTIONAL DEFINITION OF ORGANIZATIONAL CULTURE

Earlier, I asserted that there are two predominant ways to define a concept, inductively and deductively. But other methods exist as well. One other way to define something is functionally or, in Meehan's (1981) phraseology, *pragmatically*. As the name implies, a functional definition is a statement of the functions performed by the concept being defined. In the listing of points of general agreement about organizational culture was "a few functions it performs." Interestingly, general agreement about substantive functions exists across the literature of organizational culture, because they are the same regardless of how culture is defined formally. To say the same thing a different way, the substantive functions do not differ materially whether organizational culture is defined as artifacts, patterns of behavior, beliefs and values, or basic assumptions. The functional "hows" and the selection of words vary, but the basic functions do not.

There is general agreement across the literature about four functions of organizational culture, and they can be viewed as the core of a functional definition of organizational culture. These functions, as modified and extended from Siehl and Martin (1984, pp. 228–229), are listed below. Examples from cases and descriptions in Chapters 1 and 2 are noted in parentheses. It is important to remember that the functions only need to serve useful purposes *of some sort*. There is no reason to assume that they are necessarily rational or consistent with an organization's stated purposes or mission.

1. It provides shared patterns of cognitive interpretations or perceptions, so organization members know how they are expected to act and think. (At AT&T, technological superiority will prevail in the marketplace. At State Health, private health care providers will not act in the public interest. At Jones & Jones, clients are stupid.)

2. It provides shared patterns of affect, an emotional sense of involvement and commitment to organizational values and moral codes —of things worth working for and believing in—so organizational members know what they are expected to value and how they are expected to feel. (At the Community Center, it is important to keep parents of clients satisfied. When they are satisfied, life is happier for staff. At the Mountain State Chapter, the Board of Directors should function as a valued, caring extended family.)

3. It defines and maintains boundaries, allowing identification of members and nonmembers. (Only people in the EMS Office of State Health subculture believe that private physicians can and should design and implement systems of medical care. Members of Jones & Jones call clients "assholes".)

4. It functions as an organizational control system, prescribing and prohibiting certain behaviors. (At State Health, members do not permit private physicians to serve on policy-making bodies. At the Community Center, staff should evaluate proposed program changes against the criterion of respite for parents. At the Mountain State Chapter, directors should not disagree openly at Board meetings. At Jones & Jones, accountants will not waste time talking with existing clients.)

Agreement on a fifth function is not universal: organizational culture strongly affects organizational performance. Quality and quantity of organizational performance holds the most hope for truly valuable applications of the organizational culture perspective. Intuitively, there should be a relationship between organizational culture and performance. Many writers, including Allen and Kraft (1982); Davis (1984); Deal and Kennedy (1982); Kilmann (1984); Ouchi (1981); Peters and Waterman (1982); and Pascale and Athos (1981) have *assumed* the linkage exists; but, to date, there is no convincing empirical evidence to support the assumption (Wilkins 1983). The relationships between aspects, types, intensities, etc., of organizational culture and organizational performance remain to be proven.

Organizational culture can be defined functionally or pragmatically as a social force that controls patterns of organizational behavior by shaping members' cognitions and perceptions of meanings and realities, providing affective energy for mobilization, and identifying who belongs and who does not. The functional definition of organizational culture is quite straightforward. So why not use it and stop belaboring the comparatively complicated inductive/deductive approach that defines organizational culture by classifying its component elements? The answer is equally straightforward. The functional definition does not provide any direction for managing in, changing, or studying organizational culture. If John Thomas wants to strengthen or change aspects of the Mountain State Chapter's organizational culture, what does he go to work on—its symbols, artifacts, patterns of behavior, beliefs, values, assumptions, or all of them? What tools and strategies does a chief executive officer at AT&T, Jones & Jones, or the Community Center use to reinforce or change organizational culture? What does a researcher, manager, or consultant study, using what types of diagnosing/deciphering procedures and instruments?

A functional definition provides important understandings about the functions organizational culture performs and why organizational cultures continue to exist. Nevertheless, it is far from adequate by itself for those who would work with and in organizational cultures.

SUMMARY

So what is organizational culture? First, it is a concept, and there is no concrete way to "prove" what a concept is. There is no method for conclusively ending debates about "the truth." *Truth* is created rather than discovered, so there is no single true definition or concept of organizational culture. However, by creating a typology of organizational culture, the multitude of definitions that have been proposed by many writers have been collapsed into three and one-half levels.[7]

---

[7]Three and one half because Schein's Level 1 has been divided into Levels 1A and 1B.

The levels (or points on a continuum) represent theoretical constructs from Keesing (1974) and Schein (1981, 1984, 1985). Two preliminary tests of the typology (Figure 3–4 and Figure 3–5) show how it can be analytically useful.

Appendix to Chapter 3

A SAMPLING OF DEFINITIONS
OF ORGANIZATIONAL CULTURE

The following excerpted definitions are from fifty-eight books and articles on organizational culture or closely related subjects. The selections are representative of the literature but certainly are not exhaustive. Some cited authors do not use the phrase "organizational culture" but clearly are addressing the same or very similar concepts and constructs—for example, Jongeward (1976). A few definitions of general culture (rather than organizational culture) have been included because of their pertinence, and they are noted with an asterisk in Figure 3–5—for example, S. I. Hayakawa (1953).

When a definition overlaps substantially with other definitions, an incomplete definition is used in order to minimize repetition—for example, Hall (1977). The citations are not listed in any particular order. Quotations and paraphrasings are used liberally to retain the authors' color and flavor.

- Symbols, language, ideologies, rituals, and myths (Pettigrew, 1979).
- Behavioral regularities (Goffman, 1959, 1967; Van Maanen, 1979).
- Patterns of interactions, values, and attitudes, which are derived from traditions, precedents, and past practices and are most visible in the team formations within which managers work. The assumptions and beliefs people live by (Blake & Mouton, 1969).
- Organizational scripts derived from the personal scripts of the organization's founder(s) or dominant leader(s) (Jongeward, 1976).
- The philosophy that guides an organization's policy (Ouchi, 1981; Pascale & Athos, 1981).
- Beliefs, practical syllogisms, justifications for behavior (Sproull, 1981; Morley, 1984).

- Ideologies, a rationale for dos and don'ts (Harrison, 1972; Meyer, 1984).
- Core values that determine the organizational philosophy or mission (Selznick, 1957).
- Organizational climate, attitudes toward work, degree of personal responsibility for work (Lippitt, Langseth, & Mossop, 1985; Miles & Schmuck, 1971; Tagiuri & Litwin, 1968).
- Patterns of cognitive processes (Weick, 1979).
- Speech, communication patterns, language, nonverbal communication (Evered, 1983; Meissner, 1976).
- Myths, anecdotes, and stories (Cohen, 1969).
- Stories that control organizations (Wilkins, 1983).
- A belief in and a commitment to excellence (Peters & Waterman, 1982).
- The organization's ethic—for example, the "public service ethic" (Buchanan, 1975).
- Values and norms (Tichy & Ulrich, 1984; Hall, 1977).
- Symbols, language, and art (Hayakawa, 1953).
- The source of norms, rules, group attitudes, customs, and roles (Wharton & Worthley, 1983).
- The degree of consensus within consensus spheres on general values; organization goals; means, policy, and tactics; commitment to participate in the organization; performance obligations; cognitive perspectives (for example, common language, shared frame of reference, and an agreed-upon set of canons for empirical test) among the different status groups in the organization (Etzioni, 1975).
- (By inference) The who's who, what's what, why's why of an organization's informal society (Barnard, 1938, 1968).
- The *rules of the game* for getting along in an organization (Schein, 1968; Ritti & Funkhouser, 1977; Van Maanen, 1976).
- A *mind-set*—"the realm of feelings and sentiments" (p. 26). The basic values, assumptions, or expectations that have emerged from the organization's particular history, leadership, and contingency factors and that are supported by present-day management policies and practices (p. 27); also, worldview and beliefs, meanings and symbols, historical vestiges, traditions, and customs (Allaire & Firsirotu, 1985).
- "A quality of perceived organizational specialness—that it possesses some unusual quality that distinguishes it from others in the field" (Gold, 1982, pp. 571–572).

- "An amalgamation of some of the more interesting definitions would result in the following: organizational culture can be thought of as the glue that holds an organization together through a sharing of patterns of meaning. The culture focuses on the values, beliefs, and expectations that members come to share" (Siehl & Martin, 1984, p. 227).

- Familiar management tasks or practices (Martin & Siehl, 1983).

- Language or jargon (Edelman, 1977; Hirsch, 1980; Pondy, 1978).

- Organizational stories and scripts (Martin, 1982b; Wilkins, 1978, 1983). Also, to an extent, Clark (1970).

- The customary and traditional way of thinking and doing things (Jaques, 1952).

- Rituals and ceremonies (Gephart, 1978; Smircich, 1983).

- Physical arrangements (Edelman, 1971; Steele & Jenks, 1977).

- "The pattern of shared beliefs and values that give the members of an institution meaning, and provide them with the rules for behavior in their organization. Every organization will have its own words or phrases to describe what it means by culture; some of these are: being, core, culture, ethos, identity, ideology, manner, patterns, philosophy, purpose, roots, spirit, style, vision, and way. To most managers, these mean pretty much the same thing" (Davis, 1984, p. 1).

- Values, heroes, rites and rituals, and communications. "A strong culture is a system of informal rules that spells out how people are to behave most of the time" (Deal & Kennedy, 1982, p. 15).

- Values, norms, and knowledge (Clark, 1970).

- "*Culture*: The set of important assumptions (often unstated) that members of a community share in common. *Company Culture*: The culture of the corporation or the company as a whole" (Sathe, 1985, p. 2). (Emphasis in original text.)

- "A pattern of basic assumptions—invented, discovered, or developed by a given group as it learns to cope with its problems of external adaptation and internal integration—that has worked well enough to be considered valid and, therefore, to be taught to new members as the correct way to perceive, think, and feel in relation to those problems."

    "Because such assumptions have worked repeatedly, they are likely to be taken for granted and to have dropped out of awareness. Note that the definition does not include overt behavior patterns. I believe that overt behavior is always determined both by the cultural predisposition . . . and by the situational contingencies that arise from the external environment. Behavioral regularities could thus be as much a reflection of the environment as of the culture and should, therefore, not be a prime basis for defining the culture" (Schein, 1985, p. 9).

- "A standard definition of culture would include the system of values, symbols, and shared meanings of a group including the embodiment of these values, symbols, and meanings into material objects and ritualized practices. Culture governs what is of worth for a particular group and how group members should think, feel and behave. The stuff of culture includes customs and traditions, historical accounts be they mythical or actual, tacit understandings, habits, norms and expectations, common meanings associated with fixed objects and established rites, shared assumptions, and intersubjective meanings" (Sergiovanni & Corbally, 1984, p. vii).

- "The links between language, metaphor, and ritual and their celebration of particular social ideals or myths form the essential administrative culture of the school. The culture is a translation of myths into action and relationship" (Bates, 1984, p. 268).

- "This concept is close to that of enactment as described by Weick (1977). Weick argues that organizational members share perceptions of what factors comprise the environment of the organization. This process of enacting the environment in a sense creates the reality of organizational environments. This then is similar to Berger and Luckmann's (1966) concept of the social construction of reality. We would only add that the frameworks we are suggesting include the definition of the organization itself and of internal organizational processes" (Duncan & Weiss, 1979, pp. 90–91). (Duncan and Weiss do not explicitly state that the frameworks are the culture, but the linkage can be inferred.)

CHAPTER 4

Origins, Development, and Perpetuation of Organizational Culture

Where does an organizational culture come from, how does it develop, and why does it continue to exist even though organization members come and go over the years? Answers to these questions serve three useful purposes:

1. They hold the answers to how one goes about changing or strengthening aspects of an organizational culture, and why organizational cultures are very difficult to change.

2. They explain why all organizational cultures are relatively unique, and why most subcultures are either enhancing or orthogonal rather than countercultures.[1]

3. They lay the groundwork for understanding how to identify or decipher an organizational culture.[2]

Chapter 4 is organized into three major topics: organizational culture's origins or sources, how it develops or is refined within an organization, and how it is transmitted and perpetuated. The origins do not differ substantially, whether organizational culture is defined as artifacts, patterns of behavior, beliefs and values, or basic assumptions.[3] Nevertheless, this is not true for its development and perpetuation, so these two functions are analyzed in this chapter for the different levels of organizational culture.

---

[1] The three different types of subcultures are described and explained in the section of Chapter 2, entitled Subcultures.

[2] Identifying organizational culture is the subject of Chapter 5.

[3] See Chapter 3 for an analysis of the levels of organizational culture.

ORIGINS OR SOURCES OF ORGANIZATIONAL CULTURE

Organizational culture has three general sources or determinants:

1. The broader societal culture in which an organization resides.
2. The nature of an organization's business or business environment.
3. The beliefs, values, and basic assumptions held by the founder(s) or other early dominant leader(s).[4]

Thus, there are *common threads* among organizations' cultures, reflecting commonalities in the general culture and similarities in the types of business in which they engage; and there are *unique threads*, reflecting differences in the general culture, types of business, and the founder's beliefs, values, and assumptions.

The three general sources are not completely independent of one another. The founder's basic assumptions are in part shaped by the broader culture. The organization's choice of business in which to engage usually is influenced by the founder's assumptions. The business environment both affects and is affected by the societal culture. So it is more useful to think of the origins of an organization's culture as the unique sum of the composite blending of the three general sources than as competitors to shape an organizational culture.

The Broader Culture

Societal culture is such a fundamental shaper of organizational culture that it can be easy to overlook its importance. The beliefs, values, and expectations held by an organization's important internal and external constituencies are formed in the broader culture. Sooner or later, changes in societal norms, beliefs, values, and life-style patterns—such as sexual equality and wellness—find their way into organizations. At the other extreme, a few authors have tried to write off the concept of organizational culture as nothing more than a subculture of societal culture. It is my hope that this chapter will put both arguments to rest.

Most general cultural beliefs, values, and assumptions are quite

---

[4]People who have written about the origins of organizational culture place more emphasis on one or another of the sources and use slightly different groupings, but there is remarkably little conflict among their views and findings. See for example, Davis (1984); Deal and Kennedy (1982); Sathe (1985); and Schein (1983, 1985). Also, Gold (1982) adds as a source the clarity of and the organization's awareness of its mission.

stable. Japanese firms are expected to be paternalistic and compassionate sources of lifelong employment. Employees are expected to be loyal, noncompetitive internally, and relatively unquestioningly responsive to their employers' decisions (Ouchi, 1981; Pascale & Athos, 1981). These fundamental cultural expectations are neither discussed nor debated but are taken for granted by potential employees, current employees, their families, managers, customers, bankers, agencies of the government, directors, investors, business school professors, and textbooks. It would be next to impossible for the organizational culture of a Japanese firm located in Japan not to reflect these cultural traits. On the other hand, it is very difficult for a U.S. firm not located in Japan to emulate Japanese management practices, for the societal cultural assumptions differ dramatically.

What about organizations that have operations in more than one country? Can they tell us anything about the impact of societal culture on organizational culture? Hofstede (1984) studied organizational values in the subsidiaries of one multinational company with operations in forty countries. He identified elements of a common organizational culture, but, predictably, there were distinct organizational subcultures in each country. Most important for this discussion, Hofstede found that the basic characteristics of the organizational subcultures could be explained by (correlated with) dominant values of the national cultures.

We do not need to cross national boundaries in order to find societal cultures impacting on organizational cultures. Ouchi (1984, ch. 9) describes Minneapolis, Minnesota, as having a unique community culture in which there is "conscious and explicit peer pressure [on business leaders] to participate in public affairs" (p. 195). According to Ouchi, Minneapolis is a community of people who are connected to one another. In Minneapolis-based companies such as Control Data, General Mills, Pillsbury, and 3M, managers are *expected* to be active in long-term community development. Shafritz (1985) argues that the quality, style, and vigor of a local government's operations is determined primarily by the community's political culture. In order to understand the extreme variations among public bureaucracies in the United States, it is necessary to examine the cultural context of the host jurisdiction. Wilson (1968) found that the style of police operations in various jurisdictions could be explained by the communities' expressed and/or implied desires.

Many years ago, I conducted an unpublished field study of the business cultures in two small northeastern Pennsylvania towns, Coaltown and Riverton[5] (Ott 1961). The towns are only 15 miles

---

[5]Coaltown and Riverton are pseudonyms.

apart as the crow flies, but they lie in two almost parallel valleys separated by a sizeable mountain range. Coaltown's valley is full of coal seams that were mined extensively into the 1950s. Coaltown was a bastion of United Mine Workers of America strength. Intense labor-management hostilities, including violence, are integral parts of the town's history. Riverton's valley contains no coal. The town had been a retail center for farmers, and union-management conflict was un-known. The religious and ethnic compositions of the two towns also differ markedly.

Coaltown and Riverton each successfully conducted aggressive campaigns to attract garment firms that were fleeing New England and New York during the late 1950s. In Coaltown, antagonisms developed immediately between the imported managers and hourly workers in all four of the recruited firms. There were numerous grievances and instances of worker sabotage during the firms' first years. Three of the four firms were struck within two years of arriv-ing. Hostile labor-management relationships were *expected*. The town, including its only newspaper, backed the workers during dis-putes. All four recruited companies moved on within three years. The scenario was very different in Riverton, fewer than 15 miles away. All of the recruited firms stayed at least five years; there were no major labor-management conflicts, and the imported managers seemed to have been integrated into the community.

Among the organizations studied in preparing this book, Scenic Mountain State College, a small, rural, plains-state college, has been most shaped by the general culture in which it resides. The College is located in a very rural, low-income area. Mining and ranching have been the major industries. The educational level is low, and the population is aging and declining. There is a strong cultural work ethic, and unemployment is low—but so are salaries and wages. Underemployment is very high.

The College was founded as a normal school with a mission to educate local youth to be teachers in the area's one-, two-, and three-room schools. Low teacher salaries and geographic isolation have precluded the recruitment of outsiders as teachers, so the mission has been vital to the area. Although the College now has eight academic departments, all of them except Military Sciences still exist primarily to educate rural teachers. The primary focus of the Industrial Arts, Math and Science, Communications, Music, Physical Education, and Business departments is to prepare industrial arts, math and science, English, music, physical education, and business teachers, respec-tively. Although the departments have other missions—for example, the Business Department offers bachelor and associate degree pro-grams in small business management and office skills, respectively —they are secondary.

Fewer than twenty percent of the student body comes from outside of the area. The freshman year dropout rate is almost forty percent. A recent confidential College study found that most dropouts chose to leave as a result of homesickness, loneliness, family economic problems, and/or fear of social or academic failure. Many dropouts return home to live with parents or other relatives. Almost all of the College's administrators and more than two thirds of the faculty were born, raised, and educated in the state. At the time this study was being conducted, two thirds of the administrators had received undergraduate degrees from the College.

By now the extent of the area culture's shaping of the Scenic Mountain State College organizational culture should be very evident. Still, it took me about a year of involvement with the College to identify, organize, and document the basic assumptions of the College's organizational culture, because they are largely unspoken and fairly well concealed. The more important ones are:

- We must keep average and subaverage students here long enough to get degrees. They will stay and teach in the area. The College's high dropout rate is evidence of the difficulty and importance of our mission, not of our failure; our target students aren't here for academics. They are here to learn a job skill—which ought to be teaching.

- By maintaining our paternalistic College community, we'll ensure that some students will persevere and graduate. These are the people who *should* be teachers in our area. They have the proper values, are "of us," and can be trusted to shape the children's values.

- If we were academically sophisticated in our teaching, course offerings, and academic expectations, we would drive out even more of our target students than we are now, which would be counter to our mission.

- We do not recruit top students from high schools. They usually leave the area after graduating, so they aren't of any value to the area or, thus, to us.

- Research and publications detract the faculty from their primary job of preparing our target students to be teachers.

- Faculty members who publish and advocate higher academic standards do not understand our students, our area, or the College's mission. They don't make common sense decisions or stay here very long.

- We advertise nationally for faculty because we should, but we don't hire many from out of the state or the area.

- The College pays very poorly. We work here because we like living here. But with the low pay, don't expect us to do things beyond our specific classroom or administrative responsibilities. We don't get paid enough to advise students, work with student or alumni groups, participate in planning to improve the college, or what have you.

These longstanding basic assumptions of the organizational culture continue to control Scenic Mountain State College's mission, curriculum, student and faculty recruitment processes and targets, and performance expectations for students and staff. Its administrators, faculty, students, and alumni were raised in this rural, hard-working, low-income, nonmobile, common sense-oriented, survivalistic, unpretentious, nonacademic, area culture. Most faculty, administrators, and support staff members are there for their lifetimes. Both they and the college are products of and maintainers of the area culture. Changing the organizational culture would be a Herculean task and probably would have long-term impacts on the culture of the area.

Although the boundaries between organizational cultures and general societal cultures are permeable, and the cultures are intertwined, the general culture is far from being the sole—or even the primary—determinant of organizational culture. It is only one of three major shaping influences.

The Nature of the Business

The types of business in which organizations are engaged and their general business environment are the second grouping of important determinants of organizational culture[6] (Deal & Kennedy, 1982; Sathe, 1985). Despite the substantial impact of the area culture on Scenic Mountain State College's organizational culture, it is more similar to the culture of other colleges than it is to the culture of a CPA firm, an agency of state government, or a manufacturing firm situated in the same geographical area. Although several reasons can be postulated, no existing body of empirical research can explain or can be used to predict similarities and differences among organizational cultures resulting from the nature of business or the general business environment. Three important reasons include:

---

[6]Schein (1983) argues that the external environment per se does not shape organizational culture. Rather, it is the experiences organization members have had in developing solutions for coping with the environment (and problems of internal integration). This argument is expanded in the section of this chapter, "Development of Organizational Culture."

1. Some similarities among organizational cultures within an industry can be explained by the fact that many organizations are dominated by people from certain professions. Professions attract people who are predisposed to being socialized, and they consciously socialize new entrants into their system of values, beliefs, and assumptions (Becker, Geer, Hughes, & Strauss, 1961; Kaufman, 1960; Schein, 1978). New CPAs have been socialized into the accounting profession; medical group practices, hospitals, and pharmaceutical companies attract people socialized (or partially socialized) into the medical profession; and human service delivery agencies seek (and are sought by) social workers and related professionals. Additionally, many professions require continuing education, participation in which reinforces the professional cultures. To the extent that an organization (or parts of an organization) is dominated by a profession, its organizational culture will be shaped at least partially by that professional culture.

2. The nature of an organization's business determines with whom and how it must interact in the course of doing business. State Health interacts regularly with the health care providers it regulates. State Health's regulatory role and the types of organizations it regulates influence the nature of its interactions. The Community Center contracts with nonprofit agencies for the provision of human services and, because the funds are public, monitors the services they provide to clients and their use of funds. Thus the Community Center interacts with and acts as an extension of a government agency in its work with nonprofit service providers. It is reasonable to assume that these patterns of interaction strongly affect an organization's culture (Ott & Shafritz, 1986, Authors' Preface); still, there is no theory or empirical evidence to support the assumption.

The impact of business environments on organizational culture has received extensive media coverage because of continuing ethical problems between the Department of Defense and large defense contractors. According to Malcolm T. Stamper, Vice Chairman of Boeing Corporation (*Industry Week*, September 16, 1985), clashing cultural differences between commercial and defense industry practices are at the core of the difficulties.

> For example, he says, "in a commercial enterprise, it's good business practice to support the community by buying a table at the Boy Scout banquet and putting the cost in your product price. In defense work, that's considered an abuse."
> It's the same, he points out, with passing out product samples or

small gifts to stimulate customers or motivate employees—or entertaining customers.

Moreover, Mr. Stamper notes that in the commercial market, firms try to hire the most knowledgeable people to perform certain jobs.

"But that's called the 'revolving door' in defense work, and is discouraged," he says. And, he adds, "in free enterprise, if an employee misbehaves or breaks the law, he is disciplined, discharged, and/or prosecuted. In defense work, the company is often indicted or prosecuted; the perception is that the company in its entirety intentionally committed the wrongdoing" (p. 58).

3. Deal and Kennedy (1982) have concluded that general types of company cultures are determined by just two marketplace factors: the degree of risk and "the speed at which companies—and their employees—get feedback on whether decisions or strategies are successful" (p. 107). The culture of a regulated monopoly will not resemble the culture of a television network (degree of risk). The culture of a public health agency that inspects and cites nursing homes for code violations will not resemble the culture of a center that prepares people with developmental disabilities to live independently (speed of feedback).

Although the nature of an organization's business and its general business environment help shape its organizational culture, surprisingly little is known about the extent, nature, and conditions under which shaping occurs. When does the nature of an organization's business exert primary influence on (what aspects of) its culture? When secondary? How much professional density causes an organizational culture to mirror a professional culture? Does the density-domination relationship vary among the professions? Groups of professions? Why? Do the degree of risk and the speed of feedback indeed determine the type of organizational culture? The entire arena needs empirical research.

The Impacts of Founder(s)

Founders and other dominant, early organizational leaders seek out and attract people who share their views, values, beliefs, and assumptions and, through the force of their personalities, further shape the culture. Organization founders usually begin with a theory of how to succeed that originates in the societal culture in which they were raised and in their prior work experiences. Then, they tend to hire new people who share their theory. As an organization grows, compatible-theory newcomers move into management and executive positions and bring in subsequent generations of new members also with compatible outlooks. Through the organization's socialization processes, new and older upwardly mobile members learn and relearn "the organization's ropes" (Ritti & Funkhouser, 1982)—what it takes to get along and to get ahead. Those who do not come to share the cultural assumptions lose influence and/or depart. Thus the unique cultural imprint of the founder(s) and other early dominant leaders is pervasive and remains long after they leave or die.[7]

It is easy for an alert observer to identify impacts of founders and other early leaders on organizational cultures. The elder Mr. Jones, of Jones & Jones, CPAs, was an aloof, pompous, condescending person. He originated the metaphor *asshole* and, according to an often told Jones & Jones story, first used it while throwing a client out of the offices who had the audacity to question an accounting procedure he had used. In the 1930s or 1940s, a leader or group of leaders at State Health (it is not known which one or ones) came to hold the basic assumption that private health care providers would not act in the public interest and therefore could not be permitted to participate in formulating public health policy in that state.

Although the Community Center Director, Bill Snow, was not its first, his predecessors were weak leaders who surrounded themselves with equally weak managers. The Community Center did not have much of an identifiable culture prior to his being hired as Deputy Director in 1973. Mr. Snow's personality is very strong, almost dogmatic. He was selected by the Board of Directors despite strenuous objections by the then director and other senior managers. The Board had been pressured by its major source of funding to make major organizational changes, did not trust the director to make them, but did not have the courage to fire him. The directors terminated the immediate predecessor involuntarily in 1974, about seven months after Snow's arrival. The Community Center's identifiable organizational culture dates to 1973–1974.

Summary

There are three strong general determinants of organizational culture: the broader societal culture in which an organization resides, the nature of its business and business environment, and the basic assumptions of the founder or other early dominant leaders. Some

---

[7] Writing from a transactional analysis perspective, Dorothy Jongeward (1973, ch. 1) attributes the origins of organizational scripts to the personal life scripts of the founder or other early leaders. She concludes that organizational scripts are as difficult to change as personal scripts.

commonalities among organizational cultures are determined by the general culture and by similarities in the types of business in which organizations engage. Nevertheless, all organizational cultures are unique, because of differences in the general culture, types of business, and the founder's basic assumptions. The three sources of organizational culture are not independent of each other: the founder's basic assumptions are influenced by the broader culture, the organization's line of business is affected by the founder's assumptions, and the business environment both affects and is affected by the societal culture. Every organizational culture is the unique result of a composite blending of the sources of organizational cultures. Figure 4–1 is a representation of the origins of organizational culture.

Not much is known yet about the nature and extent of the impacts of the sources or about the dynamic interactions among them under different circumstances. Even when we do know the general culture, line of business, business environment, and the founder, we cannot predict the cultures of new organizations reliably. Perhaps the sources are so interdependent that attempts to separate their impacts are destined to fail. Yet intuitively we know that some professions, such as accounting, law, and medicine, tend to have greater impacts on organizational cultures than some other professions. Most of us would expect the community cultures in Coaltown and Riverton to overpower the common geographical cultures of the garment firms

FIGURE 4–1   Sources or Origins of Organizational Culture

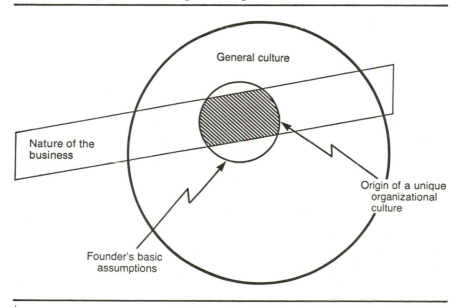

that relocated in northeastern Pennsylvania. And anyone who had met the elder Mr. Jones (of Jones & Jones) could predict the basic culture of *any* organization he formed. Empirical research into the nature, extent, and interactions of the sources of organizational culture should be very fruitful. (See Chapter 5 for more on this subject.)

THE DEVELOPMENT OF ORGANIZATIONAL CULTURE

This analysis concentrates on the ordinary or normal incremental development of organizational culture. Shifts in any of the three primary sources of organizational culture should cause at least minor alterations. Thus drifts in societal or professional cultural values, assumptions, and life-style patterns eventually creep into organizational cultures. Changes in an organization's line of business—for example, through acquisition, merger, expansion, contraction, new legislative mandates, grant awards, or budget cutting—should modify its culture; although even minor changes often happen slowly and painfully, are resisted, and typically are accompanied by conflict. New organizational leaders who ascend through evolutionary processes add their imprints to those of the founder and other early leaders. Therefore, although organizational cultures tend to be quite stable, they do not remain static. They evolve, often slowly and within limits, because their primary sources also shift.

The development of organizational culture is a more complicated process than its formation because more complex variables come into play. Organizational cultures develop as unique combinations of individuals and groups work within organizational cultures and subcultures, each with its own history of experiences with solving problems and capitalizing on opportunities. If organizational culture is defined as artifacts (Level 1A), then cultures develop primarily through the processes by which signs become symbols.[8] On the other hand, if organizational culture is defined as beliefs and values (Level 2), then cultures develop through the processes by which beliefs and values are learned.[9]

The best source of theory about the development of organizational cultures as defined as basic assumptions (Level 3) is in Schein (1985, chs. 7 and 8); moreover, the body of empirical evidence on the subject is very limited (Pettigrew, 1979; Clark, 1970; 1972). Schein

---

[8]See Chapter 2, "Artifacts."
[9]See Chapter 2, "Beliefs and Values."

(1985) postulates that it is necessary to synthesize group dynamics or *sociodynamic theory* (pp. 149–170); leadership theory; and learning theory in order to understand the dynamics of organizational culture development. Interestingly, Schein's theoretical basis draws substantially from theory on the development of patterns of behavior (Level 1B). The key theoretical points in Schein's (1985) conceptualization include:

- Organization members face difficult dilemmas because of their conflicting desires to fuse with organizational reference groups (to lose some personal identity) and retain some autonomy (and risk losing group membership and affiliation).
- Three competing basic human needs are at the core of these dilemmas: inclusion and identity; control, power, and influence; and acceptance and intimacy. The dilemmas create anxiety.
- Groups in organizations vary widely in the cultures they develop because of the unique strengths and interactions of the needs, personalities, and emotional coping styles of the leaders, members, and the circumstances.
- Despite variations among individuals' needs and solutions to the dilemmas, their solutions are influenced by group norms and shared understandings.
- Shared understandings develop from common feelings, experiences, and activities. They are transmitted and infused through a common communication system (language).
- The culture includes the "learned group repertoire of capacities to solve problems . . . and the shared cognitions that the group develops" (p. 177). Once social defense mechanisms have been learned, they will be very stable and will be repeated indefinitely.
- The interactions between leaders, members, and the organizational culture are complex. Although leaders play important roles in creating and managing organizational cultures, they become trapped in and by them and sometimes find that they cannot lead the organization in new directions.

Although organizational cultures are influenced by individual members, Schein (1985, ch. 7) argues that cultures develop from the group learning that occurs when members face problems and opportunities and "work out a solution together" (p. 183). Group solutions reflect the unique personalities, needs, and coping styles of individual members and also are shaped by leaders and by the group learning that flows from experiences specific to the group's circumstances.

Such learning requires shared understandings, and shared understandings cannot occur without common experiences and language. Thus, trying to predict how a specific organizational culture will develop requires a continuing dynamic analysis of how and what patterns of basic assumptions are

> invented, discovered, or developed by a given group as it learns to cope with its problems of external adaptation and internal integration— that has worked well enough to be considered valid and, therefore, to be taught to new members as the correct way to perceive, think, and feel in relation to those problems (Schein, 1985, p. 9).

So what? If the process of organizational culture development is as complex as Schein envisions it, isn't the study or use of it beyond pragmatic limits? Probably not. In fact, Schein's theories help divert a manager's or researcher's investigative efforts away from potentially fruitless studies of things such as artifacts, norms, beliefs, and values and into things such as patterns of historical organizational responses to critical events in their histories. Longitudinal research approaches have been used productively, for example, by Pettigrew (1979), to study the organizational culture of a British boarding school, and by Clark (1970, 1972) to understand why three colleges developed into "distinctive" institutions.

If John Thomas, the change-oriented president of the Mountain State Chapter, had studied the Chapter's historical pattern for coping with critical events, he could have observed that the absence of overt resistance to his innovations did not signify acquiescence or willingness to change. Moreover, despite formal Board decisions (votes) to make fundamental Chapter changes, those decisions would be reversed without fanfare as soon as the source of anxiety (John Thomas) departed. For years the Chapter had coped successfully with anxiety by not coping with it directly, holding conflicts in abeyance, taking and keeping disagreement underground, and waiting for the source of anxiety to disappear. The directors simply applied their learned cultural solution to an anxiety-creating problem—in other words, don't fight it overtly; stall, and ignore it until it goes away. If John Thomas had been alert, he could have predicted the failure— and the timing of the failure—of his change package. Perhaps if he had stayed long enough to engineer the replacement of a substantial number of directors and staff, he would have succeeded. As it was, as soon as he decided to rotate himself off the Board, the demise of his programs was absolutely predictable.

It required repeated failures of patterned solutions before Jones & Jones, CPAs, took steps to modify its cultural assumptions. The area's economy experienced a dramatic downturn. For the first time in its history, the firm could not replace clients who were driven away. Failure to alter the culture clearly would have led to the firm's collapse. Management and staff had to unlearn old assumptions about clients and relearn new ways of dealing with them. I do not believe that the unlearning and relearning has been truly accomplished. I predict a return to the old cultural solution patterns if Jones & Jones's ability to replace clients should return in the near future. Organizational cultures have deep roots, and they develop over long periods of time through complex individual and group mechanisms. Usually they can be altered only slowly, through painful learning processes that often are resisted by members.

TRANSMITTAL AND PERPETUATION OF ORGANIZATIONAL CULTURE

As is the case with the formation and development of organizational culture, the processes by which it is transmitted and perpetuated vary somewhat according to how the concept is defined—but they overlap. Artifacts (Level 1A) are perpetuated through the functional or symbolic meanings attributed to them by members of the culture. Symbolic attribution occurs primarily through stories, myths, metaphors, heroes, rituals, rites, and ceremonies.[10]

Basic assumptions are transmitted and perpetuated through a network of interacting processes. Figure 4–2 is an adaptation of Vijay Sathe's (1985) conceptualization of how organizational culture is perpetuated (p. 385). The diagram provides the theoretical framework for analyzing the maintenance or change of organizational culture. Managers who seek to change an organizational culture need to intervene at all numbered points in the diagram. On the other hand, managers who want to perpetuate an existing culture must "counteract any such intervention by others, and prevent any weakening of these processes by consciously attending to them" (Sathe, 1985, p. 385). Figure 4–2 serves as the outline for the remainder of this chapter.

1: Preselection and Hiring of Members

The first step in perpetuating an organizational culture should start before employees are hired. For example, Buchanan (1975) describes a public service ethic in the United States that includes an

---

[10]See Chapter 2, "Symbols: Creators and Communicators of Meaning" and "Artifacts."

FIGURE 4–2   How Culture Tends to Perpetuate Itself

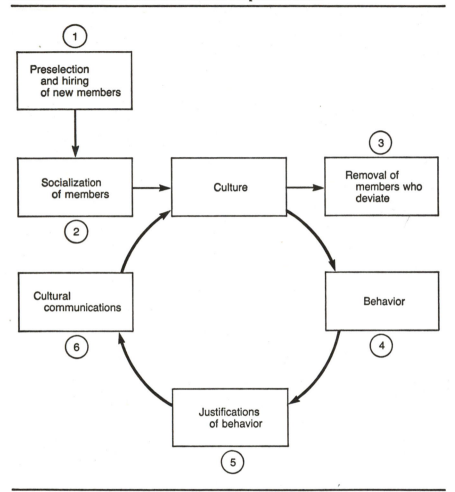

SOURCE: Reprinted from Vijay Sathe, *Culture and Related Corporate Realities: Texts, Cases, and Readings on Organizational Entry, Establishment, and Change.* Homewood, Ill.: Richard D. Irwin, Inc., 1985, p. 385. Used with permission.

expectation that public servants will have a unique sense of loyalty and a special sensitivity to the public interest.[11] If a public agency wants to perpetuate that ethic, one of its first steps should include seeking out and selecting new members who already possess it or who are strongly predisposed to accepting it. Merton (1957) calls this predisposition *anticipatory socialization* (p. 265), the process by which

---

[11]Buchanan cites Mosher (1968).

people adopt the values of a group to which they aspire to belong but have not yet joined. According to Merton, anticipatory socialization helps a person to be accepted by a group and "eases his adjustment after he has become a part of it" (p. 265). Following this line of reasoning, Popovich & Wanous (1982) advocate the use of the *Realistic Job Preview* to reduce the probability of selecting new members who will experience dissonance from unmet personal expectations (p. 571). In effect, the Realistic Job Preview screens out applicants who are not compatible with the organizational culture and may resist socialization, and it activates the presocialization process for candidates who remain in contention.

Kaufman's (1960, ch. 6) study of the U.S. Forest Service's methods for obtaining willing compliance from its forest rangers vividly demonstrates how the Forest Service sought out and selected new members who were predisposed to accommodate themselves to the demands made upon members of the Forest Service. As "willingness to conform [was] employed as an initial criterion of selection" (p. 165), the Forest Service recruited its new members from only a handful of colleges of forestry with good track records in presocializing potential rangers.

For similar reasons, most employees of the Community Center are parents of children with developmental disabilities who are served by the Center's programs. They are known to have the "right attitudes" before they are hired. State Health recruits and selects its new professional employees almost exclusively from city, county, and federal health regulating agencies known to have compatible regulatory-oriented philosophies or cultures. Scenic Mountain State College advertises for faculty and administrators nationally but almost always selects people who were raised and educated in the area. In contrast, the CPA profession to which Jones & Jones belongs was a very competitive employment industry until very recently. Jones & Jones could not preselect or presocialize new members. Over the years the firm hired many employees who were not compatible with its culture, and its new employee turnover rate has been very high. Thus preselection, presocialization, and hiring based on compatibility with the organizational culture constitute an important first step in perpetuating organizational culture.

2: Socialization of Members

Organizational socialization refers to the processes by which members learn the cultural values, norms, beliefs, assumptions, and required behaviors that permit them to participate as effective members of an organization (Van Maanen, 1976, p. 67). Organizational socialization also implies that people may need to relinquish certain of their personal attitudes, beliefs, values, and behaviors as a price of membership.

Organizational socialization, or "people processing" (Van Maanen, 1983, p. 240), is not necessarily a dangerous or coercive process of mind altering—even though coerced socialization is used in some types of total institutions (Goffman, 1961; Wallace, 1971). All societal groups socialize or enculturate their members (Kroeber, 1948). The organizational socialization process that people encounter in most employer-employee settings is a learning process. Adults continually grow, learn, and adapt; and socialization provides organization members the particular knowledge and motivation needed to learn and fill organizational roles—to become effective and productive members.

The socialization process is the way by which an individual learns the behavior appropriate to his or her position in a group "through interaction with others who hold normative beliefs about what his role should be and who reward or punish him for correct or incorrect actions" (Brim, 1966, p. 9). Becker and Strauss (1956) saw an inherent relationship between changes in social position and changes in adult identity (p. 262). And Wanous (1980) postulated that narrowing the gap between individual and organizational expectations is the key to creating employee commitment and satisfaction. Thus, people processing is neither inherently wrong nor immoral; but it can be abused, and it can contribute to overconformance and organizational rigidity. (For a more thorough discussion of this topic, see Chapter 8.)

The use of organizational socialization processes is not limited to new employees. People are most open to socialization when their anxiety level is high, particularly when they are in a state of transition—crossing or preparing to cross organizational boundaries in order to enter new working groups and/or roles. Therefore, the socialization process usually is most active when a person is entering an organization or is being promoted, demoted, or moved laterally across an organizational boundary (Van Maanen, 1983).

People processing is inevitable. However, organizations vary widely in the degrees to which they consciously or unconsciously manage their socialization processes and contents. The uniformed services tend to be most active and explicit in socializing newcomers, including agencies such as police departments (Hazer & Alvares, 1981; Van Maanen, 1975); the armed services (Stouffer, Suchman, DeVinney, Star, & Williams, 1949), and the U.S. Forest Service (Kaufman, 1960). Nonuniformed public agencies do not seem to give much thought to socialization processes, leaving them to undirected peers and immediate supervisors. Between these two extremes many companies, nonprofit organizations, and public agencies make efforts that range from token and implicit to serious and explicit. Some typical socialization activities include formal orientation sessions for new employees (Siehl & Martin, 1984); inhouse training programs for upward-moving managers (Kanter, 1983, chs. 3–5); and carefully designed formal mentoring relationships (Lunding, Clements, & Perkins, 1978).

Organizations employ a variety of socialization processes. Van Maanen (1983, pp. 243–257) has identified seven such pairs of strategies: formal (informal); individual (collective); sequential (nonsequential); fixed (variable); tournament (contest); serial (disjunctive); and investiture (divestiture).[12] Kaufman (1960) provided an unusually rich description of the U.S. Forest Service's arsenal of socialization techniques, which included training programs, identification building programs, transfer policies and practices, promotions and other rewards, reporting systems, the system of approvals and clearances, institutional advertising, and the strategic use of symbols internally and externally (ch. 6).

The organizations discussed in this book are very typical. They have left socialization of new employees pretty much to chance. State Health schedules department-wide new employee orientation sessions once or twice a year. By the time most newcomers attend an orientation session, they have already "learned the ropes" from peers and occasionally from their immediate supervisors. The Community Center encourages supervisors to take new employees out to lunch but does not reimburse them for meals. A strong and cohesive informal group takes charge of enculturating new female employees, but males are left to fend for themselves. Jones & Jones has instituted a semistructured "mentoring program" for junior accountants. Previously, socialization of new employees was done "accidentally" by the newcomers' officemates.

These same organizations are far more conscious and concerned about the match between people and organizational culture at the managerial levels, particularly when it comes time for promotion decisions at levels that provide access to policy-level influence. The State Health Division director who was over the EMS Office, told me that no one in the EMS Office would ever be promoted to a position outside of that office "because they won't accept what we are about here." The EMS Office director, the hero of its counterculture, resigned less than one year after the cessation of the federal Public

---

[12]Van Maanen (1983, pp. 241–257) also evaluates the strategies in terms of their social consequences.

Health Service categorical grant program. The assistant division director, who successfully contained and engineered the demise of the EMS counterculture, was promoted twice in the two years following the EMS Office director's resignation (and the demise of the counterculture). He now is one of two assistant state health commissioners.

With only two exceptions, every Scenic Mountain State College department chairman was educated in the state and has been on the faculty for at least fifteen years. They and their spouses had to survive extensive and extended scrutiny on the job *and* in the town before being permitted to advance. One administrator who is openly acknowledged to be the College's brightest and most able at securing and managing grants, general planning and problem-solving, starting and managing highly lucrative off-campus programs, and initiating innovative educational programs on-campus has been completely insulated from mainline College decision making. He is not permitted to meet with the President's Advisory Council or to attend Academic Division meetings—even though he reports directly to the academic vice president. His responsibilities are limited to coordinating off-campus programs (mostly for adults—not college-age youth). He is considered untrustworthy (although no one interviewed could remember why); too aggressive; and not appreciative of "our kind of" academic values and protocols. Moreover, he has a Brooklyn accent. Obviously, this is not a person who should be participating in decisions that will affect the education and future lives of the area's children!

An attractive, competent, divorced, upper-middle-class woman manager at the Community Center began wearing "suggestive" clothing to work and sometimes went bra-less. When members of the Center's cohesive, female, informal organization noticed her "leaning over" in front of the director and occasionally "brushing against him," she was immediately and totally ostracized and was denied both secretarial support and peer staff assistance. Her telephone messages did not get posted, and documents started disappearing from her desk. People began complaining to the director about her "poor work performance and bad attitude." Within three months he began to apply pressure for her to resign. She resisted for a few months while she tried to find another position but left shortly thereafter.

In the three organizations described above, only people who "live" the cultural beliefs, values, and behaviors are promoted into or allowed to remain in positions of responsibility. Professional competence and demonstrated ability to achieve were not primary deciding factors. Two of the managers who did not match with the cultures left their organizations, and the third has been excluded from all important decision-making groups and settings. Excluding unsocialized people from positions of influence serves two important organizational functions. First, it helps perpetuate the culture by preventing deviants from getting into or remaining in positions where they might be able to alter it. Second, it communicates (transmits) a clear message to all organization members that those who do not adapt to the culture will not succeed, regardless of their competence or achievements. They will exit or be rendered organizationally impotent.

In summary, organizational socialization is a most important way through which organizational culture is perpetuated and transmitted. People in a state of transition tend to be anxious and ready to be socialized—to learn the assumptions, values, beliefs, and behaviors necessary to reduce that anxiety. The culture of the person's reference group(s) determines what the person must learn to be effective in his or her new role. In organizations that socialize their members well (i.e., have a strong pervasive culture), the reference groups will require learning that is consistent with the organizational culture. Some organizations consciously plan, design, and implement socialization programs. Others seem to drift into their people-processing strategies unconsciously or implicitly. If other things are nearly equal, organizations that socialize consciously should have stronger cultures than organizations that leave their socialization processes to chance.

3: Removal of Members Who Deviate from the Culture

Members who do not match well with their organizational culture tend to exit either voluntarily or involuntarily (Wanous, 1980, ch. 4). As in the Community Center, all cultures have subtle and not-so-subtle ways to rid themselves of deviants. Such departures usually are causes for celebrations, and the circumstances leading to them become cherished organizational stories. In these ways, the departure of people who do not buy into the organizational culture transmits important symbolic messages about cultural expectations and the price of "deviance" to all who remain. An annual company party celebrates the departure of two Jones & Jones executives who challenged the prevailing cultural vision of the company's identity. When a replacement was named for the EMS Office director, the State Health newsletter carried a lead story about the priority changes he would implement. Neither the Office nor the previous director was demeaned in the article, but its message was unmistakable: the counterculture would be exorcised totally and immediately.

Thus, the first the steps in perpetuating and transmitting organizational culture are:

1. Hire people who have been presocialized.

2. Activate organizational socialization processes whenever members are preparing to or actually cross organizational boundaries. Do not permit cultural deviates to get into or remain in positions of influence.

3. Cause cultural deviates to leave the organization. Consciously celebrate their departure very visibly.

4: Behavior

Under some circumstances, organizational culture can be perpetuated by affecting the behaviors of members (Bem, 1970, ch. 6). This step in culture perpetuation has its theoretical roots in the thinking of B. F. Skinner (1953) and Leon Festinger (1957). By altering or perpetuating peoples' patterns of behavior (including the decisions they make), organizations can change or reinforce their corresponding cultural beliefs, values, and assumptions (Sathe, 1985, p. 386).

The behavior-maintaining strategies available to organizations involve rewarding and punishing conformant and deviant behaviors. Monetary and nonmonetary reward systems (including promotion policies and practices); information and control systems; and the procedures required to clear decisions provide the most obvious levers for rewarding and punishing. The importance of reward systems should be evident.

Information and control systems can be used to alter behavior in two ways. First, they dictate what and when information is available for use by decision makers and thereby communicate what information *should be* considered when one is making decisions (Stout, 1980, ch. 6). In this way, information systems—much like classroom computers—teach and reinforce desired behaviors (ways of reaching decisions). According to Skinner and Festinger, repeated behavior eventually leads to internalized thought patterns. Thus, information and control systems can control patterns of cognition in the same way that language does for the Navajo—or members of any culture.[13] Second, information and control systems provide information to executives about the nature, extensiveness, and results of members' behaviors, which can be (and often is) incorporated into decisions to reward and punish (Stout, 1980, ch. 1).

---

[13] In Chapter 2, see "The Importance of Language" and "Language."

Kaufman (1960, ch. 6) provides an excellent example of how "decision clearance procedures" were used to alter or reinforce behaviors of forest rangers located in remote outstations. Reports of rangers' decisions had to be forwarded to area or regional offices. When a ranger's decision was consistent with what would have been decided by his or her superiors, the ranger did not need to take any further actions on the issue. However, when a ranger's decision varied from the superior's expectations, a detailed written justification was required—which took hours or days of paperwork. Extra paperwork took time away from getting the ranger's job done, which quickly became visible in the Forest Service's information and control system. According to Kaufman, rangers learned the facts of life quickly—or they left the Forest Service.

In summary, organizations can perpetuate and transmit organizational culture through their systems of rewards and punishments, information and control, and decision clearances. Cultural perpetuation or change happens through reinforcement or planned alteration of members' behavior, which eventually changes or stabilizes patterns of cultural cognitions, values, and assumptions.

Interestingly, many organizations actually reward behaviors that are inconsistent with their stated cultural beliefs and values (Kerr, 1975). Such inconsistencies broadcast symbolic signals that create confusion about what the cultural values and beliefs really are and undermine efforts to perpetuate or infuse them. In fact, rewarded behaviors usually reflect the true culture, which signals discrepancies between an organization's espoused values and its values-in-fact to an astute observer (Argyris & Schön, 1978, chs. 1 and 3).

5: Justifications of Behavior: Beliefs and Values

The fifth step approaches cultural perpetuation from a different slant. Instead of reinforcing or altering behavior in order to stabilize or modify cultural assumptions, beliefs and values are reinforced or modified directly (Zimbardo & Ebbesen, 1969, chs. 5 and 6). The difference between the two approaches is very important for selecting cultural change or maintenance strategies. The behavioral approach (Step 4) *assumes* that behavioral changes will result in cognitive and affective changes. It relies on extrinsic rewards and punishments to effect those changes—an approach that works some of the time.

Nevertheless, changing behavior does not necessarily change the *justifications of behavior*—those beliefs and values that justify why things are done as they are. When behavior changes but justifications do not, people may behave (act) compliantly while they are rationalizing the discrepancies between their behavior and their beliefs and values as being temporarily necessary for personal survival. They may take their beliefs and values "underground," waiting for the extrinsic reward/punishment system to change. This is one important reason why organizational cultures are so resistant to quick-fix change efforts. Intelligently planned strategies and plenty of time and patience are needed to change beliefs and values.

John Thomas successfully changed the way many things were done (behavior) at the Mountain State Chapter—*but he did not change the culture.* As soon as he left, the "underground" basic cultural assumptions resurfaced—and the behavioral changes could not survive. Newspaper and business magazine accounts seem to say that the same thing has been happening at AT&T. Despite all the money and effort devoted to marketing, marketing research, and strategic planning since the breakup and deregulation, members may be complying with the demands of the new order while waiting for technological values to retake their "rightful place"—in the core of the organizational culture.

Sathe (1985, pp. 386–388) proposes two basic strategies for changing organizational beliefs and values. They are equally applicable for perpetuating organizational culture:

1. Minimize reliance on extrinsic motivations to change, concentrating instead on intrinsic motivations.

2. Nullify inappropriate justifications of behavior.

Techniques for implementing these two strategies are primarily those of organization development and phenomenology. These subjects are beyond the scope of this book, but readings are suggested in the chapter notes.[14]

The arguments presented in Step 5 (justifications of behavior) do not invalidate the usefulness of Step 4 (behavior) actions, particularly as they are used to perpetuate and transmit organizational culture. Perpetuating and strengthening organizational culture requires consistency between the two sets of strategies. Behavioralistic strategies (systems of rewards and punishments, information and control, and decision clearances) must be consistent with organizational assumptions, beliefs and values-in-fact. Otherwise, symbolic signals will be transmitted that counteract each other, create confusion about what the actual or desired cultural values and beliefs really are, and undermine efforts to maintain or change them.

---

[14]See Sathe (1985, pp. 386–388) for some organization development-type techniques and references to others. Symbols, the social construction of reality, and phenomenology are discussed in Chapter 2.

6: Cultural Communications

The sixth and final step in this model for perpetuating and transmitting organizational culture takes us back to the discussions of artifacts, symbols, and symbolism in Chapter 2. The most effective mediums for communicating important cultural assumptions, beliefs, values, and behaviors include an organization's language, jargon, metaphors, myths, stories, heroes, scripts,[15] sagas, legends, ceremonies, celebrations, rites, and rituals. Information transmitted through these implicit forms of communication is heard more clearly and remembered longer than through more explicit mediums. When implicitly transmitted information is at odds with explicitly transmitted information, the former usually is believed.

Summary

The adaptation of Sathe's six-step model provides a very useful framework for analyzing strategies for perpetuating and transmitting organizational culture. The model is equally applicable for changing organizational culture. Only the contents of the steps and the relative importance among them differ.

The culture perpetuation model surfaces many issues for organizational research. Three particularly obvious questions are:

1. Does conscious management of *all six steps* in fact increase the strength and pervasiveness of an organizational culture?

2. Which of the steps are most and least crucial to culture perpetuation and change? Under what circumstances?

3. At what level of strength and pervasiveness does organizational culture start to become dysfunctional, from a rational organization perspective?

By addressing cultural perpetuation, change, and transmittal, this chapter begins to answer some important practical questions about how one goes about identifying, managing, stabilizing, and changing organizational cultures. Specifically:

- Where does one begin an "attack" to identify, strengthen, or change organizational culture?

- Why are organizational cultures so difficult to change?

- Why are all organizational cultures relatively unique, even though many have similarities?

---

[15]Organizational scripts as used in the cognitive social psychology sense, not the transactional analysis sense.

• Why are most subcultures either enhancing or orthogonal rather than countercultures?

Chapter 4 has shown how levels of organizational culture relate to and impact on each other, so the importance and usefulness of the organizational culture models (Figures 3–2 and 3–3) and typologies (Figures 3–4 and 3–5) should be more evident than they were in the context of Chapter 3. Moreover, the reasons for Chapter 3's laborious attention to definitional questions should now be becoming clear. If organizational culture is defined, for example, as artifacts (Level 1A) or patterns of behavior (Level 1B), then all it takes to perpetuate or change a culture is to maintain or change peoples' behaviors. Although changing behavior isn't an easy task, it doesn't present a new challenge or require a new perspective of organizations. The same point holds if organizational culture is defined as beliefs and values. There is an enormous body of theory and empirical research to draw on. However, if organizational culture is indeed basic underlying assumptions, then managers, students, and consultants need a new theoretical perspective, all of the "old" tools, plus some practical new ones.

Although this chapter has begun to answer some important questions, many more remain unanswered.

CHAPTER 5

Methodological Approaches for Studying Organizational Culture

This and the remaining chapters address many of the questions posed at the end of Chapter 4. For example, given the complexities of organizational culture, how does one go about identifying or otherwise conducting research in organizational culture? What should be deciphered? What research strategies should be used? Does, in fact, the process of investigating an organizational culture change it or destroy it (Herbert, 1987). These are some of the subjects of Chapter 5.

It is time to assess the applicability of different approaches, tools, and methods for researching, identifying, deciphering or explaining organizational culture, for different purposes and under different circumstances. Chapter 5 begins with an analysis of the very substantial problems associated with organizational culture research. Some research needs, issues, and appropriate data collection methodologies are then reviewed for each level of organizational culture. The chapter concludes with an attempt to bridge between competing research paradigms using analytical goals as the link.

For the sake of brevity, the words *research, identify, study,* and *decipher* are used interchangeably. Words such as *explain* and *predict* have more specific implications, so their meanings are explained in the context of their use. *Measure* is carefully excluded from the lexicon of this book.

DISENCHANTMENT WITH TRADITIONAL ORGANIZATIONAL RESEARCH METHODS

Students of organizational culture almost universally reject the logical-positivist quasi-experimental designs and approaches (Cook & Campbell, 1979, pp. 10–14) that have dominated organization theory research for more than a decade (Van Maanen 1982a). Van Maanen cites numerous reasons for the growing disenchantment with quantitative quasi-experimental designs—the backbone of the research methods of the systems and "modern" structural schools.[1] They include:

> the relatively trivial amounts of explained variance, the lack of comparability across studies, the failure to achieve much predictive validity, the high level of technical and notational sophistication rendering many research publications incomprehensible. . . and the causal complexity of multivariate analysis, which. . . makes change-oriented actions difficult to contemplate (p. 13).

Goodall's (1984) study of the literature on research in organizational communication identified a body of criticisms suggesting that

> research done in the great scientific traditions tend to encourage simplistic, reductionist assumptions and explanations about human symbol-using/abusing, usually at the expense of more complex interpretive possibilities. . . . these critiques further suggest the world according to the scientific explanations of organizational behavior is, at best, incomplete, and at worst a-logical or ill-equipped to deal with the territory it purports to explain (p. 135).

Dissatisfaction with quasi-experimental designs for studying organizations is not recent; nevertheless, the organizational culture perspective has had difficulty finding adequate replacements for them. Moreover, most of the newer, mostly qualitative research methods have substantial validity, reliability, and general usefulness problems. Just as the organizational culture perspective is encountering problems of youthfulness,[2] so also are its favored research approaches.

Many of the research methods being used by students of organizational culture have warranted challenges from several points of view. First, from the logical-positivist quasi-experimental perspective, qualitative methods are not valid research and, tautologously, cannot yield valid or reliable results. Second, because there is no consensus within the organizational culture perspective about what organizational culture is, what constitutes it, and what the organizational culture perspective can reasonably expect to accomplish, it is impossible to have agreement on its research methodologies. Alternative methods for studying organizational culture must be found.

If organizational culture is defined as espoused beliefs and val-

---

[1]See Chapter 6 for discussions of "schools."
[2]See Chapter 1.

ues, myriad straightforward research tools are available for use from the human relations school. They include questionnaires, inventories, structured and unstructured individual and group interviews, and on and on. Many of these methods are amenable to quasi-experimental designs. Conversely, if organizational culture is defined as basic underlying assumptions, and if significant differences sometimes exist between espoused values and values-in-use (Argyris & Schön, 1978), then methods using questionnaires and inventories will yield misleading results. Instead, longitudinal qualitative research methods are called for, such as participant observation from the ethnographic paradigms (Sanday 1979, 1983) or from the clinician perspective (Schein 1984).

Researcher objectivity is a problematic issue for organizational research in general and organizational culture research in particular. The logical-positivists assume that researchers will (*must*) strive to be independent, neutral, dispassionate seekers of scientifically verifiable truths (Cook & Campbell, 1979). Experimental and quasi-experimental designs are protections against researcher-induced biases, such as values, hopes, feelings, preferences, and perceptions.

Nevertheless, detached objectivity in organizational research is largely a myth, no matter who conducts it. Even if one diligently seeks such objectivity, the very use of logical-positivist quasi-experimental research designs predetermines what will be looked for; the research design and instruments used; and, to a great extent, what will be found and concluded. Moreover, reflect on the "even if" assumption in the prior sentence. Since when are researchers devoid of professional hopes, emotions, and preconceptions? Why does the donning of a researcher's hat turn a person into a neutral, detached seeker of knowledge? Schools of organization theory are professional communities with shared perspectives, norms, beliefs, values, preferences, and assumptions. *Their members seek truths within the parameters of their school's perspective.* Van Maanen (1982a) describes organizational research as "inherently a social and cultural process with deeply rooted moral, political, and personal overtones" (p. 14). The assumption of researcher objectivity is a "rational" perspective— it comes from the left side of Figure 6–2 on page 145. Martin (1982a) describes that perspective of organizational research as a statement of *what should be rather than what actually happens.* Cohen, March, and Olsen's (1972) "garbage can model" much more accurately describes how most organizational research truly is conducted.

All organizational research involves "judgment calls. . . . decisions (some big, some small, but all necessary and consequential) that must be made without the benefit of a fixed, 'objective' rule that one can apply with precision" (McGrath, 1982, p. 13). The cumulative effects of judgment calls often predetermine the outcomes of research (p. 13). Moreover, judgment calls tend to be made in accord with a researcher's preconceptions, hopes, values, and perceptions. Thus, organizational culture research tends to yield results that support and substantiate the researcher's perspective of organizational culture.[3] This is an unfortunate reality—but a reality nevertheless. Yet the problem is not unique to organizational culture research or even to qualitative methodologies. It is universal to research, particularly organizational research, logical-positivist as well as qualitative.

QUALITATIVE RESEARCH METHODS

The phrase *qualitative research* has been woven into the discussion without explanation. What is it? Van Maanen's (1979, 1983a) description sounds painfully familiar: "The label qualitative methods has no precise meaning in any of the social sciences" (p. 9). In general, however, *qualitative research* describes an umbrella of interpretive techniques for "coming to terms with the meaning, not the frequency" (p. 9) of events or phenomena.[4] Qualitative research methods are best suited for seeking a thorough description within a limited sphere, such as deciphering the basic assumptions of one organization's culture. They are not applicable, however, for purposes such as describing a population from a sample or identifying covariance between variables (as, for example, between an artifact and an ideology).

Formally, qualitative research methods are axiomatic-like principles a researcher carries around with him or her; and the primary principle of qualitative organizational research is "firsthand inspection of ongoing organizational life (Van Maanen 1982a, p. 16). Four other of Van Maanen's principles are important for this analysis:[5]

- Analytic induction. Patterns and generalizations are built from specific data. Data are not used to confirm or test preexisting theories.
- Proximity. Events and things must be witnessed firsthand. Secondhand accounts are not valid data. Thus, qualitative research methods do not include interviews, questionnaires, and surveys.

---

[3] Within relatively narrow limits.

[4] *Qualitative methods* also sometimes means the use of nonquantitative data analysis methods, as in Miles and Huberman's (1984) *Qualitative Data Analysis*.

[5] With my comments added.

- Ordinary behavior. Qualitative research is interested in routine, uninterrupted activities. Disruptions of routines, including those caused by research activities, distort data and are to be avoided. Data collection must be unobtrusive.

- Descriptive focus. The first priority for qualitative research is to describe what is going on in a given place at a certain time. This purpose is more important than explaining or predicting. Obviously, a good description should help make sense out of what is described; but a good description is a prerequisite for making sense—it must come first (Van Maanen, 1982a, p. 16).

Very few techniques of social science research satisfy all of these principles. Even such well-known semiethnographic studies as Whyte's (cited in Homans 1950, ch. 7) of the Norton Street Gang; Clark's (1970) of three distinctive colleges; and Pettigrew's (1979, 1983) of a British boarding school—all violate at least one of these criteria. Van Maanen's (1982b) own methodology for studying police behavior jeopardizes his principle of "ordinary behavior." By these standards, only participant observation with the observer (or the observer's identity) concealed (Goffman, 1961; Festinger, Riecken, & Schachter 1956) and investigations of organizational archives fully satisfy the qualitative data collection principles or standards.

Participant observation and archival searches are, in fact, fundamental data-gathering tools of qualitative organizational research. One (or both) method(s) is used in most current studies. For practical and ethical reasons, the researcher's identity is concealed only rarely. In order to help negate data distortions caused by the entry and presence of a researcher, Wolcott (1975) and others argue that ethnographic studies in organizations should span at least a full year. Thus, qualitative research studies usually take a long time to complete. Not many organizations can afford to wait months or years just to find out what their organizational culture is.

Use of Multiple Research Methods or "Triangulation"

Several recent studies have supplemented participant observation and archival searches with a variety of somewhat qualitative research methods that generally satisfy the spirit if not the letter of Van Maanen's (1982a) principles (to varying degrees). A few examples include time-lapsed videotaping and photographing of peoples' activities (Dabbs, 1982); interviewing and content analyzing newspaper and business journal articles (Martin & Siehl, 1983) and speeches (Pettigrew, 1979, 1983); intentionally stimulating organizations to react (to a researcher-initiated stimulus), then observing organizational behavior (Salancik, 1979, 1983); and sequences of verbal interchanges, feedback sessions, and joint client-researcher elaborations of initial, tentative findings (Schein, 1984; 1985).

A very small number of organizational culture research efforts have combined qualitative and quantitative methodologies. One of the best of these is Siehl and Martin's (1984) two-phased investigation of organizational culture transmittal and learning processes.

The fact that multiple research methods are gaining in use probably is more important than the specific techniques selected. Clearly, designs that utilize multiple methods are becoming the hallmark of organizational culture research. The jargon is *to triangulate,* meaning to come at the same phenomenon from different angles, using several research tools (or with several researchers using the same tools), much like sailors fix their position at sea by triangulating on stars. Triangulation increases the richness and the reliability of qualitative organizational research (Campbell & Fiske, 1959; Crano, 1981; Greene & McClintock, 1985; McClintock & Greene, 1985).

Summary

The most important problems associated with studying organizational culture are:

- Because people cannot agree about what organizational culture is, they also cannot agree what should be identified or how to go about it.

- Without consensus on what organizational culture is, research in organizational culture has had difficulty advancing beyond merely identifying to explaining, predicting, and using it. Very few attempts have been made to address issues such as relationships between the content of a culture and the culture's pervasiveness; extent of member socialization; presence of different types of subcultures; and patterns of behavior (such as decision strategies and performance levels).

- Most organizational culture studies have used (and continue to use) qualitative or near-qualitative rather than quantitative research methods. Qualitative methods are excellent for describing and explaining but not for predicting and generalizing.

- Qualitative research methods are controversial enough in themselves; but Schein (1985) complicates the picture even further. He uses Lewin (1958) to support his view that ethnographic approaches to qualitative research *cannot* yield accurate information about organizational culture. Valid data can only be obtained through a *clinical perspective. The researcher must be a helper* (pp. 21–22).

- The parameters of the organizational culture perspective are not clearly established, so that the usefulness limits of organizational culture research are not known. For some areas of research interest (for example, results of conflicts between two subcultures), explanatory and predictive research from a different perspective of organization theory, such as the power and politics perspective (Shafritz & Ott, 1987, ch. V), may be able to provide better answers.

- Organizational culture research has relied on qualitative research methods for several reasons. First, it is almost impossible to use quantitative methods to study things such as forgotten basic assumptions. Second, immature scientific perspectives tend to use inductive research designs, and inductive designs in the social sciences tend to be qualitative. Qualitative methods do not meet logical-positivist quasi-experimental research design standards for ensuring validity and reliability. For all practical purposes, qualitative studies can only seldom be replicated, and confidence limits cannot be established for their findings. Thus, by tautology, almost all organizational culture research is not valid by logical-positivist standards. If studies are not valid and confidence levels are not known, they are not worth doing.

- Most qualitative research efforts take many months or even years to complete. When information about organizational culture is needed quickly—such as for input to strategy decisions—qualitative methods cannot produce. Moreover, they are expensive to conduct.

- The use of more easily measured proxy constructs such as norms, values, and beliefs for the more ethereal cultural constructs like basic underlying assumptions would solve several organizational culture research problems. Quantitative procedures and instruments such as statistical sampling, normed instruments, and quantitative data analysis techniques could be employed. Thus, the research methods could at least approximate quasi-experimental designs. As it takes less time to collect data, interpret them and produce results, research costs could be reduced. Unfortunately, there is no existing body of knowledge about when norms, beliefs, and values coincide (and fail to coincide) with basic underlying cultural assumptions; so they cannot be used as proxy indicators with any confidence.

• For those of the logical-positivist persuasion, the lack of researcher objectivity and methodological safeguards against such nonobjectivity are very serious problems. Organizational culture researchers defend themselves and their methods by admitting they are not (and cannot be) neutrally objective (Van Maanen, 1982b, p. 115) and countercharge that *neutral objective research is not conducted within any school of organizational theory.* They see themselves as at least facing up to the problem honestly—but not satisfactorily solving it.

SOME METHODOLOGICAL APPROACHES

Clearly, organizational culture research faces monumental methodological problems—and it probably will take years for some of them to be solved. On the other hand, a few of its problems appear to be resolvable now. This is the goal of Chapter 5. To start, the typologies of organizational culture (Figures 3–3 and 3–4 on pages 62 and 63) provide useful answers about what can and should be studied. Second, as is true of research in any social science, tradeoffs always can be made between the duration and costs of research and the confidence in results. For example, if information is needed quickly, methods can be selected that yield fast results but usually with low confidence levels (and vice versa). If confidence level requirements are not high, methods can be selected to minimize research costs and duration (and vice versa).

The important assumption I make here is that *the selection of research methods should be determined by how quickly results are needed and how they will be used.* In practice, these determinants will usually dictate the choice of a research design and amount of confidence that can be placed in results. With this assumption clearly stated, we proceed now to look at some alternative strategies and methods for studying organizational culture.

It should be evident that there is no one best way to study organizational culture. In fact, there probably is no single best way to study anything. Research strategies and methods must be appropriate to what is being studied (*the construct*) and the reasons why the research is being conducted (*intended uses for the results*). Even if organizational theorists cannot agree about what organizational culture is, the organizational investigator still must make decisions. For example, the approach used by a company to study the limits its own basic underlying assumptions impose on its future marketing strategies should not be the same as the methods used by a univer-sity-based theorist who wants to know if material artifacts can be used to predict the relative impacts of different sources of organizational culture. These two (hypothetical) research purposes require designs that can measure different cultural constructs, satisfy different confidence requirements, and produce results more or less rapidly.

The next few sections of this chapter analyze alternative research approaches and data sources that can be used to study elements in different levels of organizational culture. The focus is on data collection methods and sources rather than analytical techniques (Miles & Huberman, 1984). The levels of organizational culture are those presented in Figures 3–3 and 3–4. Some of my own experiences with a few of them are woven into the discussions. A reminder: Every method and source has advantages and disadvantages, so multiple research techniques should always be used to triangulate.

Artifacts: Level 1A of Organizational Culture

Wandering Around Looking at Physical Settings. Often quite a bit can be surmised quickly about an organization's culture simply by looking around at its material artifacts. Although Fritz Steele's (1973) book, *Physical Settings and Organization Development,* was not written from an organizational culture perspective, his listing of "technophysical surroundings" (p. 10) is useful for spotting clues about culture. Steele suggests looking at the exterior setting (campus-type lawns or industrial buildings); the layout of walls and walkways; enclosing structures (walls, partitions, screens, windows, and plants); things in the immediate work areas (furniture, decorations, filing cabinets, and machines); the quality of light and noise; and relative placement of things (a secretary's desk in relation to the boss's) (p. 10).

Harold Seidman (1980) observed:

> one only has to walk into the ancient [U.S.] Treasury Department building adjoining the White House to sense the atmosphere of a conservative financial institution. The money cage at the main entryway, the gilt pilasters, the gold-framed portraits on the walls, all reinforce the Treasury "image" (p. 134).

The physical facilities at Scenic Mountain State College, a small rural state college, communicate an unmistakable message about the College's identity and its compatibility with the socioeconomic status of the area. No structure on campus has even a slightly pretentious air. All buildings were designed solely for functionality. There are no arches, statues, fountains, wood, or stone trim. Even the historic, old administrative building, constructed in the 1890s, looks like an oversized country schoolhouse. Administrative offices are homey rather than officious, imposing, or "academic." Walls painted in neutral (bland) tones are dotted with old pictures of the campus, nearby farmhouses, and country schools. Nobody who goes on the campus has to wonder about Scenic Mountain State College's self-image, identity, or mission.

With increasing frequency, however, organizations are deliberately engineering their physical settings to communicate messages. Space designers are being used to create desired images. Yet even consciously engineered settings can provide important clues. The Mountain State Chapter needed larger offices at the time John Thomas became president. He proposed moving to a vacant suite of plush executive offices on the top floor of a nearby bank building. The offices were available quite inexpensively. Several members of the Board of Directors convinced him that plush offices would communicate a damaging symbolic message to volunteers and small donors, regardless of their actual cost. Instead, unpretentious basement offices were found in an industrial/commercial neighborhood. The setting was engineered to maintain a low-budget image.

When looking around, what isn't visible often is as important as what is seen. Although Martin and Siehl (1983) were writing about organizational stories rather than material artifacts, their observation is pertinent to our subject here.

> Students of Japanese corporate cultures have noted the difficulty of interpreting cultural phenomena. To appreciate the shape and placement of a rock in a Japanese garden, the educated viewer focuses on the empty spaces around the rock. Similarly, the process of "reading" the content of a culture requires attention to disruptions and to what is absent or unsaid (p. 59).

By themselves, physical settings do not provide reliable information about organizational culture. Without the benefit of other sources of information, an investigator can not differentiate between artifacts-as-symbols and merely signs. It is very difficult to know when to regard a material artifact seriously. Would an observer with no other information about the Mountain State Chapter infer the symbolism of the computer being partially covered with old posters and styrofoam coffee cups in the back of the Board of Directors' meeting room?

On the other hand, material artifacts, just as physical settings, do perform useful research functions. First, as has been mentioned, they provide quick clues about cultural patterns which then can be investigated more thoroughly with other more sensitive or reliable methods. They can help an investigator get started by pointing out potentially fruitful directions. Second, they can help establish the validity of cultural patterns as they begin to emerge from other data collection activities. For example, if interviewing indicates that an organization is loose, informal, freewheeling, interactive, and not status-conscious, then the size, layout, and access routes to work areas should reflect the culture. If instead the physical setting looks more like the U.S. Treasury Department, the investigator knows that more digging is needed to identify reasons for the incongruities.

Rummaging Through Archives and Other Records. An organization's historical records contain all sorts of invaluable information about organizational culture. Archives can help a researcher associate seemingly unrelated events—for example, by chronologically sequencing minutes of meetings, transcripts of speeches, newspaper stories, and other documents from different offices and files. Two of the best examples of this approach are by Clark (1970, 1972) and Pettigrew (1979, 1983). Anyone who contemplates using archives to study organizational culture should review their work.

I was able to identify the discrepancy between the Community Center's espoused value (programs should benefit clients) and assumption-in-use (programs should be maximally convenient for clients' parents) by examining staff meeting minutes. These minutes provided uncontestable evidence that program policy decisions *always* turned on parental impacts—not clients. I used the same approach to confirm a hunch about State Health assumptions concerning private health care providers. The hunch had been planted during several advisory and policy-formulating meetings. Not one private physician had held a leadership position nor been influential in discussions. This was a very unusual absence of deference accorded doctors in health-related meetings. All I had to do was go back through a few years of records to verify that no health care provider had chaired similar groups at State Health. With only minimal additional work, the inductive step from facts to basic assumption was easy and fairly safe to take.

Whereas organizational archives are fruitful sources of accurate information about organizational culture, investigators need to be cautious about official organizational publications such as brochures, annual reports, and press releases. These types of documents typically reflect only what a team of executives and public relations people want to convey publicly. However, just as with physical settings, official publications can provide information often by what they don't say—by what is omitted.

Books, newspaper stories, and business magazine articles are not organizational archives or artifacts, but they are related sources of valuable information about an organization's culture. Martin and Siehl (1983) note the absence of any published "prodigal son" stories at General Motors. They correlate the absence of such stories with General Motors's strong cultural value on company loyalty.

Organization Charts. Unfortunately, most organization charts are not reliable sources of information about organizational culture. Typically, they depict how someone in authority believes an organization should appear—usually, nothing more. In fact, Meyer (1984); Greenfield (1984); Weick (1976); and others contend that the primary purpose served by organization charts is to convince important constituencies that the organization knows what it is about and is under control.

Organization charts do provide some useful information about organizational culture by their tallness or flatness; clean or scrambled lines of authority; types of position titles (director versus coordinator); the presence or absence of peoples' names in position boxes; product or functional arrangements; and the placement of staff advisory and "figurehead" offices (such as EEO). The Emergency Medical Services Office is almost hidden among several other minor regulatory offices on the State Health organization chart. The chart depicts most of these offices reporting directly to the division director, and there are coordinative or advisory dotted-line relationships with the commissioner's staff. In contrast, the EMS Office reports to the director through an intermediary office and has no dotted-line relationships with any office. The organization chart accurately communicates the EMS Office's lack of standing in the division and in State Health and its absence of coordinate relationships. However, this amount of accurate information is not typical of organization charts.

Summary: Researching Material Artifacts. Information about organizational culture can be collected quickly and relatively inexpensively by looking at material artifacts such as physical settings and archives. Material artifacts often can be accessed without encountering too many barriers. On the other hand, they should only be used as clues or to confirm other findings, because they cannot be trusted to provide accurate information by themselves. The two biggest problems with using artifacts are discriminating between signs and symbols and validly inferring (piecing together) cultural patterns from them.

Listening to the Language

If an organizational investigator is privy to ongoing routine conversations, "just listening" to the language, jargon, humor, and metaphors of an organization is one of the best ways to learn about organizational culture (Boland & Hoffman, 1983; Evered, 1983; Louis, 1981; Pondy, 1978, 1983). Often, questions do not even need to be asked until after considerable information has already been gleaned. One only needs to hear two or three Jones & Jones employees call clients "assholes" before a pattern becomes evident. It only takes sitting in on two or three Scenic Mountain State College staff meetings to realize that academic jargon is not used, the language is "rural down-home," faculty research and publications are not mentioned, and influence is determined by how well people match with the College culture. The executive director of the Community Center cannot talk about his organization or its operations for ten minutes without using phrases such as "within her authority"; "didn't go through the chain of command"; "doesn't understand the principles of management"; and "I only talk with people in other organizations who are at my (organizational) level, and I expect the same from them." Military management jargon is hard to overlook in a human service-delivery agency!

Pondy (1978) has identified two categories of situations when language is not shared. These situations provide unusually valuable opportunities to collect information about organizational culture.

1. *Having different lexicons* is the easiest situation to recognize because "it carries its own signal of mismatch" (p. 93)—for example, when organization members use a phrase totally foreign to the investigator.

2. *Lexicons are identical but the meanings attached to the words differ.* This second category of situations is much more difficult to recognize (Pondy, 1978). During one visit to Scenic Mountain State College, several staff members mentioned the College's increasing numbers of "nontraditional women students." I paid no attention to the phrase the first few times I heard it used, because I have a meaning for it. Unlike the first situation mentioned above, the words themselves did not trigger recognition of a situation where language was not being shared. I erroneously assumed it meant the same thing to them that it does to me. About the fourth time, however, a light went on in my head—the people using the phrase are members of a very conservative, traditional, rural culture. If *nontraditional women students* held the same meaning for them as it does for me, there would be more emotion in their voices. So, I finally asked what it

meant. The answer was: all women students who are not single and/or do not enroll directly from high school. With additional probing, my sources added all unmarried women with children (even those who enroll directly from high school). Their language had been trying to "shout" information to me about the College's culture. I almost missed it because *the lexicons are identical, but the meanings attached to the words differ.*

3. To Pondy's two situations under which language is not shared, I add a third. *The lexicons are identical, and the meanings attached to the words are the same; but the use seems inappropriate.* This is another easy situation for an investigator to recognize. The Community Center executive director's use of military management jargon in a human service-delivery agency and Jones & Jones' "assholes" are clear examples.

These three situations when language is not shared provide excellent opportunities for an investigator to collect important information about organizational culture. Two of the three are easy to recognize; the third, however, requires sensitivity.

Interviewing is an obvious alternative way to learn about an organizational culture through its language. Still, organization members tend to adjust their language when talking with outsiders, especially in individual interviews. Most of us do not use organization jargon at home or at noncompany social gatherings. The same is true when an outsider is interviewing a member. On the other hand, organization language often creeps into group interviews because the interviewees talk with each other as well as with the interviewer.

Other techniques, such as tape recording discussions and content-analyzing meeting notes or internal memoranda, can be useful data collection methods for some purposes. In my experience, they are of questionable value for investigating culture through language. Simply listening and conducting group interviews are more productive approaches.

Myths, Stories, Sagas, and Legends. If a researcher is on-site with regularity, he or she will hear organizational stories and myths almost every time people gather informally—in the lunchroom, during coffee breaks, and always at company parties.[6] The types of more formal gatherings where stories, myths, sagas, and legends are told are very predictable. Virtually every organizational celebration,

---

[6]I have had difficulty accessing stories and myths only when they deal with issues such as serious violations of laws or societal moral codes.

recognitional event, new employee orientation session, and (non-technical) in-house training program is a seldom-missed opportunity to tell and retell organizational stories (Martin, 1982b; Martin & Powers, 1983; Wilkins, 1983).

It is quite easy to nudge people into relating organizational stories and myths in individual or group interviews. The only problem—getting people started—usually can be overcome with a lead-in statement followed with an open-ended question such as: "Every organization has faced at least one major crisis in its history. Tell me about the biggest crisis this organization has faced—when its survival or independence was in danger." After the initial responses are received, a short series of follow-up questions usually elicits an important story. For example: "How did people respond to that crisis? How did the organization deal with it?" "Who were the important actors?" Once again, I have found group interviews more productive than individual interviews.

During a group interview at the Community Center, one person alluded to a woman manager who had been forced into resigning. A second giggled and mentioned that sometimes she hadn't dressed appropriately. A third interrupted enthusiastically with, "that means she didn't always wear a bra." Then, the whole story and its moral just flowed out with excitement. Group members kept interrupting each other, almost competing to tell the particularly poignant episodes—as much to each other as to me. From there, related story after story was told, each of which fit together into a saga.

Clark (1970) and Pettigrew (1979, 1983) carried the analysis of stories one step further. They studied archives, identified periods of major organizational crisis, and focused their searches for stories and myths on the crisis periods. They then sought and found commonalities among the individual stories, sometimes in the content of the crises but more frequently in the patterns of responses to them. Clark labeled these patterned stories *sagas*.

Saga analysis is a very potent approach whose value far exceeds descriptions of organizational culture. It surfaces perceptions of how a particular organization survived serious crises; preventitive measures it *should* take to avoid similar crises (such as not borrowing for product development); and how organization members *should* solve future problems (not just crises). In short, an analysis of sagas can identify an organization's basic blueprints for making important decisions. Thus, sagas can be used not only to describe culture, but also *to predict future patterns of organizational behavior*. This ability explains why Clark's work (1970, 1972) is one of the most significant methodological contributions to the organizational culture perspective.

Patterns of Behavior:
Level 1B of Organizational Culture

The most useful methods for studying rites and rituals are similar to those for language, stories, and myths (Smircich, 1983, pp. 59–61). Norms also can be studied through observation and interviews (Davis 1984). Therefore, these investigatory approaches are not discussed again here. Instead the analysis of methods for investigating patterns of behavior proceeds directly to the use of questionnaires for studying behavioral norms.

Innumerable pencil and paper instruments, questionnaires, and surveys exist for identifying group norms in organizations. For example, Allen and Kraft (1982) fill four appendices with just some of their own instruments. The "Instrumentation" section in most issues of University Associates' *Annual Handbook for Group Facilitators* contains instruments for identifying organizational group norms and related phenomena. Some of them have the advantage of being normed for different types of organizations.[7]

It is tempting to use questionnaires to identify norms and then hope those norms reflect basic underlying assumptions. Instruments are inexpensive to acquire, administer, and analyze. Because most instrument scores are quantifiable, findings can be compared between organizational units and within units over time. (Besides, questionnaires look like research!) Repeatedly, I have found organization members wanting to believe in questionnaire findings. Even when instrument scores do not match with organizational realities, some people always search for reasons to justify discrepancies in ways that do not invalidate either the findings or the realities.

Instruments also have their problems. First, the norms that can be identified are only those included in the instrument. If a norm is not there waiting to be checked or circled, it will not appear in the results. Second, although many instruments attempt to measure the intensity of norms, few can identify whether norms are pivotal or peripheral in a given organizational culture (Schein, 1980, p. 100). Third, most instruments group items into scales or dimensions for scoring purposes, and the scales never seem to form a coherent whole

---

[7]*The Annual Handbook for Group Facilitators* is published annually by University Associates, Inc., La Jolla, California. It is edited by J. William Pfeiffer and John E. Jones, but the sequencing of the two editors alternates each year. Materials in the *Handbook* "may be freely reproduced for educational/training activities. There is no requirement to obtain special permission for such uses. . . . Systematic or large-scale reproduction for distribution—or inclusion of items in publications for sale—may be done only with prior written permission" (1978 *Handbook,* reverse side of front page).

in the organization being studied. It seems as though one always has to either go back to individual items (discard the scales) or reformulate the scales (often with no theoretical justification for doing so) in order to obtain results that have meaning. The fourth problem is so obvious that it should not need to be stated. Relationships between behavioral norms and other levels of organizational culture are at best questionable. When I survey norms, that is all I can claim to be measuring (*unless* organizational culture is defined operationally as norms).

Most questionnaires are quick, easy, and inexpensive to administer and analyze. If they could yield useful information about organizational culture, they would be ideal investigatory tools. Thus, when I was asked to identify the organizational culture at Jones & Jones, CPAs, I was handed a golden opportunity to test the correlation between an organization's culture as identified by a norms questionnaire and through other research methods.

At the start-up meeting with the Jones & Jones staff, copies of Alexander's (1978) *Organizational Norms Opinionnaire* were distributed with self-addressed return envelopes.[8] The returned envelopes remained sealed until I had spent almost three calendar months collecting information about the basic underlying cultural assumptions. I wandered around, looked, listened, and interviewed people alone and in small groups. I also spent four hours meeting with the full staff and eighteen additional hours with individuals and small groups, verifying the accuracy of the basic cultural assumptions I had identified, filling in missing pieces, and reconciling discrepancies. Only then did I open the envelopes and analyze the responses to the questionnaires.

The *Organizational Norms Opinionnaire* may be an excellent instrument for identifying norms, but it was not useful for identifying Jones & Jones's basic cultural assumptions through the company's norms. The score sheet groups the instrument's forty-two items into ten scales (Table 5–1). Only two of the ten scale scores provided accurate clues about Jones & Jones's basic underlying assumptions: Leadership/Supervision and Candor/Openness. Most of the other scale scores were misleading. Colleague/Associate Relations and Customer/Client Relations were the highest and second highest ranked scales (most positive)—neither of which has any touch with the realities of that organization's culture. Remember, Jones & Jones is where *everyone assumes* that clients are easily replaced assholes! The

---

[8]The instrument and its scoring sheet are in the first appendix to this chapter. See also Alexander (1977) and Footnote 7.

TABLE 5–1   *Organizational Norm Opinionnaire* Scales*
Rank Order of Scale Scores at Jones & Jones†

	Scale	Rank
I.	Organizational/Personal Pride	10
II.	Performance/Excellence	5
III.	Teamwork/Communication	6
IV.	Leadership/Supervision	9
V.	Profitability/Cost Effectiveness	4
VI.	Colleague/Associate Relations	1
VII.	Customer/Client Relations	2
VIII.	Innovativeness/Creativity	7
IX.	Training/Development	3
X.	Candor/Openness	8

* From Alexander (1978, pp. 85–87).

† According to Alexander, the scale scores reflect whether or not the norms "support the organization's goals and objectives . . . [or] promote behavior that works against organizational goals" (p. 81). Thus, the #1 ranking for "Colleague/Associate Relations" supposedly reflects very positive norms—norms that promote good working relations. The #10 ranking for "Organizational/Personal Pride" reportedly reflects negative norms—norms that promote behavior that works against pride in self and company.

Please try to ignore the fact that the instrument does not address organizational goals and objectives. Apparently Alexander assumes them.

lowest-ranked scale (most negative), Organizational/Personal Pride, was equally misleading.

Not all of Alexander's scale scores were misleading. The Leadership/Supervision scale's low ranking would have provided a useful clue about Jones & Jones's organizational culture. It correctly reflected basic assumptions about supervision and supervisors. The title *supervisor* is a facade. Supervisors (*seniors* and *managers* in CPA jargon) have no supervisory roles or responsibilities. All supervising is done directly by the elder Mr. Jones—a behavioral manifestation of one of his basic assumptions. Likewise, the Openness/Candor scale ranking would have been a useful direction-pointer; but any slightly astute observer could have identified Jones & Jones's norms in this area quickly and easily without using the instrument.

Alexander's scale scores provided little accurate information about Jones & Jones. (Just enough to be dangerous!) Scores on a few items would have provided helpful pointers. Some of the items appropriately scored low (negatively) include: "look on the supervisor as a source of help and development," "suggest confronting the boss about a mistake or something in the boss's style that is creating problems," "sometimes see the customer or client as a burden or obstruction to getting the job done."

In summary, Alexander's (1978) *Organizational Norms Opinionnaire* was at best minimally useful and at worst misleading for identifying basic underlying cultural assumptions through norms at Jones & Jones. Thus, this particular instrument was not even useful for spotting clues about fruitful areas to investigate. Unfortunately, it was not worth using for this purpose. (Once again, it is important to note that the instrument was designed to identify norms—not cultural assumptions. It may be an excellent instrument for its intended purpose.) I had hoped to find positive correlations between questionnaire findings and the results of other culture identifying activities. Then, the methodological advantages of questionnaires would have warranted its use on similar projects—even if only to obtain directional clues to follow-up with other more time-consuming information collecting approaches.[9]

Level 2 of Organizational Culture: Beliefs and Values

Artifacts and patterned behaviors can be seen, touched, or heard. Norms can be inferred from patterns of behavior. Beliefs, values, and ideologies are a step further removed from observable behaviors (Figure 3-3, p. 62); and relationships between what is observable and what is inside peoples' heads can be obscured by intervening factors. Thus, inferring beliefs and values from observable behavior is a risky endeavor. On the other hand, beliefs, values, and ideologies are conceptually close to basic underlying assumptions (Figure 3-3, page 62). In theory, they should be more informative than norms as proxy indicators of basic underlying assumptions.

Just as organizational norms instruments, innumerable pencil and paper questionnaires and surveys exist for identifying values and beliefs in and out of organizations (Simon, Howe, & Kirschenbaum, 1972; Superka, Johnson & Ahrens, 1975). And, once again, most issues of the *Annual Handbook for Group Facilitators* contain several instruments for identifying beliefs, values, and ideologies. Can these instruments be used as convenient proxy indicators of basic assumptions?

To answer this question, Roger Harrison's (1975) (unnamed)

---

[9]This conclusion cannot be generalized to other instruments for identifying norms or to other organizations.

instrument for diagnosing organization ideology was administered at Jones & Jones along with Alexander's *Organization Norms Opinionnaire*. The administration procedures were the same. The specific research question was: Can Jones & Jones's basic underlying cultural assumptions be identified with this questionnaire, which was designed to uncover organization ideologies? The ideology questionnaire and its scoring profiles are in the second appendix of this chapter.

The primary reason for selecting Harrison's instrument was the compatibility of his (1972) theoretical perspective with the concepts of organizational culture used in this study (Figure 3–3, p. 62). Harrison views ideology as the justification for norms and thus for organizational behavior. Ideology "establishes a rationale for these [norms] 'dos' and 'don'ts.' This rationale explains the behavior of an organization's members" (p. 120).[10]

Harrison's instrument is not normed. Its aim is to enable people to identify where their organization stands on some important ideological dimensions, and to help people identify differences between their organization's ideologies and their own (Harrison, 1975, p. 101). Unlike the *Organizational Norms Opinionnaire,* Harrison's is a forced choice questionnaire that requires respondents to choose between four ideological orientations: power, role, task, and self.

Nine Jones & Jones staff people (between one third and one half of the staff) volunteered that completing Harrison's instrument had caused them personal discomfort—not simply because it is a forced choice instrument, but also because answering it had required them to think about things they did not like to think about. The large number of strikeouts and erasures substantiated their comments. Needless to say, I explored further. An amalgamation of paraphrased statements about their discomfort was: "It is bad enough to be reminded of our—my—counterproductive behaviors (by the *Organizational Norms Opinionnaire*), but it is painful to remember *why* we do some of the things we do (while completing the ideology questionnaire)." The ideology instrument required them to consciously admit that their "silly" behaviors were natural consequences of universally held systems of beliefs in the firm. Many of the Jones & Jones assumptions had been forgotten or suppressed. Some of them are not

---

[10] Handy (1978) acknowledges Harrison as the source of his idea to use Greek gods to symbolize organizational culture (Acknowledgments, p. i). Handy slightly modified this instrument, named it *Questionnaire on the Cultures of Organisations*, and wrote Chapter 3 around it.

very noble. Yet these people continue to live in the culture, trans-mitting it to newcomers. Moreover, whereas behaviors can be modi-fied, ideologies have an aura of permanence—just as any other accepted truths.

Scores on Harrison's (1975) four orientations were somewhat revealing; but the instrument's scales were not its real value. Many individual item scores were accurate clues about organizational culture. More important, however, completing the questionnaire opened peoples' eyes to basic cultural assumptions. This made my other data collection activities much more productive.

Nevertheless, this greatest value of the instrument poses a serious methodological problem. Administration of the instrument may have influenced (biased) all subsequent data collection activities. If so, the sequence in which people completed the two instruments may account for some of the confusing-to-misleading scale scores and rankings on the *Organizational Norms Opinionnaire*. More impor-tant, the Jones & Jones people mentioned instrument items to me repeatedly in interviews and discussions. So, in addition to affecting scores on the norms instrument, the ideology questionnaire probably affected findings from all of my other data collection activ-ities—and these findings were used to gauge the accuracy of the two instruments.

The instrument's second problem is simply a limitation: it only taps four ideologies.

Harrison's instrument for diagnosing organization ideology provided some accurate information about a few basic assumptions at Jones & Jones, apparently even some forgotten assumptions. By stirring up suppressed thoughts and emotions, it also made subse-quent verbal and observational data collection activities more fruit-ful. On the other hand, it probably altered the results I would have otherwise obtained through these other activities, thereby raising serious doubts about the independence of findings.[11]

Should Harrison's instrument be used as a proxy indicator or to get directional clues about organizational culture? In a study con-ducted for purely academic inquiry purposes, no, I do not believe so. Its effect on data collected through other methods seems to have been great. On the other hand, in a study initiated by an organization's request for help, I would not hesitate to use it again. The advantages far outweigh the potential problems of interaction contamination.

---

[11] Including the findings used to assess the accuracy of the scores on the two instru-ments.

Level 3 of Organizational Culture: Basic Underlying Assumptions

How does one identify an organization's basic underlying assumptions? Because this is the newest conception of organizational culture, few organization theorists have adopted it, and fewer yet have attempted to identify it. The methodological problems are formidable. For example, although Siehl & Martin (1984) have acknowledged and accepted Schein's (1984) conceptualization of organizational culture as basic underlying assumptions, their research design did not attempt to tap basic assumptions. Instead, they used knowledge of the contents of organizational stories as a proxy measure for knowledge of organizational culture. Their methodological choice was made for practical reasons—the problems of identifying basic assumptions are imposing. Likewise, in testing two instruments to see whether basic assumptions at Jones & Jones could be identified by proxy, my first effort (norms) failed. The second (ideology) was helpful but incomplete. Although the subject needs considerably more study, my first attempt here indicates that easily administered, single-method, diagnostic tools have only limited utility. At best they can only be small parts of a more comprehensive culture-deciphering strategy.

Clearly, deciphering an organization's Level 3 basic underlying assumptions richly, thoroughly, and accurately is a substantial undertaking. Currently, such deciphering efforts require a lengthy involvement with the organization; the presence of an outside perspective; almost unrestricted access to people and records; and the use of multiple data-collection strategies (only a few of which have been described in this chapter). Three combinations of researcher roles and methodological strategies can satisfy these four requirements:

1. Participant-observation, with the identity of the researcher concealed, using ethnographic research strategies (Festinger, Riecken, & Schachter, 1956; Goffman, 1961).

2. Participant-observation and iterative interviewing, conducted jointly by an outsider who has a clinical perspective (not an ethnographic perspective) and key insider(s) (Schein, 1984; 1985).

3. Participant-observation, with the identity of the researcher revealed, using quasi-ethnographic research strategies (Kaufman, 1960; Van Maanen, 1982b).

The first role/strategy combination can be dismissed rather quickly. There are not many people who are willing to follow Erving Goffman's (1961) example and work as a custodian in a mental asylum for a year under a concealed identity.[12] How many persons would or could remain in an organization that long, pretending to be someone else, without losing their outside perspective? How many positions in an organization would give a concealed identity researcher access to the organizational culture, not just a subculture? How could one determine whether she or he was encountering the organizational culture or a subculture without "blowing cover"? Concealed identity enthography is not a feasible role/strategy, except perhaps in a few very unusual situations.

Joint Iterative Interviewing by an Outsider with a Clinical Perspective and Key Insider(s). Schein (1984, 1985) argues persuasively for the second role/strategy as *the only way* to decipher organizational culture accurately. Unless organization members have a "particular stake in the intellectual issues that may have motivated the study" (p. 21), they have no true motivation to expend the emotion, energy, or time required to dig, find, and explore forgotten basic assumptions—particularly if the assumptions are discomforting or not particularly noble, as at Jones & Jones. On the other hand, when an organization asks for help, the psychological contract between the investigator (who then fills a clinician role) and the client is entirely different. Organizations ask for assistance when they perceive they are or will be experiencing problems they cannot cope with by themselves. To withhold data, effort, or time from the clinician would be akin to a sick patient withholding information from the doctor. It happens—but not frequently nor for very long.

Even the most skilled outsider-clinician has difficulty learning the intricacies of an organization's culture. For a while, the clinician will only be exposed to its surface layers. A clinician working alone can never be sure of the accuracy of his or her interpretations of findings. A collaborating insider(s) is needed, someone who will question, challenge, and otherwise respond to the clinician's hunches and observations about cultural clues, patterns, gaps, and incongruities (Schein, 1985, p. 113).

An inside collaborator cannot do the job alone either. Just as a fish cannot describe water, an insider cannot tell an outsider "what the basic assumptions are and how they are patterned"

---

[12]Only the superintendent of the asylum knew Goffman's true identity and reasons for being there. He maintained the secret.

(Schein 1985, p. 113). A clinician-outsider *and* perceptive insiders are needed to decipher basic cultural assumptions.

It takes time and involvement to learn the right questions to ask in a given organization. The first sets of interview questions are never adequate. Moreover, even in a clinician role, few outsiders can gain the full confidence of organization members in one or two encounters. Thus, Schein (1985) proposes a ten-step iterative interviewing process to decipher organizational culture[13]:

1. Entry and focus on surprises.
2. Systematic observation and checking for patterns.
3. Locating a motivated insider.
4. Revealing the clinician's surprises, puzzlements, and hunches to the motivated insider.
5. Joint exploration to find explanations for the meaning of surprises.
6. Formalizing hypotheses and identifying data needed to test hypothesized assumptions.
7. Systematic checking, consolidating, and testing hypotheses (using questionnaires, artifacts, structured and unstructured interviews, etc.).
8. Pushing to the level of assumptions.
9. Perpetual recalibration of the cultural model.
10. Formal written description—articulating and disseminating the paradigm to help prepare the organization to use the information (pp. 114–119).

Schein's ten-step model incorporates research approaches from virtually all current organizational research perspectives. The first four steps are in the inductive, *grounded theory*-generating tradition of Glaser and Strauss (1967). The sixth and seventh steps encourage the use of designs from the *logical-positivist quasi-experimental* paradigm. The ninth step should cause any good *systems and contingency* school member to smile. Joint diagnostic roles for outsiders and insiders, and the iterative "find, piece together, clarify, verify, go find again" process are standard *organization development (O.D.)* intervention strategies (French & Bell, 1984, p. 109; French, Bell, & Zawacki, 1983, pt. 3). Schein's expansive use of *interview* to mean multiple, inductive, proximate efforts to describe organizational culture through its ordinary behaviors should at least partially

---

[13]Schein (p. 114) uses the term *interviewing* broadly to include other qualitative data-collection techniques, such as observing.

satisfy the *qualitative methodology* principles (Van Maanen, 1979, 1983a, p. 16).

Schein's ten-step model is theoretically and methodologically integrative; and it establishes a useful time, function, and role for data collection techniques from virtually every major perspective of organization theory. How can Schein's role/strategy for deciphering organizational culture be challenged?

First, as Siehl and Martin (1984) concluded, easier and faster approaches are needed sometimes. Investigators do not always have the time and/or resources needed to conduct such a comprehensive study, even if it is the *right* way. Shortcuts can be essential for some purposes.

Second, Schein's role/strategy excludes anyone who is not asked in to help, including anthropological and sociological-style investigators. The ethnographer's role and paradigm (Sanday, 1979, 1983) are excluded—not just ethnographic methods. Exclusion by role does not permit compromise. Thus, a fundamental assumption upon which Schein bases the arguments for his model is open to challenge, particularly from proponents of the ethnographic paradigms.

Identity Revealed Researcher Using Ethnographic Methods. Van Maanen (1979, 1983b) describes the ethnographic approach to the study of organizational culture as the methodology of anthropology and, to an extent, of sociology "under the stiff but precise tag, participant observation" (p. 38). Its purposes are to separate

> the facts from the fictions, the extraordinary from the common, and the general from the specific . . . by lengthy, continuous, firsthand involvement in the organizational setting under study (pp. 37–38).

The ethnographic perspective of research in organizations is embodied in Van Maanen's principles for qualitative research (enumerated earlier in this chapter on pages 102 and 103). The ethnographic perspective differs from Schein's role/strategy model in two important respects: the first is the role of the investigator; the second is the basic reason or purpose for investigating organizational culture. The ethnographic perspective gives priority to description: explanation has only secondary importance (Van Maanen, 1982a, p. 16). For Schein, thorough description is only an important beginning step toward explanation and organizational action. Van Maanen is an explorer: Schein is primarily a clinician.

Sanday (1979, 1983) groups ethnographic research methods into three major and several subsidiary styles, which she labels *paradigms*. Although the major ethnographic styles (holistic, semiotic, and behavioristic) are important for what one looks for and how one

FIGURE 5–1   Sanday's Ethnographic Substyles Organized by
Analytical Goal

	Analytical Goal	
	Diagnosis	*Explanation*
Holistic Style		
Configurationalism	Mead (1949); Benedict (1934): To describe and interpret the cultural whole.	
Functionalism		Malinowski (in Harris, 1968); Radcliffe-Brown (1952): To establish relations between things, their functions, and/or structures.
Semiotic Style		
"Thick Description"	Geertz (1973): Not to generalize across cases. Rather, to make "thick descriptions" within cases.	
Ethnoscience		Goodenough (1974): To build the whole from careful study of the parts. Find systematic rules that apply across cases.
Behavioristic Style	(No Substyle)	Whiting (1963): To uncover covarying patterns in behavioral systems.

SOURCE: Contents are from P. R. Sanday, "The Ethnographic Paradigms," in J. Van Maanen (Ed.), *Qualitative Methodology.* Beverly Hills, Calif.: Sage Publications, 1979, 1983, pp. 19–36. Used with permission.

categorizes field notes, they are not central to this analysis. What is important is Sanday's *basis* for grouping the major styles into subsidiary styles—the ethnographer's primary analytical goal. The very fact that Sanday divides the ethnographic paradigms based on research purpose helps bridge the gap between Schein's model and Van Maanen's principles.[14] Sanday's styles and substyles are presented in

---

[14]But only partially. It cannot bridge Schein's exclusion of the ethnographic role.

Figure 5–1, with some examples of representative enthnographers and very brief summaries of their perspectives.

Sanday describes the methodologies used by members of the five substyles and concludes:

> The main differences are whether the primary focus is on the whole, the meaning, or the behavior, and the degree to which the analytic goal is diagnosis or explanation. . . . Which (research methodological) mode one adopts. . . . depends on one's goals as well as one's taste (p. 34).

Sanday's statement summarizes the current status of ethnographic research in organizations. Moreover, from my perspective, it depicts the current status of organizational culture research.

CONCLUSIONS

There are three basic role/strategy combinations for thoroughly investigating organizational culture as defined as basic underlying assumptions:

1. Participant-observation, with the identity of the researcher concealed, using ethnographic research strategies.
2. Participant-observation and iterative interviewing, conducted jointly by an outsider who has a clinical perspective (not an ethnographic perspective) and key insider(s).
3. Participant-observation, with the identity of the researcher revealed, using quasi-ethnographic research strategies.

The first of these role/strategies is impractical and was discarded. The second and third represent competing perspectives or paradigms of organizational culture research. Sanday's (1979, 1983) analysis of ethnographic substyles provides a theory-of-methodology bridge between them. However, it cannot bridge Schein's (1984, 1985) role exclusion of ethnographers.

My conclusions about organizational culture research methodologies selection decisions can be summarized in seven propositions:

1. The study of organizational culture requires the use of multiple research methodologies (regardless of how organizational culture is defined).
2. Qualitative research methods in general—and ethnographic strategies in particular—are most useful for describing organizational culture. They are less useful for generalizing and useless for testing hypotheses about relationships among variables.
3. Research strategies and tools must be appropriate for what is being studied. A variety of data collection methods are suggested

FIGURE 5–2   Some Methods for Deciphering Organizational Culture
and Their Applicability to Elements in Different Levels
of Organizational Culture

	Level of Organizational Culture	
	Primary Applicability	*Secondary Applicability*
Wandering around looking at physical settings	1A	All
Rummaging through historical records	1A	All
Content analyzing publications	1A	All
Learning from organization charts	1A	All
Listening to spoken words	1A	All
Interviewing people	All	
Listening to myths, stories, sagas, and legends	1A,1B	3
Administering paper-and-pencil instruments	1B, 2	3
Combinations of the above by combination of outsider with clinician perspective and insider	3	
Combinations of the above by outsider with ethnographic perspective	3	

in this chapter. Most of them are applicable as either primary or secondary approaches for identifying and understanding elements in different levels of organizational culture. The methods and their applicabilities are summarized in Figure 5–2.

4. If one must risk using a proxy indicator of basic assumptions, the substitute should be in the level of organizational culture that is closest to Level 3. Said in a different way, elements in Levels 1A, 1B, and 2 can be measured more quickly and less expensively than basic underlying assumptions. Thus, if there is a need for rapid results, one might use, for example, norms or beliefs as proxies. The proposition states that proxies in Level 2 are preferable to proxies in Level 1B or 1A.

5. The selection of research methods also needs to reflect the purpose for the research. If the analytical goal is to provide information about basic underlying assumptions that will be used to improve

organizational functions, the clinical model probably is advantageous. If the goal is purely to describe basic cultural assumptions, one of the diagnostic ethnographic styles probably is adequate.

6. Any organizational culture research methodologies not from the logical-positivist paradigm will be challenged or impugned by logical-positivists.

7. Any organizational culture research methodologies from the logical-positivist paradigm will be challenged or impugned by qualitative methodologists.

Chapter Appendix 1

MARK ALEXANDER'S *ORGANIZATIONAL NORMS OPINIONNAIRE* WITH SCORING SHEETS AND SCORING PROFILES

Instructions: This opinionnaire is designed to help you determine the norms that are operating in your organization. The opinionnaire asks you to assess what the reaction of most persons in your organization *would be* if another person said a particular thing or behaved in a particular manner. For example, the first item reads:

"If an employee in your organization were to criticize the organization and the people in it ... most other employees would ..."

To complete this statement, choose one of the following five alternatives:

A. Strongly agree with or encourage it
B. Agree with or encourage it
C. Consider it not important
D. Disagree with or discourage it
E. Strongly disagree with or discourage it

Choose the alternative that you think would be the most common response to the action or behavior stated and place the letter corresponding to that alternative in the blank space following each item. Complete all forty-two statements in the same manner, being as honest as possible.

If an employee in your organization were to ...

Most Other Employees Would:

1. criticize the organization and the people in it ... _____

2. try to improve things even though the operation is running smoothly ... _____

Reprinted from J. William Pfeiffer and John E. Jones (Eds.), *The 1978 Annual Handbook for Group Facilitators.* San Diego, Calif.: University Associates, Inc., 1978. Used with permission.

3. listen to others and try to get their opinions . . . _____

4. think of going to a supervisor with a problem . . . _____

5. look upon himself/herself as being responsible for reducing costs . . . _____

6. take advantage of a fellow employee . . . _____

7. keep a customer or client waiting in order to look after matters of personal convenience . . . _____

8. suggest a new idea or approach for doing things . . . _____

9. actively look for ways to expand his/her knowledge in order to be able to do a better job . . . _____

10. talk freely and openly about the organization and its problems . . . _____

11. show genuine concern for the problems that face the organization and make suggestions about solving them . . . _____

12. suggest that employees should do only enough to get by . . . _____

13. go out of his/her way to help other members of the work group . . . _____

14. look upon the supervisor as a source of help and development . . . _____

15. purposely misuse equipment or privileges . . . _____

16. express concern for the well-being of other members of the organization . . . _____

17. attempt to find new and better ways to serve the customer or client . . . _____

18. attempt to experiment in order to do things better in the work situation . . . _____

19. show enthusiasm for going to an organization-sponsored training and development program . . . _____

20. suggest confronting the boss about a mistake or something in the boss's style that is creating problems . . . _____

21. look upon the job as being merely eight hours and the major reward as the month-end paycheck . . . _____

22. say that there is no point in trying harder, as no one else does . . . _____

23. work on his/her own rather than work with others to try to get things done . . . _____

24. look upon the supervisor as someone to talk openly and freely to . . . _____

25. look upon making a profit as someone else's problem . . . _____

26. make an effort to get to know the people he/she works with . . . _____

27. sometimes see the customer or client as a burden or obstruction to getting the job done . . . _____

28. criticize a fellow employee who is trying to improve things in the work situation . . . _____

29. mention that he/she was planning to attend a recently announced organization training program . . . _____

30. talk openly about problems facing the work group, including personalities or interpersonal problems . . . _____

31. talk about work with satisfaction . . . _____

32. set very high personal standards of performance . . . _____

33. try to make the work group operate more like a team when dealing with issues or problems . . . _____

34. look upon the supervisor as the one who sets the standards of performance or goals for the work group . . . _____

35. evaluate expenditures in terms of the benefits they will provide for the organization ...   _____

36. always try to treat the customer or client as well as possible ...   _____

37. think of going to the boss with an idea or suggestion ...   _____

38. go to the boss to talk about what training he/she should get in order to do a better job ...   _____

39. be perfectly honest in answering this questionnaire ...   _____

40. work harder than what is considered the normal pace ...   _____

41. look after himself/herself before the other members of the work group ...   _____

42. do his/her job even when the supervisor is not around ...   _____

ORGANIZATIONAL NORMS OPINIONNAIRE SCORE SHEET

Instructions. On the ten scales below, circle the value that corresponds to the response you gave for that item on the questionnaire. Total your score for each of the ten categories and follow the indicated mathematical formula for each. The result is your final percentage score.

I. Organizational/Personal Pride

Item	Response				
	A	B	C	D	E
1	−2	−1	0	+1	+2
11	+2	+1	0	−1	−2
21	−2	−1	0	+1	+2
31	+2	+1	0	−1	−2

Total
Score _____ ÷ 8 × 100 = [_____] %   Final Score

II. Performance/Excellence

Item	Response				
	A	B	C	D	E
2	+2	+1	0	−1	−2
12	−2	−1	0	+1	+2
22	−2	−1	0	+1	+2
32	+2	+1	0	−1	−2
40	+2	+1	0	−1	−2

Total
Score _____ ÷ 10 × 100 = [_____] %   Final Score

III. Teamwork/Communication

Item	Response				
	A	B	C	D	E
3	+2	+1	0	−1	−2
13	+2	+1	0	−1	−2
23	−2	−1	0	+1	+2

| 33 | +2 | +1 | 0 | −1 | −2 |
| 41 | −2 | −1 | 0 | +1 | +2 |

Total
Score _____ ÷ 10 × 100 = [   ] %   Final Score

IV. Leadership/Supervision

Item			Response		
	A	B	C	D	E
4	+2	+1	0	−1	−2
14	+2	+1	0	−1	−2
24	+2	+1	0	−1	−2
34	+2	+1	0	−1	−2
42	+2	+1	0	−1	−2

Total
Score _____ ÷ 10 × 100 = [   ] %   Final Score

V. Profitability/Cost Effectiveness

Item			Response		
	A	B	C	D	E
5	+2	+1	0	−1	−2
15	−2	−1	0	+1	+2
25	−2	−1	0	+1	+2
35	+2	+1	0	−1	−2

Total
Score _____ ÷ 8 × 100 = [   ] %   Final Score

VI. Colleague/Associate Relations

Item			Response		
	A	B	C	D	E
6	−2	−1	0	+1	+2
16	+2	+1	0	−1	−2
26	+2	+1	0	−1	−2

Total
Score _____ ÷ 6 × 100 = [   ] %   Final Score

VII. Customer/Client Relations

Item			Response		
	A	B	C	D	E
7	−2	−1	0	+1	+2
17	+2	+1	0	−1	−2
27	−2	−1	0	+1	+2
36	+2	+1	0	−1	−2

Total
Score _____ ÷ 8 × 100 = [   ] %   Final Score

VIII. Innovativeness/Creativity

Item			*Response*		
	A	B	C	D	E
8	+2	+1	0	−1	−2
18	+2	+1	0	−1	−2
28	−2	−1	0	+1	+2
37	+2	+1	0	−1	−2

Total
Score _____ ÷ 8 × 100 = [   ] % **Final Score**

IX. Training/Development

Item			*Response*		
	A	B	C	D	E
9	+2	+1	0	−1	−2
19	+2	+1	0	−1	−2
29	+2	+1	0	−1	−2
38	+2	+1	0	−1	−2

Total
Score _____ ÷ 8 × 100 = [   ] % **Final Score**

X. Candor/Openness

Item			*Response*		
	A	B	C	D	E
10	+2	+1	0	−1	−2
20	+2	+1	0	−1	−2
30	+2	+1	0	−1	−2
39	+2	+1	0	−1	−2

Total
Score _____ ÷ 8 × 100 = [   ] % **Final Score**

ORGANIZATIONAL NORMS OPINIONNAIRE PROFILE SHEET

Instructions. For each of the ten scales, enter your final percentage score from the score sheet and then plot that percentage by placing an "X" on the graph at the appropriate point. (Negative percentages are plotted to the left of the center line and positive percentages are plotted to the right.) Next, connect the "X"s you have plotted with straight lines. The result is your Organizational Norms profile.

Scale	Final Score	−100%	−50%	0%	+50%	+100%
I. Organizational/Personal Pride						
II. Performance/Excellence						
III. Teamwork/Communication						
IV. Leadership/Supervision						
V. Profitability/Cost Effectiveness						
VI. Colleague/Associate Relations						
VII. Customer/Client Relations						
VIII. Innovativeness/Creativity						
IX. Training/Development						
X. Candor/Openness						

Chapter Appendix 2

ROGER HARRISON'S QUESTIONNAIRE FOR DIAGNOSING ORGANIZATION IDEOLOGY WITH SCORING PROFILES

Organizations have patterns of behavior that operationalize an ideology—a commonly held set of doctrines, myths, and symbols. An organization's ideology has a profound impact on the effectiveness of the organization. It influences most important issues in organization life: how decisions are made, how human resources are used, and how people respond to the environment. Organization ideologies can be divided into four orientations: *Power* (a), *Role* (b), *Task* (c), and *Self* (d). The items below give the positions of the four orientations on a number of aspects of organization structure and functioning and on some attitudes and beliefs about human nature.

Instructions. Give a "1" to the statement that best represents the dominant view in your organization, a "2" to the one next closest to your organization's position, and so on through "3" and "4." Then go back and again rank the statements "1" through "4," this time according to *your* attitudes and beliefs.

Existing Organization Ideology **Participant's Preferred Organization Ideology**

1. A good boss is:

    ____ ____ a. strong, decisive and firm, but fair. He is protective, generous, and indulgent to loyal subordinates.

    ____ ____ b. impersonal and correct, avoiding the exercise of his authority for his own advantage. He demands from subordinates only that which is required by the formal system.

    ____ ____ c. egalitarian and capable of being influenced in matters concerning the task. He uses his authority to obtain the resources needed to complete the job.

    ____ ____ d. concerned with and responsive to the personal needs and values of others. He uses his position to provide satisfying and growth-stimulating work opportunities for subordinates.

2. A good subordinate is:

    ____ ____ a. compliant, hard working, and loyal to the interests of his superior.

    ____ ____ b. responsible and reliable, meeting the duties and responsibilities of his job and avoiding actions that surprise or embarrass his superior.

Reprinted from John E. Jones and J. William Pfeiffer (Eds.), *The 1975 Annual Handbook for Group Facilitators*. San Diego, Calif.: University Associates, Inc., 1975. Used with permission.

Existing Organization Ideology	Participant's Preferred Organization Ideology	
____	____	c. self-motivated to contribute his best to the task and is open with his ideas and suggestions. He is nevertheless willing to give the lead to others when they show greater expertise or ability.
____	____	d. vitally interested in the development of his own potentialities and is open to learning and to receiving help. He also respects the needs and values of others and is willing to help and contribute to their development.

3. A good member of the organization gives first priority to the:

____ ____ a. personal demands of the boss.

____ ____ b. duties, responsibilities, and requirements of his own role and to the customary standards of personal behavior.

____ ____ c. requirements of the task for skill, ability, energy, and material resources.

____ ____ d. personal needs of the individuals involved.

4. People who do well in the organization are:

____ ____ a. shrewd and competitive, with a strong drive for power.

____ ____ b. conscientious and responsible, with a strong sense of loyalty to the organization.

____ ____ c. technically effective and competent, with a strong commitment to getting the job done.

____ ____ d. effective and competent in personal relationships, with a strong commitment to the growth and development of people.

5. The organization treats the individual as:

____ ____ a. though his time and energy were at the disposal of persons higher in the hierarchy.

____ ____ b. though his time and energy were available through a contract with rights and responsibilities for both sides.

____ ____ c. a co-worker who has committed his skills and abilities to the common cause.

____ ____ d. an interesting and worthwhile person in his own right.

6. People are controlled and influenced by the:

____ ____ a. personal exercise of economic and political power (rewards and punishments).

____ ____ b. impersonal exercise of economic and political power to enforce procedures and standards of performance.

____ ____ c. communication and discussion of task requirements leading to appropriate action motivated by personal commitment to goal achievement.

____ ____ d. intrinsic interest and enjoyment to be found in their activities and/or by concern and caring for the needs of the other persons involved.

7. It is legitimate for one person to control another's activities if:

____ ____ a. he has more authority and power in the organization.

____ ____ b. his role prescribes that he is responsible for directing the other.

____ ____ c. he has more knowledge relevant to the task.

____ ____ d. the other accepts that the first person's help or instruction can contribute to his learning and growth.

Existing Organization Ideology	Participant's Preferred Organization Ideology

8. The basis of task assignment is the:

_____ _____ a. personal needs and judgment of those in authority.

_____ _____ b. formal divisions of functions and responsibilities in the system.

_____ _____ c. resource and expertise requirements of the job to be done.

_____ _____ d. personal wishes and needs for learning and growth of individual organization members.

9. Work is performed out of:

_____ _____ a. hope of reward, fear of punishment, or personal loyalty toward a powerful individual.

_____ _____ b. respect for contractual obligations backed up by sanctions and loyalty toward the organization or system.

_____ _____ c. satisfaction in excellence of work and achievement and/or personal commitment to the task or goal.

_____ _____ d. enjoyment of the activity for its own sake and concern and respect for the needs and values of the other persons involved.

10. People work together when:

_____ _____ a. they are required to by higher authority or when they believe they can use each other for personal advantage.

_____ _____ b. coordination and exchange are specified by the formal system.

_____ _____ c. their joint contribution is needed to perform the task.

_____ _____ d. the collaboration is personally satisfying, stimulating, or challenging.

11. The purpose of competition is to:

_____ _____ a. gain personal power and advantage.

_____ _____ b. gain high-status positions in the formal system.

_____ _____ c. increase the excellence of the contribution to the task.

_____ _____ d. draw attention to one's own personal needs.

12. Conflict is:

_____ _____ a. controlled by the intervention of higher authorities and often fostered by them to maintain their own power.

_____ _____ b. suppressed by reference to rules, procedures, and definitions of responsibility.

_____ _____ c. resolved through full discussion of the merits of the work issues involved.

_____ _____ d. resolved by open and deep discussion of personal needs and values involved.

13. Decisions are made by the:

_____ _____ a. person with the higher power and authority.

_____ _____ b. person whose job description carries the responsibility.

_____ _____ c. persons with the most knowledge and expertise about the problem.

_____ _____ d. persons most personally involved and affected by the outcome.

14. In an appropriate control and communication structure:

_____ _____ a. command flows from the top down in a simple pyramid so that anyone who is higher in the pyramid has authority over anyone who is lower. Information flows up through the chain of command.

Existing   Participant's
Organization   Preferred Organization
Ideology   Ideology

_____ _____ b. directives flow from the top down and information flows upwards within functional pyramids which meet at the top. The authority and responsibility of a role is limited to the roles beneath it in its own pyramid. Cross-functional exchange is constricted.

_____ _____ c. information about task requirements and problems flows from the center of task activity upwards and outwards, with those closest to the task determining the resources and support needed from the rest of the organization. A coordinating function may set priorities and overall resource levels based on information from all task centers. The structure shifts with the nature and location of the tasks.

_____ _____ d. information and influence flow from person to person, based on voluntary relationships initiated for purposes of work, learning, mutual support and enjoyment, and shared values. A coordinating function may establish overall levels of contribution needed for the maintenance of the organization. These tasks are assigned by mutual agreement.

15. The environment is responded to as though it were:

_____ _____ a. a competitive jungle in which everyone is against everyone else, and those who do not exploit others are themselves exploited.

_____ _____ b. an orderly and rational system in which competition is limited by law, and there can be negotiation or compromise to resolve conflicts.

_____ _____ c. a complex of imperfect forms and systems which are to be reshaped and improved by the achievements of the organization.

_____ _____ d. a complex of potential threats and support. It is used and manipulated by the organization both as a means of self-nourishment and as a play-and-work space for the enjoyment and growth of organization members.

INDIVIDUAL AND GROUP PROFILES

Sums of Ranks

	a. Power Orientation	b. Role Orientation	c. Task Orientation	d. Self Orientation
Existing Organization Ideology				
Participant's Preferred Organization Ideology				

Tally of Lowest Scores of the Group Members

	a. Power Orientation	b. Role Orientation	c. Task Orientation	d. Self Orientation
Existing Organization Ideology				
Participant's Preferred Organization Ideology				

CHAPTER 6

The Development of the Organizational Culture Perspective Within Organization Theory

Why in the world is a historical overview of the development of the organizational culture perspective essentially buried near the end of this book? Why isn't it the first or second chapter? There are several very good reasons.

First, there is no such thing as *a* historical analysis of *the* organizational culture perspective, just as there is no single organization theory. Rather, there must be multiple historical analyses of (a) the evolution of the organizational culture perspective within organization theory; and (b) of widely divergent attempts to explain and predict organizational behavior by studying and theorizing about functions and concepts, such as organizational socialization processes, norms, decision processes, climate, beliefs, values, symbols, and sagas—from within and outside of organization theory.

Second, it is very difficult to appreciate the organizational culture perspective's historical development without a grounding in its language, essence and functions (Chapter 2); composition and levels (Chapter 3); and origins, development, and perpetuation (Chapter 4). How can one understand the importance of the differences between the cognitive social psychological-phenomenological-social constructionist history of organizational symbolism, and the learning theory-group dynamics history of basic cultural assumptions without an appreciation for the differences between symbolism and cultural assumptions?

Third, the methodologies of the organizational culture perspective (Chapter 5) have been adapted from widely divergent academic disciplines and schools within those disciplines, all which have rich traditions. They have evolved from and been shaped by very different historical views of what is important to study and how to go about it.

So, after several unsuccessful attempts to force this chapter (and Chapter 7) up front, it has been pushed back to where it seems to fit most naturally and comfortably—here near the book's conclusion.

Actually, the historical analyses are presented in two chapters. This chapter traces the history of organization theory and the major "schools" that have led up to and contributed to the development of the organizational culture perspective.[1] It is a macro-level historical overview. Perspectives or schools[2] of organization theory do not just appear spontaneously. They evolve out of, borrow from, and are adaptations of their predecessors. This is not to say that the organizational culture perspective has adopted the basic assumptions and precepts of all preceding schools of organization theory. Quite the contrary is true. Nevertheless, much can be learned about the origins and reasons why the organizational culture perspective has taken the directions it has by understanding what its proponents consider the weaknesses and false assumptions of other schools of organization theory. Thus this chapter analyzes organizational culture's holistic place in the field of organization theory.

Chapter 7 follows with an analysis of the historical development of the important concepts and elements that comprise the three and one-half levels of organizational culture.[3] Chapters 1 and 3 demonstrated the diversity of views about what organizational culture is and how the organizational culture perspective can and should be applied in organizations. Many of the divergent opinions reflect different historical perspectives and roots. The typologies (Figures 3–4 and 3–5 on pages 63 and 65) provide the framework for conducting manageable analyses of the important ones. Thus, Chapters 6

---

[1]Chapter 6 has been adapted from Shafritz and Ott (1987).

[2]Several terms are used virtually interchangeably with *perspective*. For decades *schools* of organization theory was the term of standard use, and generally it still is. Thus one sees references to the *Classical School* or the *Systems School*. Quite recently, however, a few organization theorists have started to use terms such as *frame* and *framework* (Bolman & Deal 1984). Occasionally, but not often, Thomas Kuhn's "paradigm" is encountered (Hunt, 1984; Schein, 1984; Sergiovanni & Corbally, 1984).

Perspective is the term of choice in this book. It connotes a way of looking at or seeing things, in this case organizations, which I believe is most appropriate for a study of organizational culture. Metaphorically, it means looking at organizations through those special 3-D glasses to see cultural phenomena rather than such things as organization charts, matrices, linking pins, or information systems. *School* and *frame* are used purely for variety and in this study they have the same meaning.

[3]See Chapter 3.

and 7 are complementary analyses of the history of the organizational culture perspective.

ORGANIZATION THEORY REFLECTS ITS CONTEXT

Theories about organizations do not develop in a vacuum. They reflect what is going on in the world—including the existing culture. Contributions to organization theory vary over time and across cultures and subcultures. The advent of the factory system, World War II, the "flower child"/antiestablishment/self-development era of the 1960s, and the computer/information society of the 1970s all substantially influenced the evolution of organization theory. In order to truly understand organization theory as it exists today, one must appreciate the historical contexts through which it developed and the cultural milieux during which important contributions were made to its body of knowledge.

DIFFERENT PERSPECTIVES OR SCHOOLS WITHIN ORGANIZATION THEORY

Many theories attempt to explain and predict how organizations and the people in them will behave in varying organizational structures, cultures, and circumstances. Some theories of organization are compatible with and build on others in what they explain or predict, the aspects of organizations they consider to be important, their assumptions about organizations and the world at large from which they are created, and the methods they use to study organizations. They use the same language or jargon. These groupings of compatible theories and theorists usually are called alternately *schools, perspectives, traditions, frameworks, models,* or occasionally *paradigms* or *eras* of organization theory.

Organization theorists from one school quote and cite each other's works regularly. However, they usually ignore theorists and theories from other schools or acknowledge them only negatively. In 1961, Harold Koontz described management theory as a semantics jungle. In 1963, Arthur Kuriloff examined the perspectives of organization theory and found that each was at odds with others, each defended its own position, and each claimed that the others had major deficiencies. Twenty years after Kuriloff's statement, Graham Astley and Andrew Van de Ven (1983) observed that different schools of organizational thought "tend to focus only on single sides of issues and use such different logics and vocabularies that they do not speak to each other directly" (p. 246). A year later, Lee Bolman and Terrence Deal (1984) remarked:

> The field of organizational behavior has long been split into several major intellectual camps. With each camp, campers share a similar view of the world, study similar problems, use similar methods and cite one another's accomplishments. Across camps, interchange is limited and mostly combative (pp. 190–191).

Some things never change.

Just as there is disagreement among the various schools about what makes organizations tick, there also are different views about the best way to group organization theories into schools. A few examples of different views on the schools of organization theory are summarized in Table 6–1.

Each of the major perspectives or schools of organization theory is associated with a period in time. For example, classical organization theory was at its prime in the 1920s and 1930s, and neoclassical theory in the 1940s and 1950s. Each perspective had its beginnings while another was dominant, gradually gained acceptance, and eventually replaced its predecessor as the dominant school. Some years later, another perspective came along to challenge and eventually take its position. Once-dominant perspectives of organization theory may lose the center stage, but they do not die. Their thinking influences subsequent schools—even those that reject their basic assumptions and tenets.

This cycling of perspectives through struggling ascendancy, dominance, challenge by other perspectives, and reluctant decline is not unique to organization theory. Thomas Kuhn (1970) postulated that this developmental process has been common to most sciences, physical and social. It is quite common for schools close to each other chronologically to have widely divergent basic assumptions about the object of their theories.

Despite their differences, most of the approaches to grouping organization theories into perspectives (including those summarized in Table 6–1) have commonalities. First, they group theories by their basic assumptions about humans and organizations and by those aspects of organizations which they see as most important for understanding organizational behavior. Second, as was mentioned previously, they usually group the theories by the period of time during which the most important contributions were written.

However, there are notable exceptions. Graham Astley and Andrew Van de Ven (1983) use a very different logic to classify schools of organization thought into four basic views based on two analytical dimensions: *the level of organizational analysis* (micro or

TABLE 6–1   A Few Examples of How Scholars Have Grouped Schools
of Organization Theory

Author	Schools
William G. Scott (1961). Organization theory: An overview and an appraisal. *Academy of Management Journal.*	The Classical Doctrine Neoclassical Theory Modern Theory
Harold Koontz (1961). The management theory jungle. *Academy of Management Journal.*	Management Process School Empirical Approach (or Case Approach) Human Behavior School Social System School Decision Theory School Mathematics School
John G. Hutchinson (1967). *Organizations: Theory and classical concepts.* New York: Holt, Rinehart, and Winston.	Scientific Management Environmental and Human Relations School Man as a Decision Maker Current Theories 1. Operational School 2. Empirical School 3. Human Behavior School 4. Social Systems School 5. Decision Theory School 6. Mathematical School
William G. Scott and Terence R. Mitchell (1972). *Organization theory* (rev. ed.). Homewood, Illinois: Richard D. Irwin & The Dorsey Press.	The Scientific Management Movement The Human Relations and Industrial Humanism Movements Classical Theory Neoclassical Critique The Systems Concept (Unlabeled, but including Personality Dynamics and Motivation, Attitudes, and Group Dynamics) Organization Processes (Communication Processes, Decision Processes, Balance and Conflict Processes, Status and Role Processes, Influence Processes, Leadership Processes, and Technological Processes) Organization Change

Author	Schools
Claude S. George, Jr. (1972). *The History of Management Thought.* Englewood Cliffs, New Jersey: Prentice-Hall.	Traditional School: Scientific Management Behavioral School Management Process School Quantitative School
Charles Perrow (1973, Summer). The short and glorious history of organizational theory. *Organizational Dynamics.*	Scientific Management Human Relations Bureaucracy ("A Comeback") Power, Conflict, and Decisions The Technological Qualification Goals, Environments, and Systems
Jeffrey Pfeffer (1981a). *Power in organizations.* Boston: Pitman Publishing Co.	Rational Choice Models Bureaucratic Models of Decision Making Decision Process Models Political Models
Lee Bolman and Terrence Deal (1984). *Modern approaches to understanding and managing organizations.* San Francisco: Jossey-Bass.	Structural/Systems Frame Human Resources Frame Power Frame Symbolic Frame

macro), and *the emphasis placed on deterministic versus voluntaristic assumptions about human nature.* Astley and Van de Ven conclude that organization theories can be grouped into the cells of a two-by-two matrix (Figure 6–1). Their voluntaristic-to-deterministic dimension (the horizontal continuum in Figure 6–1) classifies theories by their assumptions about the autonomy and self-direction of organization members, versus the assumption that behavior in organizations is determined by structural constraints. The macro-to-micro continuum (the vertical continuum in Figure 6–1) groups organization theories by their focus on communities of organizations or single organizations.

Although nonhistorical approaches such as those of Astley and Van de Ven (1983) and Koontz (1980) are insightful and thought-provoking, a historical approach offers clear advantages for understanding how the organizational culture perspective came to be. Organization theory tends to be cumulative—but not necessarily cumulative in the sense of a straight line. Some theorists and schools of theorists learn and build from each others' works. Sometimes the

FIGURE 6–1   Astley and Van de Ven's Four Views of Organization

Macro Level • • • • • • Micro Level	Natural Selection View	Collective Action View
	System-Structural View	Strategic Choice View

Deterministic . . . . Voluntaristic
Orientation   Orientation

Examples of Some Representative Organization Theorists for
Each of the Four Views

System-Structural View: Gulick and Urwick (1937); Fayol (1916); Merton
   (1940); Blau and Scott (1962); Lawrence and Lorsch (1967); and James D.
   Thompson (1967)

Strategic Choice View: Blau (1964); Feldman and March (1981); Strauss and
   associates (1963); Weick (1979); and Bittner (1965)

Natural Selection View: Aldrich (1979); Hannan and Freeman (1977); Porter
   (1981); Pfeffer and Salancik (1978)

Collective Action View: Emery and Trist (1973); Hawley (1950, 1968); Schön
   (1971)

SOURCE: W. Graham Astley and Andrew H. Van de Ven, "Central Perspectives and Debates in
Organizational Theory," *Administrative Science Quarterly 28* (June 1983):247.

cumulative building of organization theory has been accomplished
through the adoption of prior theorists' assumptions, logic, and
empirical research methods and findings. In other instances, the
building process has advanced by rejecting prior assumptions and
theories. A historical approach permits analysis of the ebbs and flows
within and among the perspectives of organization theory that pre-
ceded organizational culture.

   The major perspectives of organization theory that have led up to
the organizational culture perspective are listed below. They are also
presented diagrammatically in Figure 6–2 in order to demonstrate
the historical ebbs and flows in the development of organization
theory:

FIGURE 6–2   The Historical Development of the Major Perspectives
of Organization Theory

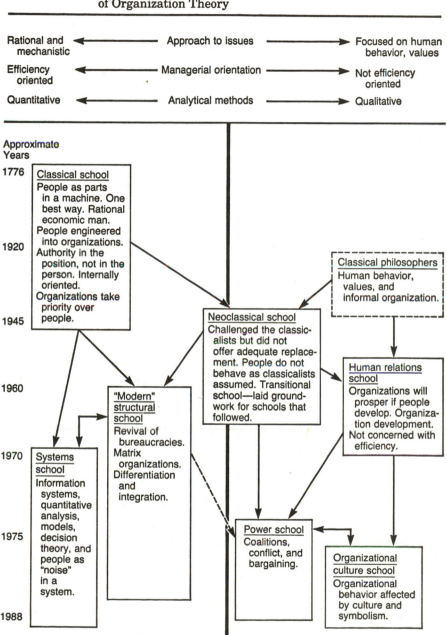

- Classical organization theory.
- The "classical philosophers."
- Neoclassical organization theory.
- The human relations perspective.
- "Modern" structural organization theory.
- The systems and contingency perspective.
- The power and politics perspective.

CLASSICAL ORGANIZATION THEORY: THE SEARCH FOR THE ONE BEST WAY TO ORGANIZE

No single date can be pinpointed as the beginning of serious thinking about how organizations work and how they should be structured and managed. One can trace writings about management and organizations as far back as the known origins of commerce. Much can be learned from the early organizations of the Egyptians, Hebrews, Greeks, and Romans. After all, it was Aristotle who first wrote of the importance of culture to management systems, and Machiavelli who gave the world the definitive analysis of the use of power. However interesting the contributions of the ancients may be, the origins of modern organization theory coincided with the beginnings of the factory system in Great Britain in the eighteenth century.[4]

The evolution of any theory must be viewed in context. The beliefs of early management theorists about how organizations worked or should work were a direct reflection of the society's cultural values of their times. And the times were harsh. It was well into the twentieth century before the industrial workers of the United States and Europe began to enjoy even limited rights as organizational citizens. Workers were not viewed as individuals but as the interchangeable parts in an industrial machine—the parts of which were made of flesh only when it was impractical to make them of steel.

The advent of power-driven machinery and the modern factory system spawned our current concepts of economic organizations and organization for production. Power-driven equipment was expensive. Production workers could not purchase and use their own equipment as they had their own tools. Increasingly, workers without their own tools, and often without any special skills, had to gather for work where the equipment was—in factories. Expensive pieces of equip-

---

[4]For a complete historical account of the origins of classical organization theory, see Daniel Wren (1972).

ment had to produce enough output to justify their acquisition and maintenance costs.

The factory system presented managers of organizations with an unprecedented array of new problems. Managers had to arrange for heavy infusions of capital; plan and organize for reliable large-scale production; coordinate and control activities of large numbers of people and functions; contain costs (this was hardly a concern under cottage industry production); and maintain a trained and motivated work force.

Under the factory system, organizational success resulted from well organized production systems that kept machines busy and costs under control. Industrial and mechanical engineers and their machines were the keys to production. Organizational structures and production systems were needed to take best advantage of the machines. Organizations, it was thought, should work like machines, using people, capital, and machines as their parts (Smith, 1776). Just as industrial engineers sought to design the best machines to keep factories productive, industrial and mechanical engineering thinking dominated theories about the best way to organize for production (Taylor, 1911; Towne, 1886). Thus, the first theories of organizations were concerned primarily with the anatomy—or structure—of formal organizations (Fayol, 1916; McCallum, 1856; Metcalfe, 1885; Weber, 1922). This was the milieu—the environment, the mode of thinking—that shaped and influenced the tenets of classical organization theory.

The classical perspective dominated organization theory into the 1930s and remains highly influential today (Merkle, 1980). Over the years, classical organization theory expanded and matured. Its basic tenets and assumptions, however, rooted as they were in the industrial revolution of the 1700s and the professions of mechanical engineering, industrial engineering, and economics, have never changed. These fundamental tenets are:

1. Organizations exist to accomplish production-related and economic goals.
2. There is one best way to organize for production, and that way can be found through systematic, scientific inquiry.
3. Production is maximized through specialization and division of labor.
4. People and organizations act in accordance with rational economic principles.

The organizational culture perspective totally rejects the basic assumptions, precepts, and tools of classical organization theory. The two schools have virtually nothing of content in common except that organizations are the focus of their attention. It can be argued that the organizational culture perspective's debts to the classical school are limited to (a) the fact that it initiated organization theory as a serious field of inquiry, and (b) the fact that its naive, oversimplistic assumptions and solutions serve as cognitive and emotional prods or motivators to find "better" answers.

Daniel A. Wren (1972) has observed:

> The development of a body of knowledge about how to manage has . . . evolved within a framework of the economic, social, and political facets of various cultures. Management thought is both a process in and a product of its cultural environment (p. 13).

Looking through today's organizational culture lenses, it is tempting to denegrate the contributions of the classicalists, to view them as narrow and simplistic. In the context of their times, however, they were brilliant analysts. Their thinking provided invaluable foundations for the field of organization theory, and their influence on organization theory and theorists continues today. However, its direct contributions to the organizational culture perspective are mostly limited to (a) contributions by rejection—there is no one best way to manage or organize, and even if there were, it could not be found through engineering or scientific methods; and (b) by establishing organization theory as a serious field of study.

The Classical Philosophers

Whereas the contributions of the classical organization theorists to the organizational culture perspective were indirect or by rejection, a few "classical philosophers" of the 1920s and 1930s provided important theoretical grounding. Therefore, Figure 6–2 places the classicalists on the left side of the central vertical dividing line and the classical philosophers on the right side (with the organizational culture perspective).

The classical philosophers were not sufficiently numerous nor coherent as a group to warrant the label *school*. During the zenith of the classical organization theory era, these few pioneers were advocating perspectives of organizations that were based on different assumptions. They saw and wrote about flaws in basic classical theory precepts, such as the ability of scientific inquiry to find the one best way and economic rationality of organization members. Instead of scientifically discovered principles of management and organization, the important things for organizational functioning were members' values, informal relationships, behavioral norms, intrinsic motivation, and the importance of feeling important. Although their stances now are quite commonplace, they were radical in their time.

Of the classical philosophers, Chester I. Barnard (1938, 1968) provided the most significant theoretical roots for the organizational culture perspective. He argued that the most critical function of a chief executive was to establish and communicate a system of organizational values among organization members. If the value system was clear and strong, the structural concerns of the classical organization theorists would, in effect, take care of themselves. In the language of organizational culture, he understood the importance of behavioral justification. Further, Barnard's conceptualization of the role of an executive implied a symbolic role for leaders. The linkages between Barnard's emphasis on values and the assumptions of the organizational culture perspective are self-evident.

According to Barnard, working relationships among organization members cannot be understood by studying formal structures. Rather, the informal structure, the interpersonal relations among members, determines and explains how people interact with whom to get work done. Although Barnard's writings do not contain the words *organizational culture*,[5] he clearly understood and appreciated the importance of group cultural norms, values, and beliefs for the functioning of organizations.[6]

The organizational culture perspective has taken concepts directly from the classical philosophers. For example, the concepts of norms (Level 1A); values (Level 2); and, to an extent, symbolism can be traced directly to the pioneering work of the classical philosophers, particularly Chester Barnard. In fact, Barnard may have been the "grandfather" of the organizational culture perspective.

NEOCLASSICAL ORGANIZATION THEORY

The neoclassical perspective modified, added to, and somewhat extended classical theory. It attempted to blend assumptions of classical theory with concepts used by organization theorists from all subsequent schools—including organizational culture. The neoclassicalists attempted to save classical theory by introducing modifications based on research findings in the behavioral sciences (March &

---

[5]Chester Barnard (1938) does employ the concept of *organization personality*, which he defines as "the private code of morals which derives from a definite formal organization" (p. 270).

[6]In addition to Barnard, some notable classical philosophers include Follett (1940); Mayo (1933); and Roethlisberger and Dickson (1939).

Simon, 1958). However, it did not have a bona fide theory of its own. To a great extent, it was an *antischool*.

Herbert A. Simon certainly was the most influential of the neoclassical organization theorists as an incisive critic of the classical perspective. His most important direct contribution to the organizational culture perspective was the concept of organizations as artificial entities (Simon, 1969). He (1946, 1947) was the first to challenge the tenets of classical organization theory comprehensively and thereby opened the way for the development of subsequent schools. Simon (1946) was particularly devastating in his criticism of the classical approach to general principles of management, like those proposed by Babbage, Fayol, McCallum, Metcalfe, and others, as being inconsistent and useless in practice.

Despite its limitations, the neoclassical school played a very significant role in the historical development of organization theory. But, like a rebellious teenager, neoclassical theory could not permanently stand on its own. It was a transitional, almost reactionary school. Why then was the neoclassical school so important? First, because it initiated the theoretical movement away from the oversimplistic mechanistic views of the classical school. The neoclassicalists challenged some of the basic tenets of the classical school head-on (Simon, 1946, 1947). And, the classical school was the *only* school at that time. Organization theory and classical organization theory were virtually synonymous.

Second, in the process of challenging the classical school, the neoclassicalists raised issues and initiated theories that became central to the foundations of the perspectives that followed it. The neoclassical school was a critically important forerunner. Most serious post-1960 articles from any school of organization theory cite neoclassical theorists. Neoclassical organization theory was an important precursor of the human relations; "modern" structural; systems; power and politics; and organizational culture perspectives of organization theory. One can argue persuasively that the organizational culture perspective originated in neoclassical organization theory, particularly in the works of Elliott Jaques and Philip Selznick.

Elliott Jaques's (1952) *The Changing Culture of a Factory* is the earliest published use of the word *culture* in an organizational context that I have been able to locate, and Jaques's use of the term is amazingly similar to current organizational culture writing. Without realizing it, he may have been the founder of the organizational culture perspective. Jaques defines the culture of a factory as:

> its customary and traditional way of thinking and of doing things, which is shared to a greater or lesser degree by all its members, and

which new members must learn, and at least partially accept, in order to be accepted into service in the firm. . . . The culture of the factory consists of the means or techniques which lie at the disposal of the individual for handling his relationships, and on which he depends for making his way among, and with, other members and groups (p. 251).

In describing the culture of a factory, Jaques identified elements of organizational culture that remain current in 1986: knowledge, attitudes, customs, habits, values, and "the less conscious conventions and taboos" (p. 251). He also alluded to socialization processes; effects of changes in culture on members' personalities; the use of culture to control behavior (p. 253); and "the sanctioning process [as] a cultural mechanism by the use of which power is linked to authority" (p. 255).

Philip Selznick (1948), a leading neoclassical sociologist, extended Chester Barnard's thinking about the importance of organizational values, norms, nonrational behavior, and discrepancies between individual and organizational goals. He also described the impacts of "co-opting" external groups in an existing organizational culture. Selznick's conceptual and methodological approaches to studying organizations, as well as his use of value systems to distinguish between organizations and institutions, have recently been lauded as models of insightfulness and usefulness by several members of the organizational culture school (Martin & Powers, 1983; Siehl & Martin, 1984; Wilkins, 1983). Other neoclassical sociologists made important contributions to the organizational culture perspective and to the general development of the field of organization theory, but none were as integral to the development of the organizational culture perspective as Philip Selznick.[7]

The neoclassical school played a very substantial role in the evolution of organization theory and the development of the organizational culture perspective. Its writers provided the intellectual, emotional, and empirical impetus to break the classicalists' simplistic, mechanically oriented, monopolistic dominance of the field. Neoclassicalists also opened the door for the soon-to-follow explosions of thinking from the human relations, "modern" structural, systems, power and politics, and organizational culture perspectives.

Among its most significant contributions to the organizational

---

[7]For example, Melville Dalton (1950, 1959) focused on structural frictions between line and staff units and between the central office of an organization and geographically dispersed facilities. His work drew attention to some of the universal ingredients of conflict within organizations and to problems of educating and socializing managers. William F. Whyte (1948) described the resultants of interrelations and status differences in the workplace. Talcott Parsons (1956) studied the contributions of organizations to the accomplishment of goals of the larger society.

culture perspective is its articulation of assumptions to counter those of classical organization theory, including:

- Organizations exist to accomplish goals other than production-related and economic goals.
- There is no one best way to organize for production, because people do not behave as classical theorists assume they do—in accordance with rational economic principles.
- For the same reason, production is not necessarily maximized through specialization and division of labor.
- The one best way to organize cannot be found through systematic, scientific inquiry.

In addition to initiating the intellectual break with classical organization theory, the neoclassicalists—most notably Elliott Jaques and Philip Selznick, who could be called the "fathers" of the organizational culture perspective—contributed concepts of organization that now are integral to the organizational culture perspective.

THE HUMAN RELATIONS PERSPECTIVE OF ORGANIZATION THEORY

The seeds of the organizational culture perspective may have been planted in the neoclassical era, but they germinated during the human relations era of the late 1950s and the 1960s. Core organizational culture concepts cannot be discussed without referencing theory and research by human relations perspective giants such as Chris Argyris, Warren Bennis, Robert Blake, Kenneth Blanchard, Leland Bradford, Fred Fiedler, Mason Haire, Paul Hersey, Frederick Herzberg, Rensis Likert, Douglas McGregor, Edgar Schein, Robert Tannenbaum, and Victor Vroom. The contents of the three and one-half levels of organizational culture shows why.[8]

- Artifacts (Level 1A).
- Patterns of Behavior (Level 1B).
- Beliefs and Values (Level 2).
- Basic Underlying Assumptions (Level 3).

The theoretical and empirical bases for patterns of behavior (Level 1B) and beliefs and values (Level 2) have been adopted virtually intact from the human relations perspective. Moreover, basic underlying assumptions (Level 3) are beliefs and values (from Level

---

[8]Refer to Chapter 3.

2) that through repeated successful use "are likely to be taken for granted and to have dropped out of awareness" (Schein, 1985, p. 9). Thus, except for (a) artifacts (Level 1A); (b) the overarching concepts of symbols and symbolism; and (c) the "dropped out of awareness" aspects of basic underlying assumptions (Level 3), virtually all of the organizational culture perspective's concepts and research data are rooted solidly in the human relations perspective. For example, the organizational culture perspective uses the human relations perspective's tools for perpetuating and changing patterns of behavior (Allen & Kraft, 1982; Davis, 1984; Sathe, 1985, ch. 11), as well as beliefs and values (Sathe, 1985, ch. 12; Schein, 1985, chs. 11–14).

Although the organizational culture school had its origins and groundings in the human relations school, the two schools' perspectives differ substantially. Bolman and Deal (1984) identify the major assumptions of the "human resource frame" as:

1. Organizations exist to serve human needs.

2. Humans do not exist to serve organizational needs.

3. Organizations and their members need each other.

4. Poor matches between individuals and organizations are detrimental to both.

5. Good matches benefit both (p. 65).

The human relations perspective is a philosophy of optimism, of faith in people. It assumes organization members should grow and develop. To the extent that organizations permit and help them to do so, personal and organizational resources and capacities are expanded. In Astley and Van de Ven's typology (Figure 6–1), the human relations perspective has a voluntaristic orientation, an orientation that implies a high degree of member free will. Organizations should consider and treat humans as capital assets (Schultz, 1971), investing resources in them just as they do with physical assets.

Compare these beliefs and values with the organizational culture perspective's assumptions: for example, people create meaning and reality so as to establish stability in the face of ever-present uncertainty; communicate by manipulation of symbols rather than through explicit media; and culture's ability to control members' behaviors. Astley and Van de Ven would classify the organizational culture perspective as having a *deterministic orientation*. Organizational culture's theories, research, and tools may have roots in the human relations school, but the two schools have widely divergent assumptions and perspectives.

The emergence of the human relations perspective was almost an inevitability. This chapter has asserted repeatedly that organization theory is shaped by the societal culture of the times (Wren, 1972, ch. 1). The human relations perspective is one of the best examples. The 1960s were a decade of optimism for humanism. It was the time of the Kennedys and Martin Luther King, Jr.; the Peace Corps and VISTA; the war on poverty; commitment to eliminate racial bigotry; the beginning of the women's rights movement; "flower children"; assertiveness training; sensitivity training; encounter groups; LSD; the legitimacy of resistance to authority in face of an unpopular war; "anti-big business-ism"; and anti-"organization man" (Whyte, 1956) mentality. This country was ripe for the human relations perspective.

Moreover, the neoclassicists had successfully pointed out the weaknesses of the bureaucratic, mechanistic, one best way-seeking, unhuman classical school; but it did not possess the body of theory needed to replace it. By the late 1950s, however, the social sciences had advanced sufficiently to cause McGregor (1960) to observe:

> [The social sciences] are still in their adolescence in comparison with the physical sciences. . . . These are relative matters however. . . . The social sciences are a rich resource today for management even though they have not reached full maturity (p. 5).

The human relations school could draw on a previously unparalleled array of theories and empirical research findings about how and why humans behave as they do. Its primary sources were psychology, social psychology, and sociology.

The emergence of the human relations school in the 1960s was inevitable. The times were right. The cause was right. And, the maturing social sciences said that optimism about humans in organizations was warranted. For many human relations school devotees, the ideology virtually became a religion. The human relations perspective moved the mainstream of organization theory almost off the right side of Figure 6–2.

The human relations school is far more concerned with organizational effectiveness than with efficiency. Effectiveness is optimistic and expansive, whereas efficiency is pessimistic and controlling. Thus, armed with its social sciences knowledge, the human relations school has focused its attention on some of the most vexing problems organizations face: how to lead effectively, how to increase employee motivation, how to gain commitment to an organization, how to manage working groups, and how to allow members to develop into better people and organizational resources.

Although the membership and focuses of the human relations perspective are broad and diverse, its philosophical basis has been articulated clearly and accepted widely. Douglas McGregor first stated it in 1957, and it was published first in *Adventures in Thought and Action, Proceedings of the 5th Anniversary Convocation of the School of Industrial Management* at the Massachusetts Institute of Technology (Bennis, Schein, & McGregor, 1966). McGregor then expanded his statement into the 1960 classic, *The Human Side of Enterprise.*

McGregor (1960) believed that managers' assumptions about the nature of man determine how they manage people and, in turn, how employees and the organization will behave. He placed these managerial assumptions at two ends of a continuum and labeled them *Theory X* and *Theory Y.* Theory X assumptions are McGregor's interpretation of classical organization theory assumptions, Theory Y of the human relations school. The two sets of assumptions are summarized in Figure 6-3. McGregor also believed that human behavior in organizations is a self-fulfilling prophecy. If managers assume people are lazy, they manage them accordingly; so employees will behave lazily. Conversely, if managers assume people want challenging opportunities for growth and self expression, they manage them accordingly; and employees will respond positively. Thus organizational effectiveness can be achieved harmoniously by changing managers' basic assumptions about human nature.

The human relations perspective has been a powerful, pervasive force within organization theory. It spawned the power and politics and organizational culture perspectives, and it has influenced the development of the "modern" structural and systems school. Since the 1960s, it has been impossible to advocate a perspective of organizations that does not at least give lip service to behavioral considerations.

However, in retrospect, the human relations perspective of the 1960s was naively optimistic. It underestimated the difficulty of changing peoples' basic assumptions and the impacts of external forces on people and organizations. It assumed that with enough time and skill, any problem between people and groups could be worked through and resolved. There wasn't, and probably still isn't, enough known about the nature of human nature to support its underlying philosophy.

Yet the human relations school provided the direct theoretical and empirical underpinnings for Levels 1B, 2, and portions of Level 3. Much of the organization development (O.D.) thinking and its values and premises were quite similar to—and contributed to—aspects of the organizational culture perspective. Many of the leading writers about organizational culture and power and politics came out of the human relations school. Some notable examples include Allen and Kraft (1982); Davis (1984); Deal (of Deal & Kennedy, 1982); Kilmann (1984, 1985); Pfeffer (1981a, 1981b); Sathe (1985); and Schein (1981,

FIGURE 6–3   Theory X and Theory Y Assumptions

Theory X Assumptions

1. Management is responsible for organizing the elements of productive enterprise—money, materials, equipment, people—in the interest of economic ends.

2. With respect to people, this is a process of directing their efforts, motivating them, controlling their actions, modifying their behavior to fit the needs of the organization.

3. Without this active intervention by management, people would be passive, even resistant, to organizational needs. They must therefore be persuaded, rewarded, punished, controlled. Their activities must be directed. This is management's task in managing subordinate managers or workers.

4. The average person is by nature indolent and works as little as possible.

5. The average person lacks ambition, dislikes responsibility, and prefers to be led.

6. The average person is inherently self-centered and indifferent to organizational needs.

7. The average person is by nature resistant to change.

8. The average person is gullible, not very bright, the ready dupe of the charlatan and the demagogue.

Theory Y Assumptions

1. Management is responsible for organizing the elements of productive enterprise—money, materials, equipment, and people—in the interest of economic ends.

2. People are not by nature passive or resistant to organizational needs. They have become so as a result of experience in organizations.

3. The motivation, the potential for development, the capacity for assuming responsibility, the readiness to direct behavior toward organizational goals are all present in people. Management does not put them there. It is a responsibility of management to make it possible for people to recognize and develop these human characteristics for themselves.

4. The essential task of management is to arrange organizational conditions and methods of operation so that people can achieve their own goals best by directing their own efforts toward organizational objectives.

SOURCE: Adapted from D. McGregor, *The Human Side of Enterprise.* New York: McGraw-Hill, 1960, ch. 7.

1984, 1985). Perhaps these two later schools are homes for older, wiser, and more realistic human relationists.

"MODERN" STRUCTURAL ORGANIZATION THEORY

The historical development of organization theory can be characterized as a series of ebbs and flows. In the 1940s and 1950s, the neoclassicalists initiated the break from the classicalists, moving organization theory toward the right side of Figure 6–2. In the 1950s and 1960s, the human relations perspective further propelled the mainstream of organization theory away from classical tenets. However, the "modern" structural perspective started a 1960s movement back toward the left side of Figure 6–2—back toward a more rational, goal-oriented, mechanistic view of organizations.

Structural organization theory is concerned with vertical differentiations—hierarchical levels of organizational authority and coordination as well as horizontal differentiations between organizational units—for example, between product or service lines, geographical areas, or skills. The organization chart is the ever-present "tool" of a structural organization theorist.

Why use the label *"modern"* to modify structural organization theory? Because most organizational theorists from the classical school were structuralists. They focused their attention on the structure or design of organizations and their production processes. The word *"modern"* (always in quotation marks) is used merely to differentiate between the structural organization theorists of the 1960s and 1970s and the pre–World War II classical school structuralists.

The "modern" structuralists are concerned with many of the same issues as were the classical structuralists, but their theories have been influenced by and have benefited greatly from advancements in organization theory since World War II. Their roots are in the thinking of Fayol, Taylor, Gulick, and Weber, and their underlying tenets are quite similar: organizational efficiency is the essence of organizational rationality, and the goal of rationality is to increase the production of wealth in terms of real goods and services. However, "modern" structural theories also have been influenced substantially by the neoclassical school, the human relations-oriented theorists, and the systems school.

Bolman and Deal (1984) identify the basic structural school assumptions as:

1. Organizations are rational institutions whose primary purpose is to accomplish established objectives; rational organi-

zational behavior is achieved best through systems of defined rules and formal authority. Organizational control and coordination are key for maintaining organizational rationality.

2. There is a "best" structure for any organization—or at least a most appropriate structure—in light of its given objectives; the environmental conditions surrounding it (for example, its markets, the competition, and the extent of government regulation); the nature of its products and/or services (the "best" structure for a management consulting firm probably is substantially different than for a certified public accounting firm); and the technology of the production processes (a coal mining company has a different "best structure" than the high-tech manufacturer of computer microcomponents).

3. Specialization and the division of labor increase the quality and quantity of production—particularly in highly skilled operations and professions; and

4. Most problems in an organization result from structural flaws and can be solved by changing the structure (pp. 31–32).

The "modern" structural and organizational culture perspectives do not have much in common. They see organizations through very different lenses. However, there are a few commonalities. For example, division of labor is an inevitable consequence of specialization by skills, products, or processes. Most "modern" structuralists now use the word *differentiation,* which means essentially the same thing as specialization but also reflects increased appreciation of the myriad rapidly changing external environmental forces with which organizations interact (for example, different markets, sociopolitical cultures, regulatory environments, technologies, competition, and the economy). Thus, complex differentiation is essential for organizational effectiveness as well as efficiency. However, differentiation *means* diverse forces that tend to pull organizations apart. Differentiation increases the need for organizational coordination and control, which, in the language of "modern" structuralists, is labeled *integration.*

Although the organizational culture perspective differs markedly from the "modern" structural perspective in its basic assumptions and views of organization, the impacts of the "modern" structuralists on the culturalists is very evident. For example, Paul R. Lawrence and Jay W. Lorsch (1967) asserted that the single most important problem all organizations must solve is achieving a balance between the conflicting needs for the demands of differentiation and integration. In 1981, Edgar Schein defined the basic content of an organizational culture as the responses learned by members in struggling to solve problems of external adaptation (differentiation) and internal integration. Despite the philosophical differences between the two perspectives, where would organizational culture be without concepts from the "modern" structural school like differentiation and integration?

SYSTEMS AND CONTINGENCY THEORIES OF ORGANIZATION

Starting in the 1960s, the "modern" classical perspective started a pendulum swing away from the humanistic orientation (the right side of Figure 6–2) back toward the rational economic views of classical organization theory (the left side of Figure 6–2). The systems and contingency perspective continued and accelerated the swing starting in the late 1960s. Just as classical organization theory was important to neoclassical theory, the systems perspective's importance to the organizational culture perspective is primarily as a focus of theoretical, empirical, and emotional dissatisfaction (Cummings, 1981; Hunt, 1984; Van Maanen, 1979, 1983). The power and politics and the organizational culture perspectives both can be viewed as antisystems schools that developed out of frustration with and rejection of systems school assumptions and methods.

Perhaps the field of organization theory was simply ripe for advancement in the late 1960s. The human relations perspective had lost much of its vigor. The cultural milieu was moving away from the introspective, self-developmentalistic optimism of the flower-child generation and the T-groups of the early 1960s. We were becoming enamored with computers, statistics, models, information systems, and measurement. Whatever the reasons, Katz and Kahn (1966) and James D. Thompson (1967) provided the intellectual basis for the systems school to emerge as the mainstream of organization theory through the 1970s and early 1980s.

The systems and contingency perspective has dominated organization theory since 1966–1967 (Hunt, 1984), when two of the most influential modern works in organization theory appeared: Katz and Kahn's (1966) *The Social Psychology of Organizations,* which articulated the concept of organizations as *open systems,* and J. D. Thompson's (1967) statement of the *rational systems/contingency approach* to organizations in *Organizations in Action.*

The systems school has two major conceptual themes or components: (a) applications of general systems theory to organizations; and (b) the use of quantitative tools and techniques to understand complex relationships among organizational variables and, thereby, optimize decisions.

The systems school views an organization as a complex set of dynamically intertwined and interconnected elements, including its inputs, processes, outputs, feedback loops, and the environment in which it operates. A change in any element of the system inevitably causes changes in its other elements. The interconnections tend to be complex, dynamic, and often unknown. When management makes decisions involving one organizational element, unanticipated impacts usually occur throughout the organization. Systems school organization theorists study these interconnections, frequently using organizational decision processes and information and control systems as their focal points for analysis. Whereas classical organization theory tends to be unidimensional and somewhat simplistic, systems theory tends to be multidimensional and complex in its assumptions about cause-and-effect relationships. The classical school viewed organizations as static structures; the systems school sees organizations as dynamic processes of interactions among elements of organizational structure, information, intelligence, decisions, and environment. Organizations are adaptive systems that must adjust to changes in their environment, if they are to survive.

Norbert Wiener's (1948) classic model of an organization as an adaptive system epitomizes these basic theoretical perspectives of the systems school (Figure 6–4). *Cybernetics,* a Greek word meaning *steersman,* was used by Wiener to mean the multidisciplinary study of the structures and functions of control and information processing systems in animals and machines. The basic concept behind cybernetics is self-regulation: biological, social, or technological systems that can identify problems, do something about them, and then receive feedback to adjust themselves automatically. Wiener, a mathematician, developed the concept of cybernetics while working on antiaircraft systems during World War II. Variations on this simple model of a system have been used extensively by systems school organization theorists (Bertalanffy, 1968; Boulding, 1956; Blumenthal, 1969; Carzo & Yanouzas, 1967; Dearden & McFarlan, 1966; Galbraith, 1973).

The organizational culture perspective does not dispute the notion of organizations as open systems. After all, the perspective acknowledges that two primary sources of organizational culture are the broader culture in which an organization resides and the nature of the business or business environment. However, the differences between the two perspectives are pronounced when it comes to issues such as controlling and predicting organizational system behavior. According to the organizational systems perspective, system behavior can be controlled through the use of feedback loops and control systems. McKelvey (cited in Lawler & Rhode, 1976) draws a graphic analogy to a thermostat. Organizations respond to discrepancies be-

FIGURE 6–4   Model of an Organization as an Adaptive System

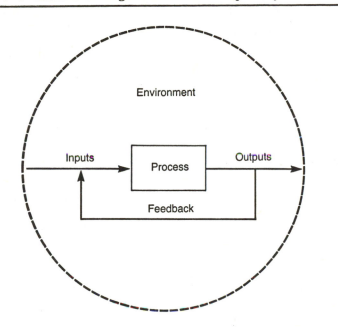

SOURCE: Based on concepts from N. Wiener, *Cybernetics*. Cambridge, Mass.: The M.I.T. Press, 1948.

tween the desired and actual status just like a thermostat turns on a furnace when the temperature falls below a desired standard.

The organizational culture perspective debunks this entire way of thinking about and viewing organizations as mythology or wishful thinking. The systems school reflects a naively arrogant belief that organizations can be controlled mechanically or electrically (Stout, 1980). Instead, organizations need to be seen as social cultures that cannot be directed, explained, or controlled by methods analogous to thermostats regulating furnaces. Organizational systems are needed to support efforts to perpetuate or change organizational culture; but when there is conflict between systems and culture, culture usually will prevail.[9]

The organizational culture perspective has even more difficulty with the systems perspective's reliance on quantitative, quasi-experimental approaches to studying and measuring organizations (Van Maanen, 1979, 1983).

The systems school's search for order among complex variables

---

[9]See Chapter 4.

has led to an extensive reliance on quantitative analytical methods and models. In these respects, the systems school has close philosophical and methodological ties to the scientific management approach of Frederick Winslow Taylor. Whereas Taylor used quantitative scientific methods to find *the one best way,* the systems school uses quantitative scientific methods to find *optimal* solutions. In this realm, the conceptual approaches and purposes between the two schools are strikingly similar. Thus, systems school theory is often called *management science* or *administrative science.*

Computers, models, and interdisciplinary teams of analysts are the basic tools of the systems school. Studies of organizations done by its members typically use the scientific method and quasi-experimental research techniques or heuristic computer models. This quantitative orientation reflects the systems school's roots in the years immediately following World War II when the first serious attempts were made to apply mathematical and statistical probability models to organizational processes and decision making. Many of the early efforts started under the label *operations analysis* or *operations research,* in defense industry-related think tanks. Operations research or operations analysis refers to the use of mathematical and scientific techniques to develop a quantitative basis for making organizational decisions. During the subsequent decades, defense and aerospace programs provided the development and testing settings for many tools and techniques of operations research, such as PERT, CPM, statistical inference, linear programming, gaming, Monte Carlo methods, and simulation.

It is important to remember and easy to forget that there is a social-systems side to the systems school, as well as a management-systems side. The social-systems side is rooted in the traditions and philosophies of social psychology, cultural anthropology, and sociology, and in the humanistically oriented classical philosophers of organization theory such as Elton Mayo (1933); Chester Barnard (1938); Roethlisberger and Dickson (1939); and Mary Parker Follett (1940). Thus Daniel Katz and Robert L. Kahn (1966) produced the first major application of existing knowledge of social systems in general to organizations in particular. Open systems theory provided the intellectual basis for merging classical, neoclassical, human relations/behavioral, "modern" structural, and systems perspectives of organizations. Katz and Kahn balance these perspectives through their use of the concept of organizations as *open systems,* systems which must adapt constantly to changing environmental factors. Once again, the organizational culture perspective has adopted the concept of organizations as open systems. The difficulties between the systems and organizational culture theories arise when the systemists put on their "thermostat-type 3-D glasses" and attempt to use quantitative methods and heuristic models to measure and control organizations.

Contingency theory, a close cousin of systems theory, provides another excellent example of how the systems and organizational culture perspectives start from the same philosophical point and progress in diametrically opposite directions. Contingency theory views the effectiveness of an organizational action (for example, a decision) as dependent upon the relationship between the element in question and all other aspects of the system—at the particular moment. Everything is situational: there are no absolutes or universals. Thus, contingency theory places high importance on rapid, accurate information systems.

The organizational culture perspective follows the same logic path until the last sentence. Actions do depend on the relationship between all elements in the cultural system at a given moment. Everything is situational. Absolutes and universals exist only as they are socially constructed in the culture and transmitted through the manipulation of symbols. However, where the contingency perspective turns to rapid, accurate information systems to deal with the lack of absolutes and uncertainties, the organizational culture perspective turns to people's anxiety-reducing mechanisms—their reliance on symbols, rites, rituals, and shared interpretations of meaning to make sense of ambiguity.

The differences both reflect and highlight the fundamentally conflicting views about people and organizations that dominate the two perspectives. The systems perspective *assumes* that people and organizations are rational and will deal with uncertainty through faster and better processing of data. Managers should have better information systems. In contrast, the organizational culture perspective *assumes* that people in organizations will use complex psychological processes to reduce the anxiety resulting from uncertainty. Thus managers should have appropriate cultural symbols to provide stability (material artifacts, language, rites and rituals, and norms).

As the systems school ascended to the center stage of organization theory during the 1960s, its focus on computers, information technology, and control systems spawned many heated debates between members of the systems school and human relations-oriented organization theorists over such philosophical issues as computer domination of social structures and irresolvable conflicts between the individual freedom of organizational members and technology-based organizational confinement. Norbert Wiener, the "father" of cybernetics and a visionary systems-oriented scientist, wrote in 1964:

> Render unto man the things which are man's and unto the computer the things which are the computer's. This would seem the intelligent

policy to adopt when we employ men and computers together in common undertakings. It is a policy as far removed from that of the gadget worshipper as it is from the man who sees only blasphemy and the degradation of man in the use of any mechanical adjuvants whatever to thoughts (p. 73).[10]

The systems and organizational culture perspectives do not like what the other assumes or stands for. The differences are intellectual, theoretical, and emotional. In large part, the organizational culture perspective represents an *antisystems school,* somewhat like the neoclassical school's relationship to classical organization theory.

However, in reflecting back on Astley & Van de Ven's (1983) continuum from voluntaristic to deterministic (Figure 6–1), there are a few notable similarities between these two basically dissimilar perspectives of organization theory. They both view the fundamental issues of organization in somewhat the same manner: for example, organizations are viewed as active and passive parts of their environments, the basic need to reduce organizational uncertainty, and the need to solve the problems of differentiation and integration. Moreover, both the systems and the organizational culture perspectives attribute minimal amounts of free will to organization members (although in very different ways). Despite the substantial differences between the two perspectives, the organizational culture perspective clearly has benefited from the systems perspective.

THE POWER AND POLITICS PERSPECTIVE
OF ORGANIZATION THEORY

In the late 1970s, the power and politics perspective of organization theory began to assert itself and to pull organization theory back away from the mechanistic rationality of the systems perspective, once again initiating a movement within organization theory toward the right side of Figure 6–2. The organizational culture perspective appeared shortly thereafter and reinforced the trend, but neither of these two recent perspectives can claim to have replaced the systems perspective's hold on the mainstream of organization theory in the 1980s.

Like the literature of the organizational culture perspective, many of the important pieces from the power school are quite recent, and the theoretical grounding of the school is not as advanced as it is in the classical, human relations, "modern" structural, and systems schools. Thus, it is useful to contrast its basic assumptions with those of its immediate predecessors, the modern classical and systems schools.

---

[10] An *adjuvant* is something that serves to help or assist.

In both the "modern" structural and the systems perspectives of organization theory, organizations are assumed to be institutions whose primary purpose is to accomplish established goals. Those goals are set by people in positions of formal authority. In these two schools, the primary questions for organization theory involve how best to design and manage organizations to achieve their declared purposes effectively and efficiently. The personal preferences of organizational members are restrained by systems of formal rules, authority, and by norms of rational behavior.

The power and politics perspective rejects these assumptions about organizations as being naive, unrealistic, and of minimal practical value. Instead, organizations are seen as complex systems of individuals and coalitions, each having its own interests, beliefs, values, preferences, perspectives, and perceptions. The coalitions compete with each other continuously for scarce organizational re- sources. Conflict is inevitable. Influence and the power and political activities through which influence is acquired and maintained, are the primary weapons for use in competition and conflicts. Power, politics, and influence are critically important and permanent facts of organizational life.

Only rarely are organizational goals established by those in positions of formal authority. Goals result from ongoing maneuvering and bargaining among individuals and coalitions. Coalitions tend to be transitory. They shift with issues and often cross vertical and horizontal organizational boundaries. Organizational goals change with shifts in the balance of power among coalitions. Baldridge (1971) found that organizations have many conflicting goals, and different sets of goals take priority as the balance of power changes among coalitions—as different coalitions gain and use enough power to control them. Organizational goals are important in the theory of organizational power and politics for a very different reason than in the systems school: they provide the *official legitimization* for resource allocation decisions, which, in fact, are made based on the relative power of competing coalitions.

Power relations are permanent features of organizations primarily because specialization and the division of labor result in the creation of many small, interdependent organization units with varying degrees of importance. Units compete with each other and with transitory coalitions for scarce resources. As Thompson (1967) points out, a lack of balance in the interdependence among units sets the stage for the use of power relations. Pfeffer (1981a, Preface) re-emphasizes this point: persons and units that have the responsibility for performing the more critical organizational tasks have a natural advantage in developing and exercising power. Power is first and foremost a structural phenomenon.

The "modern" structural school places high importance on legitimate authority (authority that flows down through the organizational hierarchy) and formal rules (promulgated and enforced by those in authority) to ensure that organizational behavior is directed toward the attainment of established organizational goals. Structuralists tend to define power synonymously with authority. In contrast, power and politics theorists such as John Kotter (1985, ch. 2) argue that in today's organizational world, the gap is increasing between the power one needs to get the job done and the power that automatically comes with position (authority). Thus the power and politics school views authority as only one of many available sources of organizational power; power is aimed in all directions, not just down through the hierarchy. Other forms of power and influence often prevail over authority-based power. A few examples include control over scarce resources (office space, discretionary funds, current and accurate information, and time and skill to work on projects; easy access to others who are perceived as having power (such as important customers or clients, members of the board of directors, or someone else with formal authority or who controls scarce resources); a central place in a potent coalition; ability to "work the organizational rules" (knowing how to get things done or to prevent others from getting things done); and credibility (for example, knowing that one's word can be trusted).

According to the power and politics perspective, conflict and the use of power often are over the choice of methods, means, approaches, and/or turf. They are not limited to battles about outcomes. This point re-emphasizes that power is primarily a structural phenomenon, a consequence of the division of labor and specialization. For example, competing organizational coalitions often form around professions: sociologists versus mathematicians at Scenic Mountain State College; public health school-educated staff specialists versus inspectors from the "school of hard knocks" at the Plains State Health Department; and social workers versus special educators at the Community Center. Organizational conflicts among people representing different professions, educational backgrounds, sexes, and ages frequently do not involve goals: they center on questions about the "right" of a profession, academic discipline, sex, or age group to exercise its perception of its "professional rights"; to control the way things will be done; or to protect its turf and status.

This point re-emphasizes the power and politics perspective's view that organizational behavior and decisions frequently are not rational—as the word is used by the "modern" structural school and the systems school to mean directed toward the accomplishment of established organizational goals. The power and politics school rejects these basic assumptions of the "modern" structural school and the systems school as naive and unrealistic and considers those theories of organization to be of minimal value.

The power and politics perspective shares fundamental views and assumptions with the organizational culture perspective. The two perspectives reject the systems school's assumptions of rational behavior in the face of organizational uncertainty; they do not believe that organizations are necessarily goal-oriented in the rational sense of the term; they do not see structural authority as controlling organizational behavior; and they both recognize that values, beliefs, and preferences of groups vitally affect organizational behavior. On this latter point, their differences appear to be more of emphasis and semantics: coalitions versus subcultures, conflict versus cultural perpetuation and transmittal.

Several leading current organization theorists have written from both perspectives (Kanter, 1977, 1979, 1983; Mintzberg, 1979, 1983; Pfeffer, 1981a, 1981b). I would not be surprised to see a merging of the power and politics and organizational culture perspectives in the near future. Their similarities exceed their differences.

CONCLUSIONS

What can be learned from this macro-level historical overview of the development of organization theory? Several important things, I hope. First, the historical development of organization theory can be viewed as cumulative (although not in the sense of a straight line). Therefore, the movement in the 1980s away from the rational-mechanistic systems and "modern" structural schools toward the non-rational organizational culture and power perspectives has been predictable. The pendulum is again swinging from the left to the right side of Figure 6–2.

Second, organization theory tends to reflect the beliefs, values, and mood of the time. The 1960s were a decade of optimism about humans and their capacity for self-development. Antiestablishment sentiments prevailed. The human relations school fit the mood of the times. In the late 1960s and 1970s, people in the United States were convinced as a nation that computers, high-tech industry, models, quantitative methods, PPBS, and ZBB could solve our basic problems. Further, we were cynical about people and basic institutions as the result of Vietnam, Watergate, and stagflation.

The 1980s have been years of uncertainty, change, and of questioning basic values, institutions, national economic and military strength, and our ability to solve fundamental problems *at all*. The organizational culture perspective fits the current national mood.

Who says rational views have solved our problems or have led us to understand organizations?

Third, the historical overview provides a fairly clear picture of how the organizational culture perspective has learned from and built upon previous schools of organization theory. It did not appear spontaneously but evolved out of a long history within organization theory.

The classical school established organization theory as a legitimate field of serious study and provided a foundation for all subsequent schools. Its overly simplistic views of organizations and people in them provide basic assumptions for other schools, such as organizational culture, to reject.

The classical philosophers were true pioneers, arguing years ahead of their time that people do not act like and cannot be treated like machines. They provided the organizational culture perspective with basic concepts such as: organizations become institutions only when they are infused with values; things happen through the informal organization as much as through the formal organization; and organizations have distinctive personalities. The most important function of an executive is to imbed a value system.

The neoclassical school provided theoretical and empirical evidence and emotional energy to refute the basic assumptions of classical organization theory. Although the neoclassical school was primarily an "anticlassical school," several basic organizational culture concepts and research methods had their origins with such neoclassicalists as Elliott Jaques and Philip Selznick.

The organizational culture perspective probably received more impetus and background from the human relations school than any other. It learned its basic assumptions, concepts, and methods for working with patterns of behavior (Level 1B); beliefs and values (Level 2); and portions of basic underlying assumptions (Level 3) directly from the human relations perspective (including organization development). Moreover, a significant number of leading organizational culture theorists came to the school from the human relations school.

Although the "modern" structural school is somewhat philosophically aligned with the classical school, it still has contributed to the development of the organizational culture perspective. It emphasized the impacts of external forces on organizations and their members as well as organizations' needs to solve the problem of differentiation and integration. These concepts are integral to the sources and development of organizational culture.

The fundamental disagreements between the systems and contingency school and the organizational culture perspective are all-pervasive. Whereas the systems school prescribes how organizations ideally should behave (rationally), the organizational culture perspective attempts to describe an entirely contrary, socially constructed world of organizational rationality. The two schools share many common views about crucial issues facing organizations but differ totally about how to deal with them. The systems school also contributed a language that is used by organizational culturists: consider, for example, Schein's model of organizational culture (Figure 3–2 on page 55). Graphic models with boxes and arrows are from the language of the systems school.

The power and politics perspective and the organizational culture perspective are cousins. They share many assumptions and originated within a few years of each other; and many current organization theorists overlap the boundaries of both schools. It would not be surprising if one day they merge into a single perspective.

Thus, the organizational culture perspective is largely a product of its time and of the history of organization theory. However, important questions remain to be answered. The next important step is to analyze the historical development of the important concepts and elements that comprise the different levels of organizational culture. This is the subject of Chapter 7.

The Origins and Development of the Major Concepts and Elements of Organizational Culture

Chapter 6 traced the history of organization theory and the major perspectives that have led to and contributed to the development of the organizational culture perspective. It offered a macro-level historical overview. This chapter, while still historical, has a different purpose and takes a very dissimilar approach. It analyzes the origins and development of the central concepts and elements of organizational culture. In doing so, Chapter 7 cuts across the perspectives of organization theory and other academic disciplines to identify where organizational culture's important concepts came from and how they developed. Thus, Chapters 6 and 7 are complementary historical analyses of the organizational culture perspective.

Some theories of organization are compatible with and build upon others in what they explain or predict; the aspects of organizations they perceive to be important; their beliefs and assumptions about organizations and the world at large from which they are created; and the methods they use to study organizations (Masterman, 1970). Organization theorists from one school quote and cite each others' works regularly; but they tend to ignore theorists and theories from other perspectives or acknowledge them only negatively (Kuhn, 1970b). These groupings of compatible theories and theorists usually are called *perspectives* or *schools*.[1]

Scientific schools serve a very useful purpose. They are profes-

---

[1] See Chapter 6, Footnote 2.

sional communities that advance knowledge within the scope of their particular perspective. On the other hand, schools tend to block the advancement of knowledge that requires crossing lines between competing or incompatible perspectives. For example, in organization theory, few systems and contingency school members cite or use information from human relations perspective writers except to note their weaknesses or inadequacies.

The same problem exists *within* perspectives that have not achieved maturity, and this clearly includes the organizational culture perspective. Theorists who define organizational culture as its beliefs and values (Level 2) justify and substantiate their basic assumptions, theories, and research methods primarily with theory and empirical findings from human relations perspective social psychologists and sociologists. In contrast, those who define organizational culture as socially constructed realities that are manifested in and perpetuated through artifacts (Level 1A) and/or patterns of behavior (Level 1B) tend to substantiate their assumptions with theory and research findings from cognitive social psychology and phenomenology—disciplines outside of organization theory. Often there is little or no basis for comparing theories or findings, and each subperspective continues merrily on its own way (Schein, 1985, p. x).

This discussion about barriers between and within perspectives of organization theory is designed to add meaning to the assertions made in Chapter 1 about the dearth of and need for comprehensive and integrative studies of organizational culture and the organizational culture perspective. Moreover, it is designed to help explain why Schein's three-level (1985) model of organizational culture and the typologies presented in Chapter 3[2] are so important for understanding and using the organizational culture perspective.

In this chapter, the typology (see Figure 3–3 on page 62) is used to organize analyses of each level of organizational culture, starting with basic underlying assumptions (Level 3); symbols and symbolism; and then the remaining levels.[3] Although this sequence may appear somewhat circular, it has the advantage of addressing the most complex and holistic concepts of organizational culture first, thus paving the way for looking at the less complex levels.

---

[2] See Chapter 3, Figures 3–2 through 3–5.

[3] An alternative way I considered for organizing this chapter—but decided against—would have started with an analysis of the historical development of the phrase *organizational culture*. This approach was not used because it only resulted in a repetition of Chapters 2 and 3, arranged chronologically.

HISTORICAL ANALYSIS: ORGANIZATIONAL CULTURE AS BASIC UNDERLYING ASSUMPTIONS

Schein's (1985) formal definition of organizational culture serves as the framework for analyzing Level 3, because his is the first and only comprehensive articulation of it:

> A pattern of basic assumptions—invented, discovered, or developed by a given group as it learns to cope with its problems of external adaptation and internal integration—that has worked well enough to be considered valid and, therefore, to be taught to new members as the correct way to perceive, think, and feel in relation to those problems (p. 9).

In an important adjunct to the formal definition, Schein (1985, p. 9) asserts that basic assumptions are likely to have moved out of members' conscious into their preconscious because they have yielded successful results repeatedly over time.

The Level 3 conceptualization of organizational culture is holistic and integrative. It incorporates, under one umbrella, theories and knowledge about:

- Beliefs.
- Values.
- Norms.
- Emotions.
- The distinction between espoused values and values-in-use.
- Coping with problems of organizational differentiation and integration.
- Social construction of perceptions of validity.
- Adult learning theory.
- Group dynamics.
- Group growth.
- Informal organization.
- Socialization processes and their impacts on individual personalities and behavior.

Where did these concepts originate and how did they develop? Within organization theory, the overarching concept of culture appears to have originated with the classical philosopher Chester I. Barnard's (1938, 1968) assertions about the importance of norms and moral codes and the responsibility of executives to infuse organizations with value systems.

Barnard saw morals as nonarguable innate convictions that are emotional rather than intellectual, provide behavioral sanctions, and, are specific to professions or organizations (ch. XVII). According to Barnard, morals are personal forces or propensities "which tend to inhibit, control, or modify inconsistent immediate specific desires, impulses, or interests, and to intensify those which are consistent with such propensities" (p. 261). In Barnard's eyes, morals are far more than behavioral norms.

One could argue that Barnard's morals are justifications of behavior (Level 2 of organizational culture); but when he linked them specifically to professions or organizations, and described them as "nonarguable, innate convictions," he placed them squarely in the realm of Level 3 assumptions. The linkage between Barnard's morals and current concepts of basic cultural assumptions is even stronger because of his (a) definition of moral codes as sets of shared or commonly held morals; (b) conclusion that publicly professed moral codes may influence members' behaviors "although the conduct affected is not necessarily in harmony with such public codes" (p. 265); (c) assertion that members who are strongly attached to an organization are "likely to have a code or codes derived from it"[4] (p. 270) that is separate and distinct from their nonorganizational moral code; and (d) belief that organizational moral codes result from intangible forces, influences, and habitual practices that must be accepted as a whole. These codes are quite different among organizations, being affected by their status and by their purposes (p. 273).[5]

Barnard's influence on current thinking about organizational culture remains very strong. It is difficult to find recent works on the subject that do not reference him and his pioneering concepts.[6] A strong argument can be made that Barnard laid the essential intellectual foundation for holistically viewing the organization culture as basic underlying assumptions. Barnard also contributed substantially to the thinking of organization theorists such as Philip Selznick (1957) and Douglas McGregor (1960), who, in turn, created and synthesized

---

[4]Barnard (1938, 1968) calls this the *organization personality* of an individual (p. 88).

[5]It is interesting to note that in Barnard's (1938, 1968) discussions of morals and moral codes (ch. XVII) and organizational personality (ch. VII), he does not cite a single reference. This is in contrast to his discussions about learning the "organization ropes," where he cites, for example, Mayo (1933); Roethlisberger and Dickson (1938); and Whitehead (1936, 1938)—and norms and roles, where he acknowledges Durkheim's concept of anomie (without a specific bibliographic reference). Perhaps, then, these concepts in fact did originate with Barnard.

[6]In a very cursory review of some current organizational culture literature, only Allen and Kraft (1982); Kilmann (1984); and Davis (1984) do not cite Barnard. However, Davis (1984) does not cite anyone.

concepts that have become fundamental to the organizational culture perspective.

Although Elliott Jaques is best known for his work with A. K. Rice, E. L. Trist, K. Bamforth, and other members of the (British) Tavistock Institute's "socio-technical systems" group,[7] his (1952) book, *The Changing Culture of a Factory,* was a true forerunner of the organizational culture perspective. Whereas Barnard appears to have originated concepts that support a holistic and culturalistic view of organizations, Jaques (1952) was the first to synthesize such concepts into a cohesive statement and to use the label "culture" in an organizational context (p. 251).[8] Table 7–1 displays the essential components of Jaques's definition side-by-side with elements from Schein's (1985) formal definition and contents of organizational culture as basic underlying assumptions.

Despite the obvious contributions Jaques made to the theoretical foundations of organizational culture, they have remained virtually unnoticed.[9] Schein (1985) is the notable exception; and Jaques's conceptual influence on Schein is unmistakable. If the conceptualization of organizational culture as basic underlying assumptions gains credence, one would expect the historical stature of Jaques's work to increase.

Selznick's (1957) primary intellectual contributions to the Level 3 concept of organization culture are centered on what he called "organization character" (pp. 15–19; 38–40) and his longitudinal organizational research methodologies. His methodologies are discussed in Chapter 5, and *organization character* receives attention here.

Selznick communicated his conception of organization character through a psychological analogy to individual personalities.

1. Organizational character is a historical product that reflects the specific experiences of an organization, much like the "ego's habitual way of reacting" (p. 38). This history is "compounded of dis-

---

[7]Most notably, connected with the Glacier Project and the longwall method of coalgetting. See, for example, Jaques (1950); Rice, Hill, and Trist (1950); and Trist and Bamforth (1950).

[8]No one should ever use absolute terms such as *the first* or *the only* when writing about the history of organization theory. The origins of its theories and concepts are too diverse to ever be certain. However, if any theorist predated Jaques, he or she was *very* obscure.

[9]For example, in five leading current works on organizational culture and symbolism, Kilmann, Saxton, Serpa, and Associates (1985); Pondy, Frost, Morgan, and Dandridge (1983); Sathe (1985); Schein (1985); and Sergiovanni and Corbally (1984b), Jaques is referenced only by Schein. And, Kilmann and associates, Pondy and associates, and Sergiovanni and Corbally are edited collections!

TABLE 7–1 Jaques's Definition of the Culture of the Factory Compared With Schein's Formal Definition of Basic Underlying Assumptions

Elements of Jaques's Definition	Elements and Contents from Schein
Its customary and traditional way of thinking and doing things. Part of second nature to those who have been with the firm for some time.	A pattern of basic assumptions that has worked well enough to be considered valid.
Shared to a greater or lesser degree by all its members	Invented, discovered, or developed by a given group.
New members must learn and, at least partially, accept in order to be accepted in the firm. Ignorance of culture marks out the newcomers. Maladjusted members are those who reject or are unable to use it.	To be taught to new members as the correct way to perceive, think, and feel.
Impacts on a wide array of • Work-related behavioral patterns. • Methods of production. • Job skills and technical knowledge. • Attitudes toward discipline and punishment. • The customs and habits of managerial behaviour. • The concern's way of doing business. • The values placed on different types of work. • Beliefs in democratic living and joint consultation. • The less conscious conventions and taboos.	Which have yielded successful results repeatedly over time in coping with problems of external adaptation and internal integration. They include assumptions about • Relationship to environment. • Nature of reality, time and space. • Nature of human nature. • Nature of human relationships.
The extent to which individuals have absorbed the culture determines • The quality of their relationships and roles within the factory's social structure. • The ability to operate within the social structure of the factory.	These assumptions define the correct way to perceive, think, and feel.

SOURCE: Adapted from E. Jaques, *The Changing Culture of a Factory*. New York: Dryden Press, 1952, p. 251; and E. H. Schein, *Organizational Culture and Leadership*. San Francisco, Calif.: Jossey-Bass, 1985, pp. 9 and 14. The components and elements are not presented in the authors' sequences.

cernible and repetitive modes of responding to internal and external pressures" (p. 16).

2. The habitual way of reacting forms an integrated pattern and social structure similar to an individual's personality character.

3. Organizational character is functional: it helps an organization adapt to its internal and external environments and, just as personality, is more than an "accidental accretion of responsive patterns" (p. 39).

4. It is dynamic "in that it generates new strivings, new needs and problems" (p. 39). The dynamics include conflicts among internal interest groups from which the organization's unique values and patterns of commitment develop and are altered.

Just as Barnard before him, Selznick believed that the infusion of values creates a distinctive identity that causes organizations to become institutions. Institutions are socially integrated organizations in which "distinctive outlooks, habits, and other commitments are unified, coloring all aspects of organizational life . . . that goes well beyond formal coordination and command" (p. 40). Selznick used the U.S. Marine Corps as one of his prime examples of a socially integrated organization (p. 19).

Selznick's influence on organization theory and organizational culture has been tremendous. It is most visible in works such as Herbert Kaufman's (1960) analysis of forest rangers' culturally molded willingness to conform, and Sergiovanni and Corbally's (1984a) assertions that organizations' battles for quality are "won or lost on the basis of individual commitment—a cultural matter and not one of bureaucratic regulation or management technique" (p. ix).

Douglas McGregor (1960) articulated *the* philosophical tenets of the human relations perspective in his descriptions of Theory X and Theory Y. He also legitimized the human relations perspective in the world of practicing managers and, in so doing, played a vital role in shaping and gaining acceptance for many organizational behavior concepts that since have become central to the organizational culture perspective. McGregor's distinction between Theory X and Theory Y management is predicated on managers' *basic assumptions* about the human nature of employees and how they view work. To McGregor, leadership style, compensation plans, employee performance reviews, and the like are simply *manifestations* of underlying managerial assumptions. In the language of organizational culture, they are artifacts.

So, McGregor made at least two outstanding contributions to the organizational culture perspective—he articulated Theory X and

Theory Y (and other related concepts); and he established the precedent of basing his theoretical distinction on basic assumptions. When Schein (1985) defined organizational culture as "a pattern of basic assumptions" (p. 9) and listed the nature of human nature, the nature of human activities, and the nature of human relationships as three out of five basic assumptions of organizational culture (p. 14), McGregor's influence was clearly evident.[10]

One of the few areas of virtual unanimity among organizational culture writers involves culture functioning as a control mechanism, requiring and prohibiting certain beliefs, assumptions, and behaviors (Allaire & Firsirotu, 1985, p. 24; Deal & Kennedy, 1982, pp. 15, 76; Sathe, 1985, p. 27; Siehl & Martin, 1984, p. 229; Tichy & Ulrich, 1984, p. 67; Van Maanen & Barley, 1984). Nevertheless, no single person can be credited for initiating or originally synthesizing this notion, particularly in the context of basic underlying cultural assumptions.

One would expect the organizational culturists to rely most heavily on cultural anthropologists for their theoretical and empirical grounding in cultural control. Instead, the intellectual heritage lies mostly in social psychology and sociology. The earliest work on the topic that is cited with any frequency is *The Human Group*, George Homans's (1950) sociological study of small group formation and dynamics.

Within the field of organization theory, the first real organizational culture mind-control and behavior-control attention getters were William H. Whyte, Jr.'s (1956) potent study of *The Organization Man* and, several years later, Becker, Geer, Hughes, and Strauss's (1961) analysis of how medical schools shape future doctors' assumptions, values, and behaviors, *Boys in White: Student Culture in Medical School.*

Probably it is not coincidental that the birth of interest in organizational mind control coincided with this nation's shock and distress caused by the relative ease with which the Chinese brainwashed U.S. prisoners of war (POWs) in Korea. Schein's interest in the subject definitely was not a coincidence. As a clinical psychologist, he had been a member of a team that interviewed defecting POWs in Korea. That experience led directly to his (1961) book, *Coercive Persuasion,* and later to his multiyear study of processes organizations use to influence or control the thinking and behavior of

---

[10]It also is worth noting that Doug McGregor and Ed Schein were colleagues in the Organization Studies Group at M.I.T.'s Sloan School of Management from the late 1950s virtually until McGregor's death.

their members (Schein, 1964, 1966, 1968, 1978; Schein & Lippitt, 1966; Schein & Ott, 1962).

Research-based theory on the control of people through management of organizational culture flowed into organization theory from many diverse streams during the late 1950s and early 1960s. A few examples include Goffman's (1961) "Chicago school of sociology" study of cultural control in a mental asylum; Festinger, Riecken, and Schachter's (1956) sociological and psychological study of mind-shaping in a religious cult that had predicted the destruction of the world; and Herbert Kaufman's (1960) sociologist-temporarily-gone-cultural-anthropologist's (p. 7) research into

> the success of the Forest Service in welding the behavior of hundreds of geographically dispersed and relatively isolated Rangers into a unified organizational pattern [which] apparently rests heavily on manipulation of the perceptions, thinking, and values of members of the Service (p. xii).

Organization theory's interest in culture's ability to control waned during the late 1960s and 1970s. The limited attention it received was directed at cultural socialization processes. A few examples include Ritti and Funkhouser (1977); Salancik (1977); and Van Maanen (1975, 1976). Interest in the topic revived once again in the 1980s, particularly with the popularization of the "Japanese style of management" (Ouchi, 1981; Pascale & Athos, 1981) and the advent of the organizational culture perspective. Two prime examples include Van Maanen and Barley (1984) and Siehl and Martin (1984).

In Chapter 2, organizational climate was defined as something akin to an "organizational mood," a phenomenon related to but separate from organizational culture. It is reintroduced here because a limited body of literature developed on the subject in the 1960s and 1970s that contributed to the holistic conceptualization of organizational culture. A few examples include Gellerman (1961); Etzioni (1961); Michael (1961); and Miles and Schmuck (1971). Gellerman portrayed organizational climate as

> the kinds of hunches a company will follow in the absence of reliable facts (or, sometimes in spite of the facts) frequently reflect *a common core of subjective attitudes among key executives toward key business problems* (p. 73). (Emphasis in original text.)

Ott (unpublished, 1964) depicted organizational climate as something similar to but not as general as the culture of the organization. It represents one area of the

> "blueprint for living" within the organization confines; it has historical continuity and origin, it is transmitted to new members through a

socialization process, and it may exist in various states of integration (pp. 1–2).

Ott identified differences among the climates in four organizations and postulated that a new employee's ability to adjust to the climate would affect his or her ability to function on the job (p. 3).

Although organizational climate is neither organizational culture nor a basic assumption, the concept has played a role in the intellectual development of organizational culture as basic underlying assumptions. Moreover, organizational climate itself is still alive in the literature of the 1980s (Davis, 1984; Sathe, 1985).

The distinction between viewing organizational culture as values and beliefs (Level 2 of organizational culture) or as basic underlying assumptions (Level 3) has both practical and theoretical importance. Basic assumptions often vary dramatically from consciously held and publicly stated organizational beliefs and values for two primary reasons:

1. The assumptions may not be rational (in the traditional sense of the word).

2. They may not be acceptable to important and powerful organizational constituencies.

Thus, assumptions can work like a person's deeply ingrained defense mechanisms, serving as secret coping devices to help organizations cope with problems of external adaptation and internal integration. Beliefs and values are what people are aware of and will admit to—so, they may be rationalizations. In contrast, basic assumptions are what people truly believe and feel and what determine their patterns of behavior—*whether or not the people are aware of them*. Argyris and Schön (1978) are the acknowledged sources of this fundamental distinction, which they labeled "espoused theory" and "theory-in-use" (and, the close parallel concepts, espoused values and values-in-use) (p. 11).

Although the conceptualization of organizational culture as basic underlying assumptions (Level 3) is quite recent, its major components, assumptions, and perspectives have long histories. This chapter's analysis of the history is designed to serve three purposes:

1. To make Schein's (1985) careful distinction between beliefs and values (Level 2 of organizational culture) and basic assumptions (Level 3) much more significant.

2. To give credibility to Level 3 by demonstrating that it has evolved out of a long and rich tradition in both theory and in research.

3. To remove the aura of mystique inherent in ethereal concepts such as beliefs and values "that have tended to drop out of awareness."

TABLE 7–2   Basic Assumptions of the Symbolic Frame Grouped into
Three Categories

Bolman & Deal's Assumptions	*Categories*
1. What is most important about any event is not what happened but the meaning of what happened.	Social Construction of Reality and Meaning
2. The meaning of an event is determined by the ways that humans interpret what happened.	
3. Many important organizational events and processes are ambiguous or uncertain. It is often difficult to know what happened, why, or what will happen next.	Justification for the Frame and when It Is Most Applicable
4. Ambiguity and uncertainty render useless rational approaches to problem solving and decision making.	
5. When faced with uncertainty and ambiguity, humans create symbols to reduce the ambiguity, resolve confusion, increase predictability, and provide direction.	Symbols and Symbolism

SOURCE: The left side of Table 7–2 has been adapted from L. G. Bolman and T. E. Deal, *Modern Approaches to Understanding and Managing Organizations*. San Francisco, Calif.: Jossey-Bass, 1984, pp. 149–150.

HISTORICAL ANALYSIS: ORGANIZATIONAL CULTURE FROM THE SOCIAL CONSTRUCTION OF REALITY AND SYMBOLIC PERSPECTIVE

The preceding section's historical look at organizational culture as basic underlying assumptions used Schein's formal definition as its analytical framework. There is no equally cogent conceptual statement we can use with the social construction of reality and symbolic perspectives of organizational culture.[11] Bolman and Deal's (1984, pp. 149–150) statement of the symbolic frame's basic assumptions does a reasonable job of helping one to organize a confusing array of views, so it has been selected as the framework for this analysis.

Bolman and Deal saw the symbolic frame as resting on five basic assumptions about the nature of organizations and human behavior.

---

[11]Sergiovanni and Corbally's (1984a) statement is the best I have found, but it is too cumbersome for use as an analytical framework.

For this analysis, the five assumptions have been grouped into three categories that are displayed in Table 7–2.

The "Justifications for the Frame and when It Is Most Applicable" are discussed extensively in Chapters 1 and 2, and they are not repeated here. Yet two categories from Table 7–2 do warrant attention: "The Social Construction of Reality and Meaning" and "Symbols and Symbolism."

Social Construction of Reality and Meaning

For some branches of archaeology and cultural anthropology, the study of culture is the study of meanings created, maintained, and transmitted by people. For example, the *normative approach* to archaeology (Hodder, 1982, p. 5) defines culture as the body of meanings held by a society and transmitted by tradition (Martin, Lloyd, & Spoehr, 1938; Rouse, 1939). Psychological cultural anthropology sees culture as distinctive constellations and personality determinants consisting of patterned worldviews and values ideals. These perspectives and ideals are internalized so deeply by members of a culture that they determine behavior and feelings (Jacobs, 1964, pp. 34–37). Sociocultural anthropology conceptualizes culture as the totality of the biological, psychological, and social products of a people that are created, learned, and transmitted to new generations through social interaction (Kroeber, 1948, sect. 6).

By synthesizing perspectives from these three branches of archaeology and cultural anthropology, culture can be conceptualized in this way:

1. It is a holistic set of patterned physical, psychological, and social products.

2. It is anchored in a shared body of meaning (or an ideology), views about world realities, perceptions, and values.

3. It is created by a society's members in the course of their social interactions.

4. It determines specific patterns of behavior and feelings.

5. It is transmitted to new generations through traditions.[12]

This amalgamated statement *is* the core of the social constructionistic conceptualization of culture and its role in organizations.

---

[12] Note that very little needs to be changed or added in order to once again arrive at Schein's (1985) definition of organizational culture. Despite the differences within the organizational culture school, there are strong threads of consistency.

Organizational culture *is* the shared set of meanings and perceptions of realities that are created and learned by organization members in the course of their social interactions. Four of the frame's leading proponents state these fundamental perspectives most clearly and forcefully.

> Despite the fact that objective reality exists and is worth pursuing, reality is also a state of mind whose validity and meaning are determined by the private worlds within which each of us lives. Reality is also created and validated in our interaction with others and this interaction network constitutes a cultural web (Bates 1984, p. 278).
>
> We consider organizations to be snapshots of ongoing processes, these snapshots being selected and controlled by human consciousness and attentiveness. . . . [which], in turn, can be seen as . . . processes where the mind acquires knowledge about its surroundings. In these . . . processes, both knowledge and the environment are constructed by the participants interactively (Weick, 1979, p. 42).
>
> The idea of organizations as nonnatural realities[13] means that they are founded in meanings, in human intentions, actions, and experience. Organizations are therefore . . . systems of meaning that can be understood only through the interpretation of meaning (Greenfield, 1984, p. 150).
>
> There is no separate reality in organizational behavior and administrative functioning. Objectivity and truth are evasive and no order exists beyond that which is created in the minds of persons and that which is imposed upon the organization by persons (Sergiovanni, 1984, p. 2).

The social construction view of organization has been receiving quite a bit of attention in the literature from members of what L. L. Cummings (cited in Hunt 1984) labeled the *radical camp* of organizational behavior and leadership theory and research.[14] According to Cummings, the radical camp is calling for a "paradigm shift" in the 1980s, a complete abandonment of traditional ways of seeing and studying organizational behavior and leadership (p. 275). The new direction will treat "organizations as social constructions of reality. Applied to leadership, this means treating it as a perceptual or attributional phenomenon" (p. 276).

Where did social construction notions—such as separate realities and socially constructed and individually perceived meanings and realities—come from? Although they have parallels in sociocultural

---

[13] Greenfield's reference to organizations as nonnatural orders or realities is made in the same sense that Simon (1969) called the study of organizational behavior the artificial sciences.

[14] In comparison with the *conservative camp*.

anthropology and archaeology, they did not originate there. Once started, an analysis of the historical development of the social constructionist perspective is very straightforward. The problem is choosing a place to begin, for there has been so much diverse writing in it recently. However, it almost does not matter. Whether one starts with the sociologically oriented reality constructionists such as Bates (1984); Foster (1984); Benson (1977); Greenfield (1980, 1984); and Ranson, Hinings, and Greenwood (1980)—or the cognitive social psychologically oriented organization theorists such as Bougon, Weick, and Binkhorst (1977); Duncan and Weiss (1979); Eiser (1980); Mitroff (1974); Pfeffer (1981); Pondy (1978); Pondy and Mitroff (1979); and Weick (1979)—both groups build from Berger and Luckmann's 1966 classic, *The Social Construction of Reality.*

Berger and Luckmann form the intellectual wellspring of these emerging camps. *The Social Construction of Reality* is the tip of a funnel: virtually every historical stream that leads to the social construction perspective of organizations flows through this work. Berger and Luckmann *are* the frame of reference for reality constructionism.

Interestingly, Berger and Luckmann's interests were in the sociology of knowledge, not organizations. The object of their inquiry —what they were seeking to discover—was how people in social settings reach conclusions about, transmit, and maintain what we call knowledge, reality, and truth. How do we know what we know? Berger and Luckmann (cited in Holzner and Marx 1979) were trying to find out how

> a taken-for-granted "reality" congeals for the man in the street. In other words, we contend that *the sociology of knowledge is concerned with the analysis of the social construction of reality* (p. 86). (Emphasis is in original text.)

This same quest is still being pursued actively by the cognitive scientists of the 1980s (Gardner, 1987).

Social constructionists acknowledge that the focus of their quest for understanding is similar to and has been the subject of extensive research by cultural anthropologists (particularly relating to religious systems of meaning); but their primary line of theoretical and empirical reference lies in the field of phenomenological sociology. The most important of these writers was Alfred Schutz, whose best known work was not translated into English until 1970, *On Phenomenology and Social Relations.* However, Schutz's most fundamental work appeared in 1932, *Der Sinnhafte Aufbau der Socialen Welt,* or "the meaningful construction of social reality" (Schutz, 1970, p. 1). Schutz was deeply influenced and inspired by such pioneering sociologists as Max Weber, William James, John R. Dewey, George Herbert Mead, and William I. Thomas. (Thomas is best known for his observation that when situations are perceived and experienced as real, they are real in their consequences for what people do [Holzner & Marx, 1979, p. 82].) It is paradoxical that the intellectual genealogy of the social constructionist camp—the most radical of the "radical camps" —includes Max Weber (1947), the archetypal classical organization theorist.

In comparison with the history of the holistic, basic underlying assumptions (Level 3 of organizational culture), the ancestry of the social construction of reality perspective of organizations can be traced back into antiquity. The perspective may be radical to organization theory; but its history virtually is the history of modern sociology, interspersed with a liberal sprinkling of cultural anthropology and archaelogy.

Symbols, Symbolism, and Artifacts

An analysis of symbols and symbolism follows very naturally from a discussion of social construction of reality, for the only true importance of symbols to the organizational culture perspective involves their functions: creating, changing, maintaining, and/or transmitting socially constructed organizational realities. These functions make symbols truly important, as they imply that symbols can be manipulated (*symbolism*) and, thereby, can be used to create or impede organizational change.[15] Artifacts also are included in this analysis because they are of no interest to organizational culture unless they are more than just "signs"—unless they have become symbols.[16]

These assertions can be substantiated with a three-step argument:

1. Organization members create symbols to reduce uncertainty and ambiguity, resolve confusion, increase predictability, and provide direction (Bolman & Deal, 1984, p. 150).

2. The content of organizational culture can be communicated best symbolically through artifacts—such as language, jargon, metaphors, humor, organizational stories, myths, sagas,

---

[15]They also serve as easily observable clues from which an organizational culture may be inferred. See Chapter 5.

[16]For a discussion of artifacts as signs and symbols, see Chapter 2. The same is true for rites and rituals.

legends, scripts, ceremonies—and physical arrangements, such as dress and decor (Siehl & Martin (1984, p. 235).[17]

3. Allaire and Firsirotu (1985) carry the argument to its logical conclusion.

> Changes at that (cultural) level . . . must be effected in part through symbolic management. . . . In order for this to happen, management must understand and make a conscious attempt to channel the complex social processes through which symbols, meanings, and values are created.
>
> Effective changes in culture and structure must be carried out in a well-coordinated sequence of actions, which mutually reinforce, legitimate, and aim to cognitively reorient and restructure the mind-sets of management and employees (p. 31).

The lineage of organizational symbols and symbolism largely overlaps the genealogies of basic cultural assumptions and social construction of reality. For example, in the field of organization theory, the management of symbols can be traced directly to the thinking of Philip Selznick and Chester Barnard, especially its importance for effective organizational leadership. Herbert Simon contributed the privotal concept of organizations as artificial entities and, thus, the study of organizations as the science of the artificial. And, Clark's (1970, 1972) saga-based study of three distinctive colleges and Pettigrew's (1979) focus on the functions of symbolic management during critical turning points in the history of a British boarding school were substantial contributions to the theoretical and methodological advancement of organizational symbolism.

It almost goes without saying that symbols and symbolism have extensive histories outside of organization theory. Since the birth of archaeology, archaeologists have *assumed* the existence of predictive relationships among material artifacts (tangible symbols); patterns of adaptive behavior; and culture (Hodder, ch. 1). Archaeologists then take to the field, searching for artifacts and attempting to interpret relationships between what is found and the culture they symbolize (Tainter, 1978). In this context, artifacts-as-symbols are merely reflective products of a culture. Their function is to provide clues about the culture.[18] This *passive reflective use* of artifacts is similar to an organizational researcher trying to identify an organizational culture by studying office arrangements and the physical placement of computers.

---

[17]Siehl and Martin substantiate their conclusion with empirical findings.
[18]For more on this, see Chapter 2.

The more important function of symbols for organization theory involves their ability to create and perpetuate systems of meaning and reality. The intellectual history of this *active use* of symbols (symbolism) goes back to the origins of ethnoarchaeology or, as it is often called, "action archaeology" (Kleindienst & Watson, 1956). According to Hodder (1982), action archaeology views artifacts as "symbols in action" (p. 12)—as more than passive reflections of culture: "they play an active part in forming and giving meaning to social behaviour" (p. 12). For example, in the Baringo tribes of north central Kenya, particular spears have a symbolic meaning that allows young men to empower themselves psychologically to act in defiance of tribal elders. Similarly, wearing the calabash decoration allows Baringo women to challenge established social controls (p. 75). Thus, ethnoarchaeological symbols do more than just reflect a culture—they actively help change realities and influence behaviors. If symbols can be manipulated, human behavior can be managed.

Action symbols have equally distinguished intellectual traditions in cultural anthropology[19] and political science (Edelman, 1964, 1971, 1977). In addition, the secondary or symbolic meaning of words is the primary interest of the field of general semantics.

> In symbols the idiosyncratic and personal are always intermingled with the general and universal. Precisely this interplay constitutes symbols and prescribes meaning. . . . Not only does the human being use and create symbols, but *the individual is also made and created by symbolism*" (S. I. Hayakawa, 1953, p. vi). (Emphasis added.)

Within organization theory, symbols, symbolism, and symbolic management views originated with the thinking of Barnard (1938, 1968) and Selznick (1957). Simon (1969) and Clark (1970, 1972) added major impetus. Current activity in the symbolic camp is at a very high level, and it is predicted to continue. Outside of organization theory, the origins of symbolism are similar to those of social constructionism; but symbolism probably owes a bit more to political science and ethnoarchaeology.

The origins of organizational culture's symbolic camp may be diverse; but they are not dissimilar from those of social construction and basic assumptions (Level 3). Despite differences among these camps within the organizational culture perspective, they share many commonalities including large segments of their histories. By now the reasons should be obvious. Without social constructionist concepts, there would be no reason for the symbolic management

---

[19]See this chapter's earlier analysis of the social construction of reality.

frame to exist. There would be no reason to manage symbols. If there were, in fact, universally perceived absolute realities and meanings, symbols would not have any "action" functions and would disappear. Without symbols and their potential for changing meanings and behaviors, artifacts are irrelevant except to archaeologists, anthropologists, and historians.

A HISTORICAL LOOK AT PATTERNS OF BEHAVIOR, AND BELIEFS AND VALUES

Basic cultural assumptions (Level 3 of organizational culture) start out as beliefs and values (Level 2). Symbols both reflect and help shape perceptions of cognitive and emotional meaning (beliefs and values). Patterns of behavior (Level 1A) are determined and reinforced by beliefs and values; and they produce artifacts. Obviously, beliefs, values, and patterns of behavior are essential pieces of the core of organizational culture. (Why then only a brief look at the historical development of these central concepts? Because the essence of their histories has already been analyzed in Chapter 5 and earlier sections of this chapter.)

The origins of rites and rituals as a component of organizational culture are the same as for the social construction of reality and symbols. The history of organizational culture as norms, beliefs, and values starts with the classical philosophers, works its way through the neoclassicalists, and achieves maturity in the human relations perspective.[20] These elements of organizational culture have not advanced substantially since the 1960s, except as they have been refined and incorporated into more holistic perspectives—just as culture's basic underlying assumptions and symbolism. Numerous texts exist on these subjects, and there is no reason to repeat what has been done already (Bell, 1967; French & Bell, 1984; Longenecker, 1973; Miles, 1975; Wren, 1972).

SOME UNANSWERED QUESTIONS

These two historical chapters have tried to answer many questions about the origins, development, and rationale for organizational culture's perspectives and concepts. Nevertheless, dozens of questions

---

[20]To a great extent, the organization development movement within the human relations perspective has attempted to address organizations holistically. Many of the organizational tools for working with norms, beliefs, and values originated here. See, for example, Beckhard (1969); Bennis (1969); Burke (1982); French and Bell (1984); and French, Bell, and Zawacki (1983).

remain unanswered about organizational culture and the organizational culture perspective. The unanswered questions range from the most macro to the most micro levels, from conceptual to methodological and pragmatic, from historical impacts to organizational culture's future, from the content of specific cultures to processes by which a particular culture evolves from competing sources. Otherwise, all is clear.

Chapter 8 addresses some of the unanswered questions but does not even come close to answering all of them. For example, Chapter 6 concludes that the organizational culture perspective is essentially a descriptive theory of organization. If that is true, why bother with it? Does it really have practical uses? Consider, too, a series of corollary questions: To date, socializing employees, leadership effectiveness, and radical organizational change are the only applications of the organizational culture perspective to receive serious attention in the literature. Do these applications represent the extent of the perspective's usefulness? For a specific example, how can the organizational culture perspective be used to improve productivity, quantitatively, and/or qualitatively? Or can it?

Chapter 8 focuses on questions such as these, but numerous questions will remain unanswered even after the final pages of this book have been read.

CHAPTER 8

Conclusion

Chapter 8 tries to close the subject of organizational culture, first by reviewing what this book set out to accomplish. Second, the chapter looks at what remains to be learned—what we need to know—about organizational culture and the organizational culture perspective. What is the "research agenda" for the organizational culture perspective? Third, the chapter and the book conclude with what I consider some of the most important issues involving organizational culture for practitioners, for organizations, and for students of organizations.

PURPOSES

The overall purpose for this book has been to help make usable sense out of organizational culture and the organizational culture perspective by analyzing and synthesizing information from published sources and field data collected in several organizations. Accomplishment of the overall purpose has required tackling smaller tasks, one at a time. These subpurposes and where they are addressed are:

1. *To clarify what organizational culture (and subculture) is, what comprises it, and the functions it performs.*

Chapter 2 examines the structural elements that comprise the three and one-half levels of organizational culture, the functions they perform, and their relationships to other elements of organizational culture. Chapter 3 compares and contrasts, analyzes, and synthesizes divergent viewpoints about the essence of organizational culture and the organizational culture perspective. A classification system (a typology) is presented and is used to sort through different concepts, elements, and functions of organizational culture.

Functionally, organizational culture is seen as something that serves as a source of energy and focus; provides meaning and direction for organization members; easily identifies members and nonmembers; and functions as an organizational control mechanism, informally approving and prohibiting behaviors. Organizational culture not only *gives* an organization its unique identity, it *is* the unique character or personality of an organization and, simultaneously, *the justification* for that identity/character.

In my opinion, the most important themes from Chapters 2 and 3 are:

- Organizational culture is a dynamic social construction. It is a reality created by its members. It is a concept rather than a thing. Thus, there is neither an ultimate authority to turn to for answers nor ultimate truths to be "found" or "discovered"—particularly not by using the scientific method.

- Organizational culture is holistic. Trying to think about organizational culture reductionalistically is like trying to appreciate a painting by analyzing its stroke patterns or its chemical content. "Organizational culture is not just another piece of the puzzle, it is the puzzle. . . . a culture is not something an organization has; a culture is something an organization is" (Pacanowsky & O'Donnell-Trujillo, 1983, p. 126).

- Organizational culture needs to be examined both structurally and functionally (dynamically). Structural analysis alone leads to static reductionism; functional analysis alone usually comes up empty.

2. *To analyze how organizational cultures form, develop, are perpetuated and changed, and are transmitted to new organization members.*

Chapter 4 explores where organizational culture comes from and why, for example, cultures differ between organizations engaged in the same line of work. Organizational culture originates in the general culture, the nature of the business; and the beliefs and values (or the *script*) of the founder and/or early dominant leader(s). It develops and is refined through the learning members share from experiences encountered while solving problems of organizational (or organizational identity) survival.

Chapter 4 also examines how organizational culture is changed, maintained, and transmitted to new organization members through combinations of processes:

- Preselection and hiring of new members.
- Socialization or enculturation of new and older members who

are in the process of crossing (or are preparing to cross) organizational boundaries.

- Removal of members who deviate from the culture, either physically from the organization or from positions of influence.
- Reinforcing or changing members behaviors.
- Altering or reinforcing peoples' beliefs, values, and ideologies —their perceptions of truth and reality.
- Communicating through verbal, behavioral, and material symbols (Sathe, 1985).

3. *To assess the applicability of different tools and methods for identifying and deciphering organizational culture, for different purposes and under different circumstances.*

Chapter 5 is about identifying and deciphering organizational culture. Virtually all methods for studying organizational culture have problems and limitations, whether they are from the qualitative (ethnographic or helper) or quantitative tradition. The chapter demonstrates why the selection of investigative methods needs to consider the purposes for the investigation and the specific concept of organizational culture that is operational. The choice of methods should be driven by (a) the intended use for the findings; (b) how quickly an identification is needed; and (c) whether culture is defined operationally as artifacts, patterns of behavior, beliefs and values, or basic assumptions.

4. *To trace and analyze the historical evolution of the organizational culture perspective, its concepts, assumptions, methods, and language.*

In order to appreciate the depth, richness, and applicability of the organizational culture perspective, it is necessary to understand its roots and developmental history. Chapter 6 recounts the history of organizational culture within organization theory, while Chapter 7 traces the genealogy of major themes and concepts through the disciplines of anthropology, sociology, social psychology, speech communication and, most recently, what Gardner (1987) calls the cross-disciplinary *cognitive sciences* or *the new science of the mind.*

WHAT REMAINS TO BE LEARNED ABOUT ORGANIZATIONAL CULTURE AND THE ORGANIZATIONAL CULTURE PERSPECTIVE?

Most managers, consultants, and students of organizations know that they must pay attention to organizational culture—just as they must be on top of strategic management, strategic planning, human resources management, and all of today's other management issues, trends, and tools. It is now generally accepted that while organizational culture can provide its members with socially constructed shared perceptions and expectations, define and maintain organizational boundaries, function as a control system prescribing and prohibiting behaviors—and provide security, direction, meaning, reduce ambiguity, and increase personal commitment—it also can cause overconforming behavior, maladaptive attitudes, and organizational rigidity. Despite this acknowledged importance of organizational culture, we lack practical information about identifying, understanding, managing, and otherwise gaining control of it.

Some questions remain unanswered because of the limits of the organizational culture perspective. It only has so much to offer. On the other hand, many questions reflect the limits of what is known today about effective research methodologies; about organizational culture theory—relationships between culture and other aspects of organizations, such as productivity and quality of output; about organizational culture itself—for example, its structure and functions; and, about how to use the organizational culture perspective in organizations.

Methodological Issues

Some of the most important unanswered questions are methodological, and without methodological advancement, the perspective will not achieve maturity. Thus, one of the high priority tasks for the organizational culture perspective is to pursue the many research agendas raised in Chapter 5. For example, practicing managers need to know where and how to start examining the culture of an organization in order to predict culture-related production or quality problems or spot functional or dysfunctional subcultures. Organizational consultants need ways to identify the limits and the pervasiveness of organizational culture; for example, to help choose cultural change or maintenance strategies or help select an effective new chief executive officer. Researchers need to understand why data collection and analytical methods borrowed from different schools of organization theory will or will not work under different theories and for different purposes. Figure 5–2 is repeated below as a review of "where we are" methodologically with identifying organizational culture.

Because organizational culture is a construct rather than a thing, it feels ethereal. Thus, of necessity, most efforts to decipher (not measure) organizational culture utilize several (triangulating)

FIGURE 5–2 Some Methods for Deciphering Organizational Culture and Their Applicability to Elements in Different Levels of Organizational Culture

	Level of Organizational Culture	
	Primary Applicability	*Secondary Applicability*
Wandering around looking at physical settings	1A	All
Rummaging through historical records	1A	All
Content analyzing publications	1A	All
Learning from organization charts	1A	All
Listening to spoken words	1A	All
Interviewing people	All	
Listening to myths, stories, sagas, and legends	1A,1B	3
Administering paper-and-pencil instruments	1B, 2	3
Combinations of the above by combination of outsider with clinician perspective and insider	3	
Combinations of the above by outsider with ethnographic perspective	3	

longitudinal (over extended periods of time) qualitative research techniques (techniques for coming to terms with the meaning but not the frequency of events or phenomena). Triangulating is an expensive process; longitudinal studies do not yield quick results; and qualitative research techniques are difficult to verify (validate and replicate), and confidence limits cannot be established for their findings —so it is often hard to defend them against challenges.

On the other hand, the more traditional quantitative research approaches (methods that use quasi-experimental designs) are simply not effective for finding such "things" of organizational culture as forgotten basic assumptions. If qualitative methods are not defensible, and quantitative methods aren't able to cope with the truly important variables, how is one supposed to proceed?

Practicing managers, consultants, and students of organizations need "road maps" of practical methods and tools for deciphering organizational culture—along with warnings about methods and approaches that cannot work. For example, *practicing managers* need to know where and how to start examining the culture of a recently acquired organization; for example, to predict culture-related production or quality problems, to spot functional or dysfunctional countercultures, or to accept or reject staff or consultant recommendations. *Organizational consultants* need ways to identify the limits and pervasiveness of an organizational culture; for example, to help choose cultural change or maintenance tools and strategies or select an effective new executive. *Academic researchers* need to understand why data collection and analytical methods and tools borrowed from different schools or perspectives of organization will and will not work under different theories and for different purposes.

Theoretical Learning

On the surface, it appears that there *ought to be* relationships between organizational culture and such important things as productivity levels, quality of output, etc. And many proponents of the organizational culture perspective have assumed the existence of such relationships. What is the nature—the characteristics—of those relationships? Under what circumstances do they come into play?

Applications

Assuming that we knew how to identify organizational culture and understood the theoretical relationships between culture and organizational functioning, what specifically should a manager or a consultant *do* with that information? In what sequence? Should a manager consciously work to manage the organizational culture? Are there limits to be observed for the protection of the organization, its identity, its ability to function or adapt, the integrity of the people in it, or the culture itself? At what point and under what dynamics does organizational culture require overconformance, place "blinders" on members, and create rigidity?

SOME IMPORTANT CONCERNS

Continue to assume for the moment that we understand the relationships between organizational culture and desired aspects of organizational functioning, such as quantity and quality levels of productivity. What can and should a forward-looking manager do to change (or maintain) it?

According to the McKinsey & Company findings (Peters &

Waterman, 1982; Deal & Kennedy, 1982), some companies have been successful in using organizational culture to their long-term business advantage: McDonald's, Disney, and 3M are among those cited most frequently. Deal and Kennedy (pp. 193–196) present several models as possibly providing guidance for future use of organizational culture. The essential elements of their three models are:

- *Heroes and ceremonies to celebrate heroes* who live the cultural values, (as at McDonald's).
- *Planned enculturation,* reinforced with education and visible symbols (as epitomized in Kaufman's 1960 description of the U.S. Forest Service).
- *"Soul, spirit, magic, heart, ethos, mission, saga,"* founded on the "bedrock of a set of meaningful beliefs and values" (Deal & Kennedy, p. 195), as with the Catholic Church, IBM, Mary Kay, and the Polaris submarine project.

Let's build from Deal and Kennedy's concepts, and look at some other useful things we know.

Necessity of Using Holistic Approaches

From what we know about organizational culture being holistic and about the dynamics of organizational culture change (from Chapter 4), any actions intended to alter a culture must be parts of a multifaceted, ongoing strategy. That strategy needs to address the organization's processes for preselecting, selecting, socializing, exiting, affecting behaviors, altering values and beliefs, and communicating (Sathe, 1985).

Selecting and Shaping Organizational Leadership

From the work of Schein (1985); Sergiovanni (1984); Tichy & Devanna (1987) and others about the inseparable connectedness between leadership and organizational culture, we know that culture cannot be dealt with independent of organizational leadership. In other words, if the culture is to be modified, leadership cannot be an interested observer, because it is both an artifact of and a prime shaper of the culture. Thus, it appears that any serious effort to alter the culture of an organization requires planned interventions in the leadership selection, development and retention processes. Are we willing to do so? On one hand, it appears that there is no choice: as responsible managers, we must.

On the other hand, I cannot suppress my mental images of the men who were carefully socialized into corporations in the 1950s (Whyte, 1956). They march past in their nearly identical gray flannel suits, white shirts, and striped ties. Maybe I should not be concerned about those images. That type of conformant behavior happened thirty years ago. Still, my concerns have been revived by reports that the Levi-Strauss Foundation has funded a follow-up on the subjects from the original *Organization Man* study (Whyte, 1956). The follow-up study's limited, preliminary, follow-up findings (which led to the decision to fund a thorough study) reportedly show devastatingly negative lifelong impacts of organization man-type thinking and behavior.

Clearly, today's "yuppies" are not cut from the same cloth as were the willing-and-ready-to-be-socialized organization men of the 1950s. Society and societal views have changed. Even the most fervent pro-big business advocate of 1988 knows not to argue that "what is good for General Motors is good for America." (Perhaps the same argument would generate public support today if made on behalf of Chrysler!) Yet, I cannot help but wonder whether the late 1980s yuppie system of beliefs and values does in fact leave individuals highly susceptible to carefully designed and executed organizational enculturation processes. Young managers' receptivity to specific socialization approaches and methods certainly must differ from their 1950s counterparts—but does their overall susceptibility?

> Our country was born as a series of highly communal enterprises, and though the individualist may have opened the frontier, it was the co-operative who settled it. So throughout our history. Our national genius has always lain in our adaptability, in our distrust of dogma and doctrine, in our regard for the opinion of others, and in this respect the organization people are true products of the American past (Whyte, 1956, p. 395).

As managers, do we really want to accept the potential long-term consequences to our people of taking conscious steps to clarify and/or strengthen the links between organizational culture and leadership?

Rigidity and Overconformance

The potential negative consequences of engineering organizational culture are not limited to organizational members: they extend to the organization itself. Organizations of all types must be receptive to divergent information, viewpoints, realities, and value systems. In fact, "receptive" isn't strong enough: organizations must actively seek diversity and must reward people (and units) who are able and willing to inject diversity into the broader institutional strategic decision processes—as well as those who take the corporate risks associated with hunting-out and nurturing these sources of diverse input.

Although this may sound good, it isn't easy to achieve in practice. Systems of homogeneous organizational values, beliefs, and basic assumptions are functional. Multiple viewpoints may be desirable for long-term flexibility and adaptability, but they often create short-term inefficiencies and divisiveness.

Of the many unanswered questions associated with organizational culture, this one may have the most immediate need for answers. Especially considering our social constructionist leanings, how can an organization balance its simultaneous needs for a strong pervasive culture and diverse realities?

Predicting Organizational Decision Patterns

Bertram Clark's (1970, 1972) assertions about the potency of saga analysis for predicting organizational decision patterns raise interesting questions. First, his assessment has high surface validity. If we know an organization's basic assumptions (or scripts), it should be relatively easy to predict how the organization will behave (what decisions it will make) under certain circumstances. How to learn the assumptions takes us back to Chapter 5. Whether the answer lies in saga analysis, the ethnographic paradigms, or the helper's role, is immaterial to this issue. What is important here is the acknowledgment that a strategy may exist for predicting organizational decisions. When decisions can be predicted, advance steps can be taken to negate or enhance their impacts, whether they are corporate or governmental. Consider the enormity of the implications if we should become able to predict another nation's international policy decisions—and vice versa. Or, to predict a competitor firm's product mix strategy. I do not find this possibility at all far-fetched.

CONCLUSION

With organizational culture, it seems as though every issue raised or question asked only generates one more set of unanswered questions or one more chain of related issues to ponder. Some of the questions raised above in the discussions about "Selecting and Shaping Organizational Leadership" and "Rigidity and Overconformance" almost seem to argue for leaving culture alone. Yet the potential implications of being able to predict organizational decision patterns are too great—too heady—to permit blissful ignorance of the subject.

When the subject is organizational culture, few things or assertions are absolute. Nevertheless, there is one such certainty. Regardless of the future of the organizational culture perspective, organizational cultures themselves are and will remain permanent parts of organizations' realities. Organizational culture is here to stay. It serves necessary purposes. People in organizations need culture for identity, purpose, feelings of belongingness, communication, stability, and cognitive efficiency.

If I have successfully presented the organizational culture perspective as a needed and useful alternative to other perspectives of organization theory, I have accomplished my primary reasons for writing this book. If I have kindled any sparks of interest or provided any direction that reduces some of the perspective's knowledge gaps, I will have exceeded my purposes.

References

Abelson, R. P. (1972). Psychological status of the script concept. *American Psychologist, 36,* 715–729.

Abelson, R. P. (1976). Script processing in attitude formation and decision making. In J. S. Carroll & J. W. Payne (Eds.), *Cognition and social behavior.* Hillsdale, NJ: Erlbaum.

Ackoff, R. L., & Emery, F. E. (1972). *On purposeful systems.* Chicago: Aldine-Atherton.

Akin, G., & Hopelain, D. (1986). Finding the culture of productivity. *Organizational Dynamics, 14*(3), 19–32.

Aldrich, H. (1979). *Organizations and environments.* Englewood Cliffs, NJ: Prentice-Hall.

Alexander, M. (1977). Organizational norms. In J. E. Jones & J. W. Pfeiffer (Eds.), *The 1977 annual handbook for group facilitators* (pp. 123–125). La Jolla, CA: University Associates.

Alexander, M. (1978). Organizational Norms Opinionnaire. In J. W. Pfeiffer & J. E. Jones (Eds.), *The 1978 annual handbook for group facilitators* (pp. 81–88). La Jolla, CA: University Associates.

Allaire, Y., & Firsirotu, M. (1984). Theories of organizational culture. *Organization Studies, 5,* 193–226.

Allaire, Y., & Firsirotu, M. (1985, Spring). How to implement radical strategies in large organizations. *Sloan Management Review, 26*(3), 19–34.

Allen, R. F., & Kraft, C. (1982). *The organizational unconscious: How to create the corporate culture you want and need.* Englewood Cliffs, NJ: Prentice-Hall.

Almirall, S. (1984, February). Colorado companies seek cultural roots. *Colorado Business,* 22–26.

Argyris, C. (1976). Theories of action that inhibit individual learning. *American Psychologist, 39,* 638–654.

Argyris, C., & Schön, D. A. (1974). *Theory in practice.* San Francisco: Jossey-Bass.

Argyris, C., & Schön, D. A. (1978). *Organizational learning: A theory of action perspective.* Reading, MA: Addison-Wesley.

Astley, W. G. (1985). Administration science as socially constructed truth. *Administrative Science Quarterly, 30,* 497–513.

Astley, W. G., & Van de Ven, A. H. (1983, June). Central perspectives and debates in organization theory. *Administrative Science Quarterly, 28,* 245–270.

Babbage, C. (1832). *On the economy of machinery and manufactures.* Philadelphia, PA: Carey & Lea.

Baldridge, J. V. (1971). *Power and conflict in the university*. New York: John Wiley & Sons.

Ball, D. W. (1972). The definition of situation: Some theoretical and methodological consequences of taking W. I. Thomas seriously. *Journal for the Theory of Social Behavior, 2*, 61–82.

Barley, S. R. (1983). Semiotics and the study of occupational and organizational cultures. *Administrative Science Quarterly, 28*, 393–413.

Barnard, C. I. (1938, 1968). *The functions of the executive*. Cambridge, MA: Harvard University Press.

Barney, J. B. (1986). Organizational culture: Can it be a source of sustained competitive advantage? *Academy of Management Review, 11*, 656–665.

Barnouw, V. (1985). *Culture and personality* (4th edit.). Chicago: The Dorsey Press.

Barnouw, V. (1987). *Ethnology: An introduction to anthropology* (vol. 2, 5th edit.). Chicago: The Dorsey Press.

Bates, R. J. (1984). Toward a critical practice of educational administration. In T. J. Sergiovanni & J. E. Corbally (Eds.), *Leadership and organizational culture* (pp. 260–274). Urbana, IL: University of Illinois Press.

Becker, H. S., Geer, B., Hughes, E. C., & Strauss, A. L. (1961). *Boys in white: Student culture in medical school*. Chicago: University of Chicago Press.

Becker, H. S., & Strauss, A. (1956). Careers, personality and adult socialization. *American Journal of Sociology, 62*, 404–413.

Beckhard, R. (1969). *Organization development: Strategies and models*. Reading, MA: Addison-Wesley.

Belcher, D. W., & Atchison, T. J. (1976). Compensation for work. In R. Dubin (Ed.) *Handbook of work, organization, and society* (pp. 567–611). Chicago: Rand McNally.

Bell, G. D. (Ed.). (1967). *Organizations and human behavior*. Englewood Cliffs, NJ: Prentice-Hall.

Bem, D. J. (1970). *Beliefs, attitudes, and human affairs*. Monterey, CA: Brooks-Cole.

Benedict, R. (1934). *Patterns of culture*. New York: Houghton Mifflin.

Bennis, W. G. (1969). *Organization development: Its nature, origins, and prospects*. Reading, MA: Addison-Wesley.

Bennis, W. G. (1984). Transformative power and leadership. In T. J. Sergiovanni & J. E. Corbally (Eds.), *Leadership and organizational culture* (pp. 64–71). Urbana, IL: University of Illinois Press.

Bennis, W. G., & Nanus, B. (1985). *Leaders: The strategies for taking charge*. New York: Harper & Row, Publishers.

Bennis, W. G., Schein, E. H., & McGregor, C. (Eds.). (1966). *Leadership and motivation: Essays of Douglas McGregor* (pp. 3–20). Cambridge, MA: The M.I.T. Press.

Benson, J. K. (1977). Innovation and crisis in organizational analysis. In J. K. Benson (Ed.), *Organizational analysis: Critique and innovation* (pp. 5–18). Beverly Hills, CA: Sage Publications.

Berger, P. L., & Luckmann, T. (1966). *The social construction of reality*. Garden City, NY: Doubleday.

Berne, E. (1964). *Games people play*. New York: Gove Press.

Bernstein, B. (1975). *Class, codes and control vol. 3: Towards a theory of educational transmissions*. London: Routledge & Kegan Paul.

Bertalanffy, L., von. (1951, December). General systems theory: A new approach to unity of science. *Human Biology*, *23*, 303–361.

Bertalanffy, L., von. (1968). *General systems theory: Foundations, development, applications*. New York: George Braziller.

Bittner, E. (1965). The concept of organization. *Social Research*, *32*, 239–255.

Blake, R. R., & Mouton, J. S. (1969). *Grid organization development*. Reading, MA: Addison-Wesley.

Blau, P. M. (1964). *Exchange and power in social life*. New York: John Wiley & Sons.

Blau, P. M., & Scott, R. G. (1962). *Formal organizations*. San Francisco: Chandler.

Bleicher, J. (1980). *Contemporary hermeneutics: Hermeneutics as method, philosophy and critique*. London: Routledge & Kegan Paul.

Block, P. (1987). *The empowered manager*. San Francisco: Jossey-Bass.

Bluhm, W. T. (1974). *Ideologies and attitudes*. Englewood Cliffs, NJ: Prentice-Hall.

Blumenthal, S. C. (1969). *Management information systems*. Englewood Cliffs, NJ: Prentice-Hall.

Boland, R. J., & Hoffman, R. (1983). Humor in a machine shop: An interpretation of symbolic action. In L. R. Pondy, P. J. Frost, G. Morgan, & T. C. Dandridge (Eds.), *Organizational symbolism* (pp. 187–198). Greenwich, CT: JAI Press.

Bolman, L. G., & Deal, T. E. (1984). *Modern approaches to understanding and managing organizations*. San Francisco: Jossey-Bass.

Bougon, M., Weick, K. E., & Binkhorst, D. (1977). Cognitions in organizations: An analysis of the Utrecht Jazz Orchestra. *Administrative Science Quarterly*, *22*, 606–639.

Boulding, K. E. (1956, April). General systems theory—the skeleton of science. *Management Science*, *2*, 197–208.

Boulle, P. (1959). *S.O.P.H.I.A.* New York: Bantam Books.

Bower, G. H. (1976). Experiments on story understanding and recall. *Quarterly Journal of Experimental Psychology*, *28*, 511–534.

Brim, O. G. (1966). Socialization through the life cycle. In O. G. Brim & S.

Wheeler (Eds.), *Socialization after childhood*. New York: John Wiley & Sons.

Brunsson, N. (1985). *The irrational organization: Irrationality as a basis for organizational action and change*. Chichester, UK: John Wiley & Sons.

Buchanan, B., II. (1975, February). Red tape and the service ethic: Some unexpected differences between public and private managers. *Administration and Society, 6*, 423–444.

Burke, W. W. (1982). *Organization development principles and practices*. Boston: Little, Brown and Company.

Campbell, D. T., & Fiske, D. W. (1959). Convergent and discriminant validation by the multitrait-multimethod matrix. *Psychological Bulletin, 56*, 81–105.

Carzo, R., Jr., & Yanouzas, J. N. (1967). *Formal organizations: A systems approach*. Homewood, IL: Richard D. Irwin.

Castaneda, C. (1971). *A separate reality: Further conversations with Don Juan*. New York: Simon & Schuster.

Clark, B. R. (1970). *The distinctive college: Antioch, Reed and Swarthmore*. Chicago: Aldine.

Clark, B. R. (1972). The organizational saga in higher education. *Administrative Science Quarterly, 17*, 178–184.

Cohen, D., March, J. G., & Olsen, J. P. (1972). A garbage can model of organizational choice. *Administrative Science Quarterly, 17*, 1–25.

Cohen, P. S. (1969). Theories of myth. *Man, 17*, 1–25.

Cook, T. D., & Campbell, D. T. (1979). *Quasi-experimentation: Design & analysis issues for field settings*. Boston: Houghton Mifflin.

Crano, W. D. (1981). Triangulation and cross-cultural research. In. M. B. Brewer & B.E. Collins, (Eds.), *Scientific inquiry and the social sciences* (pp. 317–344). San Francisco: Jossey-Bass.

Cummings, T. G. (1981). Designing effective work groups. In P. Nystrom & W. Starbuck (Eds.), *Handbook of organizational design* (vol. 2). Oxford, UK: Oxford University Press.

Dalton, M. (1950, June). Conflicts between staff and line managerial officers. *American Sociological Review*, 342–351.

Dalton, M. (1959). *Men who manage*. New York: John Wiley & Sons.

Davis, S. M. (1984). *Managing corporate culture*. Cambridge, MA: Ballinger.

Deal, T. E., & Kennedy, A. A. (1982). *Corporate cultures: The rites and rituals of corporate life*. Reading, MA: Addison-Wesley.

Dearden, J. F., & McFarlan, F. W. (1966). *Management information systems*. Homewood, IL: Richard D. Irwin.

Digman, L. A. (1986). *Strategic management*. Plano TX: Business Publications, Inc.

Duncan, R., & Weiss, A. (1979). Organizational learning: Implications for organizational design. In B. M. Staw (Ed.), *Research in organizational behavior* (vol. 1) (pp. 75–123). Greenwich, CT: JAI Press.

Durkheim, E. (1893). *De la division du travail social.* Paris: F. Alcan. [translated by G. Simpson (1947) as *The division of labor in society.* New York: The Free Press, 1947].

Dyer, W. G., Jr. (1986). *Cultural change in family firms.* San Francisco: Jossey-Bass.

Edelman, M. (1964). *The symbolic uses of politics.* Urbana, IL: University of Illinois Press.

Edelman, M. (1971). *Politics as symbolic action: Mass arousal and quiescence.* Chicago: Markham.

Edelman, M. (1977). *Political language: Words that succeed and policies that fail.* New York: Academic Press.

Eiser, J. R. (1980). *Cognitive social psychology: A guide to theory and research.* London: McGraw-Hill.

Emery, F. E., & Trist, E. L. (1973). *Towards a social ecology: Contextual appreciations of the future in the present.* New York: Plenum.

Etzioni, A. (1975). *A comparative analysis of complex organizations* (rev. ed.). New York: The Free Press.

Evered, R. (1983). The language of organizations: The case of the Navy. In L. R. Pondy, P. J. Frost, G. Morgan & T. C. Dandridge (Eds.), *Organizational symbolism* (pp. 125–143). Greenwich, CT: JAI Press.

Fayol, H. (1916). *General and industrial management* (trans. by C. Storrs, 1949). London: Pitman Publishing, Ltd.

Feldman, M. S., & March, J. G. (1981). Information in organizations as signal and symbol. *Administrative Science Quarterly, 26,* 171–186.

Festinger, L. (1954). A theory of social comparison processes. *Human Relations, 7,* 117–140.

Festinger, L. (1957). *A theory of cognitive dissonance.* Evanston, IL: Row-Peterson.

Festinger, L., Riecken, H. W., & Schachter, S. (1956). *When prophecy fails: A social and psychological study of a modern group that predicted the destruction of the world.* Minneapolis, MN: The University of Minnesota Press.

Follett, M. P. (1940). *Dynamic administration: The collected papers of Mary Parker Follett* (Ed. by E. M. Fox and L. Urwick). New York: Hippocrene Books.

Foster, W. P. (1984). Toward a critical theory of educational administration. In T. J. Sergiovanni & J. E. Corbally (Eds.), *Leadership and organizational culture* (pp. 240–259). Urbana, IL: University of Illinois Press.

French, W. L., & Bell, C. H., Jr. (1984). *Organization development: Behavioral science interventions for organization improvement.* Englewood Cliffs, NJ: Prentice-Hall.

French, W. L., Bell, C. H., Jr., & Zawacki, R. A. (1983). *Organization development: Theory, practice, and research*. Plano, TX: Business Publications.

Galbraith, J. (1973). *Designing complex organizations*. Reading, MA: Addison-Wesley.

Gardner, H. (1987). *The mind's new science: A history of the cognitive sciences*. New York: Basic Books.

Geertz, C. (1973). *The interpretation of cultures*. New York: Basic Books.

Gellerman, S. W. (1961). *People, problems, and profits*. New York: McGraw-Hill.

George, C. S., Jr. (1972). *The history of management thought*. Englewood Cliffs, NJ: Prentice-Hall.

Gephart, R. P. (1978). Status degradation and organizational succession: An ethno-methodological approach. *Administrative Science Quarterly, 18*, 553–581.

Gioia, D. A. (1986). Symbols, scripts, and sensemaking. In H. P. Sims, D. A. Gioia, & Associates (Eds.), *The thinking organization: Dynamics of organizational social cognition* (pp. 49–74). San Francisco: Jossey-Bass.

Glaser, B. G., & Strauss, A. L. (1967). *The discovery of grounded theory: Strategies for qualitative research*. New York: Aldine.

Goffman, E. (1959). *The presentation of self in everyday life*. New York: Doubleday.

Goffman, E. (1961). *Asylums: Essays on the social situation of mental patients and other inmates*. Garden City, NY: Anchor Books.

Goffman, E. (1967). *Interaction ritual*. Garden City, NY: Anchor Books.

Gold, K. A. (1982, November–December). Managing for success: A comparison of the private and public sectors. *Public Administration Review*, 568–575.

Goodall, H. L., Jr. (1984, Spring). The status of communication studies in organizational contexts: One rhetorician's lament after a year-long odyssey. *Communication Quarterly, 32*(2), 133–147.

Goodenough, W. (1974). On cultural theory. *Science, 186*, 435–436.

Gortner, H. F., Mahler, J., & Nicholson, J.B. (1987). *Organization theory: A public perspective*. Chicago: The Dorsey Press.

Gouldner, A. W. (1954). *Patterns of industrial bureaucracy*. Glencoe, IL: Free Press.

Greene, J., & McClintock, C. (1985). Triangulation in evaluation: Design and analysis issues. *Evaluation Review, 9*(5), 523–545.

Greenfield, T. B. (1980). The man who comes back through the door in the wall. *Educational Administration Quarterly, 16*, 97–112.

Greenfield, T. B. (1984). Leaders and schools: Willfulness and nonnatural order in organizations. In T. J. Sergiovanni & J. E. Corbally (Eds.), *Leadership and organizational culture* (pp. 142–169). Urbana, IL: University of Illinois Press.

Guillemin, J. H., & Holmstrom, L. L. (1986). *Mixed blessings: Intensive care for newborns*. New York: Oxford University Press.

Gulick, L. (1937). Notes on the theory of organization. In L. Gulick & L. Urwick (Eds.), *Papers on the science of administration* (pp. 3–13). New York: Institute of Public Administration.

Gulick, L., & Urwick, L. (Eds.). (1937). *Papers on the science of administration*. New York: Institute of Public Administration.

Hall, R. H. (1977). *Organizations: Structure and process* (2nd ed.). Englewood Cliffs, NJ: Prentice-Hall.

Handy, C. (1978). *Gods of management: Who they are how they work and why they fail*. London: Souvenir Press.

Hannan, M., & Freeman, J. (1977). The population ecology of organizations. *American Journal of Sociology, 82*, 929–964.

Harris, M. (1968). *The rise of anthropological theory*. New York: Crowell.

Harris, P. R. (1985). *Management in transition*. San Francisco: Jossey-Bass.

Harris, S. G., & Sutton, R. I. (1986). Functions of parting ceremonies in dying organizations. *Academy of Management Journal, 29*, 5–30.

Harris, T. A. (1969). *I'm OK—you're OK*. New York: Harper & Row.

Harrison, R. (1972, May–June). Understanding your organization's character. *Harvard Business Review*, 119–128.

Harrison, R. (1975). Diagnosing organization ideology. In J. E. Jones & J. W. Pfeiffer (Eds.), *The 1975 annual handbook for group facilitators* (pp. 101–107). La Jolla, CA: University Associates.

Hawley, A. (1950). *Human ecology: A theory of community structure*. New York: Ronald Press.

Hawley, A. (1968). Human ecology. In D. L. Sills (Ed.), *The international encyclopedia of the social sciences* (vol. 4) (pp. 328–337). New York: Crowell-Collier & Macmillan.

Hayakawa, S. I. (1953). *Symbol, status and personality*. New York: Harcourt, Brace & World.

Hayakawa, S. I. (1961). The word is not the thing. In P. R. Lawrence, J. C. Bailey, R. L. Katz, J. A. Seiler, C. D. Orth III, J. V. Clark, L. B. Barnes & A. N. Turner (Eds.), *Organizational behavior and administration* (pp. 397–400). Homewood, IL: The Dorsey Press.

Hazer, J. T., & Alvares, K. M. (1981). Police work values during organizational entry and assimilation. *Journal of Applied Psychology, 66*, 12–18.

Herbert, N. (1987). *Quantum reality: Beyond the new physics*. Garden City, NY: Anchor Books.

Hickman, C. R., & Silva, M. A. (1984). *Creating excellence: Managing corporate culture, strategy, and change in the new age*. New York: NAL Books/ New American Library.

Hicks, H. G., & Gullett, C. R. (1975). *Organizations: Theory and behavior*. New York: McGraw-Hill.

Hirsch, P. (1980, August). Ambushes, shootouts, and knights of the round-table: The language of corporate takeovers. Paper presented at the meeting of the Academy of Management, Detroit.

Hodder, I. (1982). *Symbols in action: Ethnoarchaeological studies of material culture*. Cambridge, UK: Cambridge University Press.

Hofstede, G. (1984). *Culture's consequences: International differences in work-related values* (vol. 5) (abr. ed.). Beverly Hills, CA: Sage Publications.

Holzner, B., & Marx, J. H. (1979). *Knowledge application: The knowledge system in society*. Boston: Allyn and Bacon.

Homans, G. C. (1950). *The human group* (pp. 156–189). New York: Harcourt, Brace and Company.

Hunt, J. G. (1984). Integrative comments: Managerial behavior from a "radical" perspective. In J. G. Hunt, D. M. Hosking, C. A. Schriesheim, & R. Stewart (Eds.), *Leaders and managers: International perspectives on managerial behavior and leadership* (pp. 275–277). New York: Pergamon Press.

Hutchinson, J. G. (1967). *Organizations: Theory and classical concepts*. New York: Holt, Rinehart and Winston.

Iacocca, L. (1984). *Iacocca: An autobiography*. Toronto: Bantam Books.

Jacobs, M. (1964). *Pattern in cultural anthropology*. Homewood, IL: The Dorsey Press.

James, M., & Jongeward, D. (1971). *Born to win*. Reading, MA: Addison-Wesley.

Jaques, E. (1950). Collaborative group methods in a wage negotiation situation (The Glacier Project—I). *Human Relations, 3*(3).

Jaques, Elliott. (1952). *The changing culture of a factory*. New York: Dryden Press.

Jongeward, D. (1973). *Everybody wins: Transactional analysis applied to organizations*. Reading, MA: Addison-Wesley.

Kanter, R. M. (1977). *Men and women of the corporation*. New York: Basic Books.

Kanter, R. M. (1979, July/August). Power failure in management circuits. *Harvard Business Review*.

Kanter, R. M. (1983). *The changemasters*. New York: Simon and Schuster.

Kanter, R. M., & Stein, B. A. (Eds.). (1979). *Life in organizations: Workplaces as people experience them*. New York: Basic Books.

Katz, D., & Kahn, R. L. (1966). *The social psychology of organizations*. New York: John Wiley & Sons.

Kaufman, H. (1960). *The forest ranger*. Baltimore, MD: Johns-Hopkins University Press.

Keesing, R. M. (1974). Theories of culture. *Annual Review of Anthropology, 3*, 73–79.

Keesing, R. M. (1976). *Cultural anthropology: A contemporary perspective*. New York: Holt, Rinehart and Winston.

Kerr, S. (1975). On the folly of rewarding A, while hoping for B. *Academy of Management Journal, 18*, 769–782.

Kets de Vries, M. F. R., & Miller, D. (1986). Personality, culture, and organization. *Academy of Management Review, 11*, 266–279.

Kilmann, R. H. (1984). *Beyond the quick fix.* San Francisco: Jossey-Bass.

Kilmann, R. H., Covin, T. J., & Associates. (Eds.). (1988). *Corporate transformation.* San Francisco: Jossey-Bass.

Kilmann, R. H., Saxton, M. J., Serpa, R., & Associates (Eds.). (1985). *Gaining control of the corporate culture.* San Francisco: Jossey-Bass.

Kimberly, J. R., & Quinn, R. E. (1984). *Managing organizational transitions.* Homewood, IL: Richard D. Irwin.

Kleindienst, M., & Watson, P. J. (1956). Action archaeology: The archaeological inventory of a living community. *Anthropology Tomorrow, 5*, 75–78.

Kohlberg, L. (1968). The child as a moral philosopher. *Psychology Today, 7*, 25–30.

Kohlberg, L. (1969). Stage and sequence: The cognitive-developmental approach to socialization. In D. Goslin (Ed.), *Handbook of socialization theory and research* (ch. 6). Chicago: Rand McNally.

Koontz, H. (1961). The management theory jungle. *Academy of Management Journal, 4*, 174–188.

Koontz, H. (1980). The management theory jungle revisited. *Academy of Management Review, 5.*

Kotter, J. P. (1985). *Power and influence: Beyond formal authority.* New York: The Free Press.

Kotter, J. P., Schlesinger, L. A., & Sathe, V. (1986). *Organization: Text, cases, and readings on the management of organizational design and change* (2nd edit.). Homewood, IL: Richard D. Irwin.

Kroeber, A. L. (1948). *Anthropology* (rev. edit.). New York: Harcourt, Brace & World.

Kroeber, A. L., & Kluckhohn, C. (1952). *Culture: A critical review of concepts and definitions.* New York: Vintage Books.

Kuhn, T. S. (1970a). *The structure of scientific revolutions.* Chicago: University of Chicago Press.

Kuhn, T. S. (1970b). Reflections on my critics. In I. Lakatos & A. Musgrave (Eds.), *Criticism and the growth of knowledge.* London, UK: Cambridge University Press.

Lawler, E., & Rhode, J. (1976). *Information and control in organizations.* Pacific Palisades, CA: Goodyear Publishing Co.

Lawrence, P. R., & Lorsch, J. W. (1967). *Organization and environment.* Cambridge, MA: Harvard University Press.

Leavitt, H. J. (1986). *Corporate pathfinders: Building vision and values into organizations.* Homewood, IL: Dow Jones-Irwin.

Levi-Strauss, C. (1963). *Structural anthropology.* New York: Basic Books.

Levi-Strauss, C. (1978). *Myth and meaning*. Toronto: University of Toronto Press.

Lewin, K. (1947). Frontiers in group dynamics. *Human Relations, 1*, 5–41.

Lewin, K. (1958). Group decision and social change. In E. E. Maccoby, T. M. Newcomb, & E. L. Hartley (Eds.), *Readings in social psychology* (pp. 197–211). New York: Holt, Rinehart and Winston.

Lippitt, G. L., Langseth, P., & Mossop, J. (1985). *Implementing organizational change*. San Francisco: Jossey-Bass.

Longenecker, J. G. (1973). *Principles of management and organizational behavior* (3rd edit.). Columbus, OH: Charles E. Merrill Publishing Company.

Louis, M. R. (1981). Culture in organizations: The need for and consequences of viewing organizations as culture-bearing milieux. *Human Systems Management, 2*, 246–258.

Lucas, R. (1987). Political-cultural analysis of organizations. *Academy of Management Review, 12*, 144–156.

Lunding, F. J., Clements, G. E., & Perkins, D. S. (1978, July). Everyone who makes it has a mentor. *Harvard Business Review*, 89–100.

March, J. G., & Simon, H. A. (1958). *Organizations*. New York: John Wiley & Sons.

Martin, J. (1982a). A garbage can model of the research process. In J. E. McGrath, J. Martin, & R. A. Kulka (Eds.), *Judgment calls in research* (pp. 17–39). Beverly Hills, CA: Sage Publications.

Martin, J. (1982b). Stories and scripts in organizational settings. In A. H. Hastorf & A. M. Isen (Eds.), *Cognitive social psychology* (pp. 255–305). New York: Elsevier / North-Holland.

Martin, J., & Powers, M. E. (1983). Truth or corporate propaganda: The value of a good war story. In L. R. Pondy, P. J. Frost, G. Morgan, & T. C. Dandridge (Eds.), *Organizational symbolism* (pp. 93–107). Greenwich, CT: JAI Press.

Martin, J., & Siehl, C. (1983, Autumn). Organizational culture and counterculture: An uneasy symbiosis. *Organizational Dynamics*, 52–64.

Martin, P. S., Lloyd, C., & Spoehr, A. (1938). Archaeological works in the Ackman-Lowry area, southwestern Colorado, 1937. *Field Museum of Natural History Anthropological Series, 23*, 217–304.

Masterman, M. (1970). On the nature of a paradigm. In I. Lakatos & A. Musgrave (Eds.), *Criticism and the growth of knowledge*. London, UK: Cambridge University Press.

Mayo, E. (1933). *The human problems of an industrial civilization*. New York: Macmillan.

McCallum, D. C. (1856). Superintendent's report, March 25, 1856. In *Annual report of the New York and Erie Railroad Company for 1855*. In A. D. Chandler, Jr. (Ed.), (1965), *The railroads* (pp. 101–108). New York: Harcourt, Brace & World.

McClintock, C., & Greene, J. (1985). Triangulation in practice. *Evaluation and Program Planning, 8*(4), 351–357.

McGrath, J. E. (1982). Introduction. In J. E. McGrath, J. Martin, & R. A. Kulka (Eds.), *Judgment calls in research* (pp. 13–16). Beverly Hills, CA: Sage Publications.

McGregor, D. (1960). *The human side of enterprise.* New York: McGraw-Hill.

McKillip, J. (1987). *Need analysis: Tools for the human services and education.* Beverly Hills, CA: Sage Publications.

Mead, G. H. (1934). *Mind self and society: From the standpoint of a social behaviorist.* Chicago: University of Chicago Press.

Mechanic, D. (1962). Sources of power of lower participants in complex organizations. *Administrative Science Quarterly, 7*, 349–364.

Meehan, E. J. (1981). *Reasoned argument in the social science.* Westport, CT: Greenwood Press.

Meissner, M. (1976). The language of work. In R. Dubin (Ed.), *Handbook of work, organization, and society* (pp. 205–279). Chicago: Rand McNally.

Merkle, J. A. (1980). *Management and ideology: The legacy of the international scientific management movement.* Berkeley, CA: University of California Press.

Merton, R. K. (1940). Bureaucratic structure and personality. *Social Forces, 18*, 560–568.

Merton, R. K. (1957). *Social theory and social structure* (rev. ed.). Glencoe, IL: The Free Press.

Metcalfe, H. (1985). *The cost of manufactures and the administration of workshops, public and private.* New York: John Wiley & Sons.

Meyer, J. W. (1984). Organizations as ideological systems. In T. J. Sergiovanni & J. E. Corbally (Eds.), *Leadership and organizational culture: New perspectives on administrative theory and practice* (pp. 186–205). Urbana, IL: University of Illinois Press.

Meyer, J. W., & Rowan, B. (1977). Institutionalized organizations: Formal structure as myth and ceremony. *American Journal of Sociology, 83*, 340–363.

Meyer, J. W., & Rowan, B. (1978). The structure of educational organizations. In M. W. Meyer & Associates (Eds.), *Environments and organizations* (pp. 78–109). San Francisco: Jossey-Bass.

Michael, J. A. (1961). High school climates and plans for entering college. *Public Opinion Quarterly, 25*, 585–602.

Miles, M. B., & Huberman, A. M. (1984). *Qualitative data analysis: A sourcebook of new methods.* Beverly Hills, CA: Sage Publications.

Miles, M. B., & Schmuck, R. A. (1971). Improving schools through organization development: An overview. In R. A. Schmuck & M. B. Miles (Eds.), *Organization development in schools* (pp. 7–27). Palo Alto, CA: National Press Books.

Miles, R. E. (1975). *Theories of management: Implications for organizational behavior and development.* New York: McGraw-Hill.

Mintzberg, H. (1979). *The structuring of organizations.* Englewood Cliffs, NJ: Prentice-Hall.

Mintzberg, H. (1983). *Power in and around organizations.* Englewood Cliffs, NJ: Prentice-Hall.

Mitroff, I. I. (1974). *The subjective side of science: A philosophical inquiry into the psychology of the Appollo moon scientists.* Amsterdam: Elsevier.

Mitroff, I. I. (1983). *Stakeholders of the organizational mind.* San Francisco: Jossey-Bass.

Mitroff, I. I. (1987). *Business not as usual.* San Francisco: Jossey-Bass.

Morgan, G. (1986). *Images of organization.* Beverly Hills, CA: Sage Publications.

Morgan, G., Frost, P. J., & Pondy, L. R. (1983). Organizational symbolism. In L. R. Pondy, P. J. Frost, G. Morgan & T. C. Dandridge (Eds.), *Organizational symbolism* (pp. 3–35). Greenwich, CT: JAI Press.

Morley, I. E. (1984). On imagery and the cycling of decision making. In J. G. Hunt, D. M. Hosking, C. A. Schriesheim, & R. Stewart (Eds.), *Leaders and managers: International perspectives on managerial behavior and leadership* (pp. 269–274). New York: Pergamon Press.

Mosher, F. C. (1968). *Democracy and the public service.* New York: Oxford University Press.

Murray, D. W. (1977). Ritual communications: Some considerations regarding meaning in Navajo ceremonials. In J. L. Dolgin, D. S. Kemnitzer, & D. M. Schneider (Eds.), *Symbolic anthropology.* New York: Columbia University Press.

Nietzsche, F. (1968). *The will to power.* New York: Vintage Books.

Ott, J. S. (1961). The impact of two community climates on organizational climates. Unpublished paper. Cambridge, MA: Massachusetts Institute of Technology, Sloan School of Management.

Ott, J. S. (1964). *A questionnaire study of organizational climate.* Unpublished master's thesis. Cambridge, MA: Massachusetts Institute of Technology, Sloan School of Management.

Ott, J. S. (Ed.). (1989, forthcoming). *Classic readings in organizational behavior.* Chicago: The Dorsey Press.

Ott, J. S., & Shafritz, J. M. (1986). *The Facts on File dictionary of nonprofit organization management.* New York: Facts on File.

Ott, K. K. (1987). The interpretive paradigm and organizational culture: A history in social anthropology. Paper presented at the 1987 ICA Conference, Organizational Communications Division.

Ouchi, W. G. (1981). *Theory Z: How American business can meet the Japanese challenge.* Reading, MA: Addison-Wesley.

Ouchi, W. G. (1984). *The M-form society.* Reading, MA: Addison-Wesley.

Ouchi, W. G., & Wilkins, A. L. (1985). Organizational culture. *Annual Review of Sociology, 11*, 457–483.

Pacanowsky, M. E., & O'Donnell-Trujillo, N. (1983, June). Organizational communication as cultural performance. *Communication Monographs, 50*, 126–147.

Parsons, T. (1956, June). Suggestions for a sociological approach to the theory of organizations. *Administrative Science Quarterly, 1*, 63–85.

Pascale, R. T., & Athos, A. G. (1981). *The art of Japanese management: Applications for American executives.* New York: Simon and Schuster.

Pastin, M. (1986). *The hard problems of management: Gaining the ethics edge.* San Francisco: Jossey-Bass.

Perrow, C. (1973, Summer). The short and glorious history of organizational theory. *Organizational Dynamics.*

Peters, T. J. (1981). Putting excellence into management, Unpublished manuscript, Stanford University, Stanford, CA.

Peters, T. J., & Waterman, R. H., Jr. (1982). *In search of excellence.* New York: Harper & Row.

Pettigrew, A. M. (1979). On studying organizational cultures. *Administrative Science Quarterly, 24*, 579–581.

Pfeffer, J. (1981a). *Power in organizations.* Boston: Pitman Publishing Co.

Pfeffer, J. (1981b). Management as symbolic action: The creation and maintenance of organizational paradigms. In L. L. Cummings & B. M. Staw (Eds.), *Research in organizational behavior* (vol. 3) (pp. 1–52). Greenwich, CT: JAI Press.

Pfeffer, J., & Salancik, G. R. (1974). Organizational decision making as a political process: The case of a university budget. *Administrative Science Quarterly, 19*, 135–151.

Pfeffer, J., & Salancik, G. R. (1978). *The external control of organizations: A resource dependence perspective.* New York: Harper & Row.

Piaget, J. (1973). *The child and reality: Problems of genetic psychology* (trans. by A. Rosin). New York: Grossman Publishers. (Original work published in 1972).

Pondy, L. R. (1978). Leadership is a language game. In M. W. McCall, Jr. & M. M. Lombardo (Eds.), *Leadership: Where else can we go?* (pp. 87–99). Durham, NC: Duke University Press.

Pondy, L. R. (1983). The role of metaphors and myths in organization and in the facilitation of change. In L. R. Pondy, P. J. Frost, G. Morgan, & T. C. Dandridge (Eds.), *Organizational symbolism* (pp. 157–166). Greenwich, CT: JAI Press.

Pondy, L. R., Frost, P. J., Morgan, G., & Dandridge, T. C. (Eds.). (1983). *Organizational symbolism.* Greenwich, CT: JAI Press.

Pondy, L. R., & Mitroff, I. I. (1979). Beyond open systems in organizations. In B. M. Staw (Ed.), *Research in organizational behavior* (vol. 1) (pp. 3–39). Greenwich, CT: JAI Press.

Popkewitz, T. S. (1982). Educational reform as the organization of ritual: Stability as change. *Journal of Education, 164*, 5–29.

Popovich, P., & Wanous, J. P. (1982). The realistic job preview as a persuasive communication. *The Academy of Management Review, 7*, 570–577.

Porter, M. E. (1981). The contributions of industrial organization to strategic management. *Academy of Management Review, 6*, 609–620.

Radcliffe-Brown, A. R. (1952). *Structure and function in primitive society.* London, UK: Oxford University Press.

Raelin, J. A. (1985, 1986). *The clash of cultures: Managers and professionals.* Boston: Harvard Business School Press.

Ranson, S., Hinings, R., & Greenwood, R. (1980). The structuring of organizational structures. *Administrative Science Quarterly, 25*, 1–17.

Rice, A. K., Hill, J. M. M., & Trist, E. L. (1950). The representation of labour turnover as a social process (The Glacier Project—II). *Human Relations, 3*(4).

Ritti, R. R., & Funkhouser, G. R. (1982). *The ropes to skip and the ropes to know: Studies in organizational behavior* (2nd ed.). New York: John Wiley & Sons.

Roethlisberger, F. J., & Dickson, W. J. (1939). *Management and the worker.* Cambridge, MA: Harvard University Press.

Rosenberg, M. J., & Hovland, C. I. (1960). Cognitive, affective and behavioral components of attitudes. In M. J. Rosenberg, C. I. Hovland, W. J. McGuire, R. P. Abelson, & J. W. Brehm (Eds.), *Attitude organization and change: An analysis of consistency among attitude components.* New Haven, CT: Yale University Press.

Rouse, I. (1939). *Prehistory of Haiti, a study in method.* New Haven, CT: Yale University Press.

Salancik, G. R. (1977). Commitment and the control of organizational behavior and belief. In B. M. Staw &. G. R. Salancik (Eds.), *New directions in organizational behavior* (pp. 1–54). Chicago: St. Clair Press.

Sanday, P. R. (1979, 1983). The ethnographic paradigm(s). In J. Van Maanen (Ed.), *Qualitative methodology* (pp. 19–36). Beverly Hills, CA: Sage Publications.

Sathe, V. (1985). *Culture and related corporate realities: Text, cases, and readings on organizational entry, establishment, and change.* Homewood, IL: Irwin.

Schein, E. H. (1961). *Coercive persuasion.* New York: Norton.

Schein, E. H. (1964). How to break in the college graduate. *Harvard Business Review, 42*, 68–76.

Schein, E. H. (1966). The problem of moral education for the business manager. *Industrial Management Review, 8*, 3–14.

Schein, E. H. (1968). Organizational socialization and the profession of management. *Industrial Management Review, 9*, 1–15.

Schein, E. H. (1978). *Career dynamics: Matching individual and organizational needs.* Reading, MA: Addison-Wesley.

Schein, E. H. (1980). *Organizational psychology* (3rd edit.). Englewood Cliffs, NJ: Prentice-Hall.

Schein E. H. (1981). Does Japanese management style have a message for American managers? *Sloan Management Review, 23,* 55–68.

Schein, E. H. (1983, Summer). The role of the founder in creating an organizational culture. *Organizational Dynamics,* 13–28.

Schein, E. H. (1984). Coming to a new awareness of organizational culture. *Sloan Management Review, 25,* 3–16.

Schein, E. H. (1985). *Organizational culture and leadership.* San Francisco: Jossey-Bass.

Schein, E. H., & Lippitt, G. L. (1966). Supervisory attitudes toward the legitimacy of influencing subordinates. *Journal of Applied Behavioral Science, 2,* 199–209.

Schein, E. H., & Ott, J. S. (1962). The legitimacy of organizational influence. *American Journal of Sociology, 67,* 682–689.

Schmuck, R. A. (1971). Developing teams of organizational specialists. In R. A. Schmuck & M. B. Miles (Eds.), *Organization development in schools* (pp. 213–230). Palo Alto, CA: National Press Books.

Schön, D. A. (1971). *Beyond the stable state.* New York: Basic Books.

Schultz, T. W. (1971). *Investment in human capital.* New York: The Free Press.

Schutz, A. (1932). *Der sinnhafte aufbau der sozialen welt.* Vienna: Springer.

Schutz, A. (1970). *On phenomenology and social relations.* Chicago: University of Chicago Press.

Scott, W. G. (1961, April). Organization theory: An overview and an appraisal. *Academy of Management Journal,* 7–26.

Scott, W. G., & Mitchell, T. R. (1972). *Organization theory* (rev. ed.). Homewood, IL: Richard D. Irwin and The Dorsey Press.

Seidman, H. (1980). *Politics, position, and power* (3rd ed.). New York: Oxford University Press.

Selznick, P. (1948). Foundations of the theory of organization. *American Sociological Review, 13,* 25–35.

Selznick, P. (1949). *TVA and the grass roots.* Berkeley, CA: University of California Press.

Selznick, P. (1957). *Leadership in administration: A sociological interpretation.* New York: Harper & Row.

Sergiovanni, T. J. (1984). Cultural and competing perspectives in administrative theory and practice. In T. J. Sergiovanni & J. E. Corbally (Eds.), *Leadership and organizational culture: New perspectives on administrative theory and practice* (pp. 1–11). Urbana, IL: University of Illinois Press.

Sergiovanni, T. J., & Corbally, J. E. (1984a). Preface. In T. J. Sergiovanni & J. E. Corbally (Eds.), *Leadership and organizational culture* (pp. vii–x). Urbana, IL: University of Illinois Press.

Sergiovanni, T. J., & Corbally, J. E. (1984b). Theory of practice in educational administration and organizational analysis. In T. J. Sergiovanni & J. E. Corbally (Eds.), *Leadership and organizational culture* (pp. 207–213). Urbana, IL: University of Illinois Press.

Shafritz, J. M. (1985). *The Facts on File dictionary of public administration*. New York: Facts on File.

Shafritz, J. M., & Ott, J. S. (1987). *Classics of organization theory*. Chicago: The Dorsey Press.

Siehl, C., & Martin, J. (1984). The role of symbolic management: How can managers effectively transmit organizational culture? In J. G. Hunt, D. M. Hosking, C. A. Schriesheim & R. Stewart (Eds.), *Leaders and managers: International perspectives on managerial behavior and leadership* (pp. 227–269). New York: Pergamon Press.

Simon, H. A. (1946, Winter). The proverbs of administration. *Public Administration Review*, 6, 53–67.

Simon, H. A. (1947). *Administrative behavior*. New York: Macmillan.

Simon, H. A. (1969). *The sciences of the artificial*. Cambridge, MA: M.I.T. Press.

Simon, S. B., Howe, L. W., & Kirschenbaum, H. *Values clarification: A handbook of practical strategies for teachers and students*. New York: Hart.

Sims, H. P., Jr., Gioia, D. A., & Associates. (1986). *The thinking organization: Dynamics of organizational social cognition*. San Francisco: Jossey-Bass.

Skinner, B. F. (1953). *Science and behavior*. New York: Macmillan.

Smircich, L. (1983). Organizations as shared meanings. In L. R. Pondy, P. J. Frost, G. Morgan, & T. C. Dandridge (Eds.), *Organizational symbolism* (pp. 55–65). Greenwich, CT: JAI Press.

Smircich, L. (1985). Is the concept of culture a paradigm for understanding organizations and ourselves? In P. J. Frost, L. F. Moore, M. R. Louis, C. C. Lundberg, & J. Martin (Eds.), *Organizational culture* (pp. 55–72). Beverly Hills, CA: Sage Publications.

Smircich, L., & Calas, M. B. (1987). Organizational culture: A critical assessment. In F. M. Jablin, L. L. Putnam, K. H. Roberts, & L. W. Porter (Eds.), *Handbook of organizational communication*. Beverly Hills, CA: Sage Publications.

Smith, A. (1776). *The wealth of nations*. New York: Modern Library.

Spriegel, W. R., & Myers, C. E. (Eds.). (1953). *The writings of the Gilbreths*. Homewood, IL: Richard D. Irwin.

Sproull, L. S. (1981). Beliefs in organizations. In P. C. Nystrom & W. H. Starbuck (Eds.), *Handbook of organizational design*. London: Oxford University Press.

Steele, F. I. (1973). *Physical settings and organization development*. Reading, MA: Addison-Wesley.

Steele, F. I., & Jenks, S. (1977). *The feel of the work place*. Reading, MA: Addison-Wesley.

Stouffer, S. A., Suchman, E. A., DeVinney, L. C., Star, S. A., & Williams, R. M. (1949). *The American soldier: Adjustments during army life*. Princeton, NJ: Princeton University Press.

Stout, R., Jr. (1980). *Management or control?* Bloomington, IN: Indiana University Press.

Strauss, A., Schatzman, L., Erlich, D., Bucher, R., & Sabshin, M. (1963). The hospital and its negotiated order. In E. Friedson (Ed.), *The hospital in modern society* (pp. 147–169). New York: Free Press.

Superka, D., Johnson, P. L., & Ahrens, C. *Values education: Approaches and materials*. Boulder, CO: ERIC Clearinghouse for Social Studies/Social Science Education and the Social Science Education Consortium.

Tagiuri, R., & Litwin, G. H. (Eds.). (1968). *Organizational climate: Exploration of a concept*. Boston: Harvard University, Graduate School of Business, Division of Research.

Tainter, J. A. (1978). Mortuary practices and the study of prehistoric social systems. In M. B. Schiffer (Ed.), *Advances in archaeological method and theory, I*. New York: Academic Press.

Taylor, F. W. (1911). *The principles of scientific management*. New York: Norton.

Taylor, W. (1984). Organizational culture and administrative leadership in universities. In T. J. Sergiovanni & J. E. Corbally (Eds.), *Leadership and organizational culture: New perspectives on administrative theory and practice* (pp. 125–141). Urbana, IL: University of Illinois Press.

Thompson, J. D. (1967). *Organizations in action*. New York: McGraw-Hill.

Tichy, N. M. (1983). *Managing strategic change: Technical, political, and cultural dynamics*. New York: John Wiley & Sons.

Tichy, N. M., & Devanna, M. A. (1986). *The transformational leader*. New York: John Wiley & Sons.

Tichy, N. M., & Ulrich, D. O. (1984). The leadership challenge—a call for the transformational leader. *Sloan Management Review, 26*, 59–68.

Towne, H. R. (1886, May). The engineer as an economist. *Transactions of The American Society of Mechanical Engineers, 7*, 428–432.

Toynbee, A. (1956) *The industrial revolution*. Boston: Beacon Press. (Original publication was in 1884).

Trist, E. L., & Bamforth, K. (1950). Social and psychological consequences of the longwall method of coal-getting. *Human Relations, 3*(4).

Urwick, L. (1956). *The golden book of management*. London: Newman, Neame.

Van Maanen, J. (1975). Police socialization. *Administrative Science Quarterly, 20,* 207–228.

Van Maanen, J. (1976). Breaking in: Socialization to work. In R. Dubin (Ed.), *Handbook of work, organization, and society* (pp. 67–130). Chicago: Rand McNally.

Van Maanen, J. (1979). The self, the situation, and the rules of interpersonal relations. In W. G. Bennis et. al. (Eds.), *Essays in interpersonal dynamics.* Homewood, IL: The Dorsey Press.

Van Maanen, J. (1979, 1983a). Reclaiming qualitative methods for organizational research: A preface. In J. Van Maanen (Ed.) *Qualitative methodology* (pp. 9–18). Beverly Hills, CA: Sage Publications.

Van Maanen, J. (1979, 1983b). The fact of fiction in organizational ethnography. In J. Van Maanen (Ed.), *Qualitative methodology* (pp. 37–55). Beverly Hills, CA: Sage Publications.

Van Maanen, J. (1982a). Introduction. In J. Van Maanen, J. M. Dabbs, Jr., & R. R. Faulkner (Eds.), *Varieties of qualitative research* (pp. 7–10). Beverly Hills, CA: Sage Publications.

Van Maanen, J. (1982b). Fieldwork on the beat. In J. Van Maanen, J. M. Dabbs, Jr., & R. R. Faulkner (Eds.), *Varieties of qualitative research* (pp. 103–151). Beverly Hills, CA: Sage Publications.

Van Maanen, J. (1983). People processing: Strategies of organizational socialization. In R. W. Allen & L. W. Porter (Eds.), *Organizational influence processes* (pp. 240–259). Glenview, IL: Scott, Foresman and Company.

Van Maanen, J., & Barley, S. (1984). Occupational communities: Culture and control in organizations. In B. M. Staw and L. L. Cummings (Eds.), *Research in organizational behavior* (vol. 6). Greenwich, CT: JAI Press.

Van Maanen, J., Dabbs, J. M., Jr., & Faulkner, R. R. (Eds.). (1982). *Varieties of qualitative research.* Beverly Hills, CA: Sage Publications.

Wallace, S. E. (Ed.). (1971). *Total institutions.* Chicago: Aldine Publishing Company.

Wanous, J. P. (1980). *Organizational entry: Recruitment, selection, and socialization of newcomers.* Reading, MA: Addison-Wesley.

Weber, M. (1922). Bureaucracy. In H. Gerth & C. W. Mills (Eds.), *Max Weber: Essays in sociology.* Oxford, UK: Oxford University Press. 1946.

Weber, M. (1947). *Wirtschaft und gesellschaft* (3rd ed.). Tuebingen: J. C. B. Mohr.

Weick, K. E. (1976). Educational organizations as loosely coupled systems. *Administrative Science Quarterly, 21,* 1–19.

Weick, K. E. (1977). Enactment processes in organizations. In B. M. Staw & G. Salancik (Eds.), *New directions in organizational behavior* (pp. 267–300). Chicago: St. Clair Press.

Weick, K. E. (1979). *The social psychology of organizing* (2nd ed.). Reading, MA: Addison-Wesley.

Weick, K. E. (1979). Cognitive processes in organizations. In B. M. Staw (Ed.), *Research in organizational behavior* (vol. 1) (pp. 41–74). Greenwich, CT: JAI Press.

Weick, K. E. (1982, June). Administering education in loosely coupled schools. *Phi Delta Kappan*, 673–676.

Wharton, J. W., & Worthley, J. A. (1983). A perspective on the challenge of public management: Environmental paradox and organizational culture. In J. L. Perry and K. L. Kraemer (Eds.), *Public management: Public and private perspectives* (pp. 126–142). Palo Alto, CA: Mayfield Publishing.

Whitehead, T. N. (1936). *Leadership in a free society*. Cambridge, MA: Harvard University Press.

Whitehead, T. N. (1938). *The industrial worker*. Cambridge, MA: Harvard University Press.

Whiting, B. (Ed.). (1963). *Six cultures*. New York: John Wiley.

Whyte, W. F. (1943). *Street corner society*. Chicago: Chicago University Press.

Whyte, W. F. (1948). *Human relations in the restaurant business*. New York: McGraw-Hill.

Whyte, W. H., Jr. (1956). *The organization man*. New York: Simon and Schuster.

Wiener, N. (1948). *Cybernetics*. Cambridge, MA: The M.I.T. Press.

Wiener, N. (1950). *The human use of human beings*. Boston: Houghton Mifflin.

Wiener, N. (1964). *God and Golem, Inc.* Cambridge, MA: The M.I.T. Press.

Wildavsky, A. (1987, March). Choosing preferences by constructing institutions: A cultural theory of preference formation. *American Political Science Review, 81*(1), 3–20.

Wilkins, A. L. (1983). Organizational stories as symbols which control the organization. In L. R. Pondy, P. J. Frost, G. Morgan & T. C. Dandridge (Eds.), *Organizational symbolism* (pp. 81–92). Greenwich, CT: JAI Press.

Wilson, J. Q. (1968). *Varieties of police behavior*. Cambridge, MA: Harvard University Press.

Witherspoon, G. J. (1971). Navajo categories of objects at rest. *American Anthropologist, 73*(1), 110–117.

Wolcott, H. (1975). Criteria for an ethnographic approach to research in schools. *Human Organization, 34*, 111–128.

Wren, D. A. (1972). *The evolution of management thought*. New York: The Ronald Press Company.

Zimbardo, P., & Ebbesen, E. B. (1969). *Influencing attitudes and changing behavior*. Reading, MA: Addison-Wesley.

Index

ABOUT THE AUTHOR

J. Steven Ott is a faculty member at the university of Maine where he teaches courses in management, organization theory, health care policy and administration, and nonprofit organization management. Prior to 1987, he was Executive Vice President of a Denver-based management consulting firm where he assisted a variety of organizations on problems and opportunities involving organizational culture. He is a frequent speaker at executive seminars and conferences. Dr. Ott has written or co-authored numerous books and articles including, most recently, *Classics of Organization Theory*, *The Facts on File Dictionary of Health Care Management*, and *Classic Readings in Organizational Behavior*. Professor Ott received his master's degree from the Sloan School of Management at the Massachusetts Institute of Technology, and his doctorate from the University of Colorado at Denver.

A NOTE ON THE TYPE

The text of this book was set via computer-driven cathode-ray tube in 10/12 Century Schoolbook, a typeface based on a design drawn in 1894 by L. B. Benton and T. L. DeVinne for the *Century* magazine. Century Schoolbook is an excellent example of a refined Egyptian typeface. The Egyptian family of faces is characterized by thick slab serifs and little contrast between thick and thin strokes. The large x-height and simple letter forms of Century Schoolbook make it very legible.

Composed by Eastern Graphics, Binghamton, New York.

Printed and bound by Malloy Lithographing, Inc., Ann Arbor, Michigan.